Unbelievably Good Deals and Great Adventures That You Absolutely Can't Get Unless You're Over 50

Joan Rattner Heilman

Contemporary Books

Chicago New York San Francisco Lisbon London Madrid Mexico City Milan New Delhi San Juan Seoul Singapore Sydney Toronto

The McGraw-Hill Companies

Library of Congress Cataloging-in-Publication Data

Heilman, Joan Rattner.
Unbelievably good deals and great adventures that you absolutely can't get unless you're over 50, 2003-2004 / Joan Rattner Heilman.
p. cm.

1. Travel. 2. Discounts for the aged.

G151 .H44 2002
910'.84'6—dc21 2003040921

2 3 4 5 6 7 8 9 0 DOC/DOC 2 1 0 9 8 7 6 5 4 3

This book is printed on acid-free paper.

Contents

1

Introduction to Good Deals and Great Adventures

This book is a guide to the perks, privileges, discounts, and special adventures that are now yours simply because you've been around for at least 50 years.

On your 50th birthday (or on your 60th, 62nd, or 65th), you qualify for hundreds of special opportunities and money-saving offers that make younger people wish they were older—all for a couple of good reasons. First, as a person in your prime, you deserve them.

Second, as part of the fastest-growing segment of the American population, you represent an enormous market of potential consumers, a fact that has become quite apparent to the business community. More than a quarter of the U.S. population today is over 50. By 2020, that proportion is expected to increase to a third as the baby boomers turn 50 (one every 7 seconds). About 35 million Americans—

almost 13 percent of the total population—are now over 65, and it is estimated that by 2030 that number will double. Besides, life expectancy is higher today than ever before (today, more than four million Americans are 85 and older), and most of us can expect to live a long, healthy, interesting, and active life.

Those of us over 50 control most of the nation's wealth, including half of the discretionary income (the money that's left over after essentials have been taken care of) and almost 80 percent of its financial assets. Very often, the children have gone, the mortgage has been paid off, the house is fully furnished, the goal of leaving a large inheritance is not a major concern, and the freedom years have arrived at last.

As a group, we're markedly different from previous older generations who pinched pennies and saved them all. We, too, know the value of a dollar, but we feel freer to spend our money because we're better off than our predecessors, a significant number of us having accumulated enough resources to be reasonably secure. We also are far better educated than those before us, and we have developed many more interests and activities. Besides, we have more time to enjoy ourselves. The average age of retirement has dropped to 61.

Most important, we as a group are remarkably fit, healthy, and energetic. We're living longer and feeling better. In fact, a survey has shown that most of us feel at least 15 years younger than our chronological age and rate our health as good or excellent.

The business community is actively courting the mature population because now many of us have the time to spend our money doing all the things we've always put off before. With the recognition of our numbers and financial power, our flexible schedules, and our vast buying power, we are finally being taken very seriously. To get our attention, we are increasingly presented with some real breaks and good deals, all detailed on these pages. We are also invited on trips and adventures specifically tailored to suit our interests, needs, and abilities.

In this book, you will learn how to get what's coming to you—the discounts and privileges that are among the advantages of getting older. Here are some that you absolutely couldn't get if you were younger:

- Discounts at hotels and motels; at car-rental agencies; and on buses, trains, and boats
- Price breaks on airfares
- Colleges and universities that offer you an education at bargain rates
- Travel adventures all over the world designed specifically for older travelers
- Clubs, trips, and services for mature singles
- Resorts where you can ski for half price—or nothing
- Tennis tournaments, golf vacations, walking trips, bike tours, and senior softball leagues designed for you
- And much more!

Because every community in this country and abroad has its own special perks to offer you, make a practice of *asking* if there are breaks to which you are entitled, from movies to museums, concerts to historic sites, hotels to ski resorts, restaurants to riverboats. Don't expect clerks, ticket agents, tour operators, restaurant hosts, or even travel agents to volunteer them to you. First of all, they may not think of it. Second, they may not realize you have reached the appropriate birthday. And third, they may not want to call attention to your age, just in case that's not something you would appreciate. You never know if you're being offered the best possible deal unless you ask. Many bargains and privileges are available only to people who speak up.

Remember to request your privileges *before* you pay or when you order or make reservations, and always carry proof of age or an over-50 club membership card or, better yet, both. Sometimes the advantages come with membership in a senior club, but usually they are available to anyone over a specified age.

To make sure you're getting a legitimate discount when you're using your special privileges, call the hotel, airline, car-rental company, or tour operator and ask what the regular or normal prices are. Find out if there's a special sale or promotion going on. Ask about other discounts—corporate, weekend, government, auto-club membership breaks, for example. Most important, always ask for *the lowest available rate* at the time you plan to travel and compare that with the discounted senior rate. Then decide whether you are getting a good deal. Sometimes you'll find that even better specials are available.

With the help of this guidebook, completely revised and updated at least once a year, you will have a wonderful time and save money too.

2

Travel: Making Your Age Pay Off

People over 50 are the most ardent travelers of all. We travel more often, farther, more extravagantly, and for longer periods of time than anybody else. Since the travel industry discovered these facts, it's been going after our business.

The travel industry has fallen in love with our age group because we have more discretionary income than people of other ages and more time to spend it. Besides, we are remarkably flexible. Many of us no longer have children in school, so we're free to travel off-peak or whenever we feel the need for a change of scenery. In fact, we much prefer spring and fall to summer. Some of us have retired, and others have such good jobs that we can make our own schedules. We can take advantage of midweek or weekend slack times when the industry is eager to fill space.

But, best of all, we are energetic, and we're not about to stay home too much. People over 50 account for about one-third of all domestic travel, overseas packaged tours, and hotel/motel nights, as well as 70 percent of bus trips and cruises.

Contrary to what a younger person might think, people in the mature generation aren't content with watching the action. Instead, we like to get right into the middle of it. There's not a place we won't go or an activity we won't try. Though many of us prefer escorted tours, almost half of us choose to travel independently.

Not only that, but we're shrewd—we look for the best deals to the best places. We are experienced comparison shoppers and want the most for our money.

For all of these reasons, we are now offered astonishing numbers of travel-related discounts, reduced rates, special tour packages, and other perks. Many agencies and tour operators have designed all or at least part of their trips to appeal to a mature clientele. Others include older travelers along with everyone else but offer us special privileges.

So many good deals and great adventures are available to you when you are on the move that we'll start off with travel.

But, first, keep in mind:

- Rates, trips, and privileges tend to change at a moment's notice, so check out each of them before you make your plans. Airlines are particularly capricious, and it's hard to tell what they offer from one week to the next. The good deals in this guidebook are those that are available as we go to press.

- Many airlines, cruise lines, tour operators, and travel agencies have gone out of business recently, and others are struggling to stay afloat. Protect yourself by charging your travel expenses to a major credit card and purchasing comprehensive travel insurance that covers carrier default and trip cancellation as well as other potential problems.
- Always ask for your discount or special privilege when you make your reservations or at the time of purchase, order, or check-in. If you wait until you're checking out or settling your bill, it may be too late.
- Remember that your privileges may apply only between certain hours, on certain days of the week, or during specific seasons of the year. Research this before making reservations, and always remind the clerk of the discount when you check in or pay your fare. Be flexible when you can, and travel during the hours, days, or seasons when you can get the best deals.
- When traveling, it's particularly important to carry identification with proof of age or membership in a senior club. In most cases, a driver's license or passport does the job. In some cases, the organization's membership card, a birth certificate, a resident alien card, or any other official document showing your date of birth will suffice. If you're old enough for a Medicare card or Senior ID card, use that.
- Look before you book. Don't always spring for the senior discount without checking out other rates. Sometimes special promotional rates or discounts that are available to anybody of any age turn out to be better deals. The

car-rental companies and airlines, for example, are famous for this. Ask your travel agent or the ticket seller to figure out the *lowest possible available rate* for you at the time you want to travel.

- Some senior privileges are available whether you make reservations by telephone or online, but frequently they are not to be found on the websites. If you want them, you or your travel agent must call. On the other hand, you may find that Web fares or prices are the lowest, beating the price you would get on the telephone. The only solution is to try it both ways before you make your a reservation.
- Pay for all travel with a major credit card if possible. If there are problems or disputes, you will have less difficulty resolving them.
- Some of these bargains are yours at age 50, usually but not always tied to membership in a senior organization. Others come along later at varying birthdays, so watch for the cutoff points. Also, in most cases, if the person purchasing the ticket or trip is the right age, the rest of the party, a traveling companion, or the people sharing the room are entitled to the same reduced rates.

3

Airfares: Improving with Age

One thing that improves with your age is airfare. That's still true today although the largest U.S. airlines, in dire financial straits, have abandoned the money-saving senior coupons we had come to love and the standard 10 percent discount on just about all fares for senior travelers. A few foreign carriers have followed along and done away with their senior discounts too.

So what's left for us older travelers? Happily, a few good deals are still out there.

Most of the major U.S. airlines have a new senior offer—a senior fare for people 65 and older that provides a 10 percent discount if they book tickets 14 days in advance and include a Saturday stay. That means you must plan ahead and accept fares that are much more restrictive. The good news is that the maximum stay has, in most cases, been extended to 180 days, making life easier for those who spend significant time in different places. And US Airways remains a bright spot by continuing to offer its AARP Saver fares, available at age 50. Some of the smaller airlines continue to give us a break.

But, first, look before you book:

- Note that the largest airlines have imposed new rules upon us. One is that most lower-priced tickets are now really nonrefundable. If you do not plan to use your ticket, you must notify the airline before the time and day of your reservation and then rebook for a specific date in the future. In addition, you must pay a sizable service charge per ticket plus the difference in the cost of the tickets. The second rule is that many of the big airlines charge a fee to fly standby on an earlier or later flight on the same day that you are ticketed. Each airline has its own caveats and exceptions, so check them out before you make an expensive booking that may need to be changed. Besides, the rules may change again at any time.
- Make sure you are getting the *lowest possible fare* to your destination at the time you want to fly. Ask about senior discounts and senior fares, but be prepared to jump ship if you can get a better deal with a short-term sale rate or a supersaver fare.
- Always check out airline websites and the many travel sites, or talk to a travel agent before purchasing airline tickets. Often, the lowest fares are available only online. On the other hand, you may not be able to get a senior discount on a senior fare website. To get Southwest's spe-

cial fares for travelers 65 and up, for example, you must make your reservations by phone.

- Keep in mind that the restrictions you must fly by may not be worth the savings. Always examine the fees and conditions and decide whether you can live with them. There may be blackout periods around major holidays when you can't use your privileges, departures only on certain days or hours, restrictions on the season of the year, or stiff penalties for flight changes. It's not always easy to sort out the offers.
- Be prepared to present valid proof of age at the check-in counter. It's possible that your discount will not be honored if you don't have that proof with you, and you will have to pay the difference.
- Almost all airlines that continue to offer senior discounts extend the courtesy to a younger companion when you fly together.
- Book your travel as early as possible for the best fares and the most available seats. Discounted seats are limited and may not be reserved at all on some flights.
- Be flexible. To get seats and the best fares, plan to fly at off-peak times when the rest of the population isn't rushing off to faraway places. For example, noontime or late-night flights can be much cheaper than early-morning or dinnertime flights. Consider leaving on a different day—fares are often lower midweek or on Saturday. Avoid Monday mornings and Friday afternoons. And fly off-season, when children aren't on vacation and there are no major holidays, to get with better prices.
- For cheaper airfares, check out the many rapidly proliferating low-cost airlines, such as Southwest, American Trans Air, and JetBlue. They all have limited routes and

may not fly out of a city or airport that's convenient for you—and they may not feed you more than a minor snack—but they usually offer other important advantages besides cheap tickets. For example, on some of these niche airlines, you may fly only one way, paying just half the round-trip fare, book your trips at the very last minute without penalty, and have no worries about Saturday-night or minimum stays. Some offer special senior fares that can't be beat.

- Membership in a private airline VIP club means you can spend your waiting time at the airport in comfort, complete with snacks and free drinks, copy machines, private telephones, luggage storage areas, and sometimes even showers. At this writing, you can buy a lifetime club membership at age 62 or more from three airlines—America West, Continental, and Northwest—for less than half what other adults pay. The break applies to single memberships as well as those that include your spouse. Not only that, but you may also bring guests to the lounges and sometimes use the clubs even when you are not ticketed for a flight that day.
- Some European airlines give senior discounts on fares for domestic flights within their borders or to other cities in Europe. To get the breaks, it is usually necessary to book these flights at the same time and in conjunction with your international ticket.

Be advised that airfares and airline policies can change overnight—and often do—so always call the airline that interests you for an update.

U.S. AIRLINES

ALASKA AIRLINES

Fly on Alaska Airlines if you're 62 or older and you'll get 10 percent off on almost every published fare as will a traveling companion of any age. However, special discounted senior fares, which give you more than 10 percent off, are often posted on certain routes by this airline that serves 45 cities mainly on the West Coast from Alaska all the way to Mexico. Recent additions are daily flights from Seattle to Denver, Boston, and Washington, D.C. By the way, this is the only airline with vacation packages to Nome, Pt. Barrow, and Kotzebue above the Arctic Circle.

For information: 800-426-0333; www.alaskaair.com.

AMERICA WEST AIRLINES

America West is the only domestic carrier—at least at this writing—that retains its senior coupons and its 10 percent discount on almost all of its fares. The discount is available to you at 62 or more and to a younger companion who travels with you on the same flight. The Senior Saver Pack, also for passengers 62-plus, gives you four one-way coupons good for coach travel on any of the airline's flights within the U.S. and to Canada and Mexico. The coupons must be exchanged for tickets within a year. Two coupons are required for flights to Alaska.

On this airline, which flies to 93 U.S. cities, you may use your coupons for one or two grandchildren between the ages of 2 and 12 when they travel with you. Also included in the packet are coupons for bonus miles and discounts on land packages and car rentals. You may fly any day, anytime if seats are available. Reservations must be made at least 14 days in advance, although you may use your tickets to fly standby on valid travel days. You're entitled to frequent-flyer points for your miles.

Another perk for seniors is a break on a lifetime membership in the America West Club, the company's private airport lounge facility. If you've reached age 62, you'll pay less than half of what younger adults pay for the same privilege.

For information: 800-235-9292; www.americawest.com. For the America West Club: 800-406-6501.

AMERICAN AIRLINES (AA)

On some routes, AA now offers special senior fares to passengers 65 or over. These give you a 10 percent discount on a 14-day advance-purchase nonrefundable booking with a Saturday-night stay. They must be booked using the reservations number and are not available online, although sometimes you can find an even better deal on the airline's website. Senior fares are also usually available on American Eagle flights, including the Business Express shuttle that links New York, Boston, and Washington, D.C.

For information: 800-433-7300; www.aa.com.

AMERICAN TRANS AIR (ATA)

A low-fare nationwide airline based in the Midwest, ATA operates scheduled service from Chicago-Midway and Indianapolis to 44 vacation and business destinations including Las Vegas, New York, six cities in Florida, San Francisco, Phoenix, Boston, Hawaii, and the Caribbean. It not only offers low-cost tickets, even at the last minute, but you may

purchase one-way tickets and will never have to stay over a Saturday night. It also gives special senior fares to passengers 62 or older on all flights at all times, although the savings vary according to market conditions. Senior fares are not available online and must be reserved by phone.
For information: 800-435-9282; www.ata.com.

CONTINENTAL AIRLINES

Continental, having forsaken its coupons and senior club, still offers a few good deals for travelers 65 and over. First, there are special senior fares on most domestic routes. These give you a savings of approximately 10 percent off the lowest available 14-day advance-purchase fares. On international routes, a discount of about 10 percent comes off all fares, again for those 65-plus. Both may be booked by telephone or online.

Finally, a lifetime membership in Continental's Presidents Club, its airport lounges, costs those over 62 less than half of the regular fee. Join and you can wait for your departures in comfort.
For information: 800-525-0280; www.continental.com. For the Continental Presidents Club, call 800-322-2640.

DELTA AIRLINES

Delta once offered wonderful privileges to senior travelers but no more. Its special discounts, senior coupons, and senior clubs are gone. You may, however, find that Delta sometimes offers some nice low promotional fares available to everybody.
For information: 800-221-1212; www.delta.com.

FRONTIER AIRLINES

This affordable airline, with service to 40 cities from its Denver hub, has not only not cut back on its offers to seniors, but has made them a little better. It gives passengers age 62 and older and a travel companion a discount of 10 percent off the lowest available fare, even on its Web fares that are generally the lowest. Frontier, which has one of the youngest fleets today and features live TV on many of its aircraft, has no Saturday-night stay requirement and does not charge for same-day standby on earlier flights. You will get your discount whether you book by telephone or online.

For information: 800-432-1359; www.frontierairlines.com.

GREAT PLAINS AIRLINES

A new regional jet airline based in Tulsa, Great Plains offers the only direct jet service to several midsize cities, currently Tulsa, Nashville, Oklahoma City, Colorado Springs, Albuquerque, and Washington, D.C., and through an affiliate, Durango and Alamogordo. One class with a simplified fare structure, it sells one-way tickets with no round-trip requirements on its 32-seat jets and charges only $25 for changes made 72 hours or more before departure. Great Plains has a special lower fare for children younger than 12 who travel with an adult. And what's more, it takes 10 percent off the cost for passengers 62 and over on the lowest available fares.

For information: 866-929-8646; www.gpair.com.

HAWAIIAN AIR

Passengers over the age of 60 and their younger companions are offered special flat-rate senior fares that are about 10

percent less than the normal excursion fares on flights from West Coast cities to Hawaii. These fares are the best you can get except for the occasional promotional seat sale. Seniors also get 10 percent off the published (nonpromotional) rates for the Hawaiian Island Pass that allows unlimited 5- to 15-day travel between the islands.
For information: 800-367-5320; www.hawaiianair.com.

HORIZON AIR

A regional airline, Horizon Air serves 42 western destinations from Alberta to Arizona. It offers a 10 percent discount on most fares—sometimes even on seasonal sales or Web fares—to travelers 62 or older and a companion of any age. And, occasionally, it also has special senior fares that may be even better, so if you are 62, always ask what's available for you.
For information: 800-547-9308; www.horizonair.com.

MIDWEST EXPRESS

Midwest Express, one of the few carriers that still offer senior discounts, caters to upscale travelers and flies out of Milwaukee to many cities around the country. The new flat-rate senior fare is different from those of all of the other airlines because you can get the discount at age 55. The fare applies to 14-day advance-purchase flights and requires a Saturday-night stay. It also allows a maximum stay of 180 days, handy for customers who spend extended time away from home. At this writing, it is not available online but requires a telephone call.
For information: 800-452-2022; www.midwestexpress.com.

NORTHWEST AIRLINES

At age 65, you become eligible for Northwest Airlines' Senior Fare for flights within the U.S. or to Canada, Mexico, or the Caribbean. This fare is priced at about 10 percent less than the standard leisure fares and allows a stay for up to 180 days, a bonus for snowbirds and others who like to go somewhere and stay put for a while.

A lifetime membership in Northwest's World Club costs people who are 62 or more just half of what it costs their younger friends and relatives. Join as an individual or with a spouse.

For information: 800-225-2525 for domestic flights, 800-447-4747 for international flights; www.nwa.com. Northwest Airlines World Club, 800-692-3788.

SOUTHWEST AIRLINES

Southwest Airlines, a low-cost carrier known for its bargain fares, flies coast to coast to and from 58 cities. It offers even better bargains—discounted 20 to 70 percent off full fare and capped at $129 each way—on every flight, every day of the week, to people who are 65 or older. There are few restrictions on tickets, which are fully refundable, exchangeable, and changeable. Advance booking isn't required (meaning you won't have to pay exorbitant last-minute rates), and you may buy a one-way or round-trip ticket. All seats are coach. Senior fares vary from city to city and change frequently, however, and the number of senior seats is limited on each flight, so reserve your passage as early as possible.

Keep in mind though that sometimes the regular advance-purchase fares are even less expensive than the senior fares, so check them out too. And remember that they have more restrictions. For example, these tickets are not refundable.

The bad news is that few long-haul flights are nonstop, no meals are served, the senior fares are not available to younger travel companions, and the senior fares are not available online.

For information: 800-435-9792; www.southwest.com.

UNITED AIRLINES

UAL has discontinued its former good deals, such as coupons and the 10 percent discount on almost all fares for 62-plus passengers. Replacing them are its special senior rates for travelers 65 or older that offer 10 percent off 14-day advance-purchase fares. The good news is that the maximum stay has been extended to 180 days.

Meanwhile, the United Airlines Silver Wings Plus program is still flourishing. Join the club at age 55 or over, and you can get periodic zone-based fares that are usually better than other available rates. A two-year membership costs $75, or you may join for life for $225. Members ages 55 through 61 may fly a total of 8 round trips per year on United at the special rates, while those 62 or more may fly 16 round trips a year. Each may fly with a travel companion of any age at the same cost.

The special zone-based fares are especially useful on flights to and from small cities that are usually bypassed by fare sales.

Other benefits include offers of discounted vacation packages, cruises, hotel deals, and rental-car discounts and upgrades.

For information: 800-241-6522; www.united.com. For United Silver Wings Plus, call 800-720-1765; www.silver wingsplus.com.

US AIRWAYS

Fifty is the magic age at US Airways because the airline's AARP Savers fares are offered exclusively to members. The fares, which may save you a significant sum, are zone-based and used for travel within the U.S. and to Canada, the Caribbean, and Europe plus special weekend rates on the US Airways Shuttle that flies between New York, Boston, and Washington, D.C. To purchase tickets for yourself and one travel companion, you must contact the US Airways reservation center at 866-886-2277 at least 14 days in advance of travel and be ready to present your membership number. Reservations are not available online or through travel agents.

A Saturday-night stay is required, and there are some blackout dates around major holidays, but there is no maximum stay and you earn mileage credits for your flights. Peak fares are slightly higher than off-peak (Monday through Thursday). The special fares for the Shuttle are valid for travel all day Saturday and until 3 P.M. Sunday.

US Airways also has its own Senior Fares to offer you at age 65 on 14-day advance-purchase fares. These vary by the season and the market and may or may not be better than the AARP Savers fares. And neither may be better than the airline's seasonal promotional sale fares.

So here's the bottom line. Before booking a flight, check out the Senior Fares, the AARP Savers Fares, and any available promotional fares.

For information: 800-428-4322; www.usairways.com. Call 866-886-2277 for AARP Savers Fares.

US AIRWAYS SHUTTLE

On the US Airways Shuttle that operates round trips between New York LaGuardia, Boston Logan, and Reagan Washington National Airports, mature travelers have two ways to save. First, if you're a member of AARP, you and a companion can get special weekend rates that are valid for travel all day Saturday and until 3 P.M. on Sunday.

Second, you can take advantage of the Senior Fares offered at age 65. With them, you may fly off-peak weekdays between 10 A.M. and 2 P.M., and 7 P.M. and midnight, Monday through Friday and anytime on Saturday and Sunday. Again, check the fares against one another and with the regular fares to see which is lower.

For information: 800-428-4322; www.usairways.com. For the AARP Savers Fares, call 866-886-2277.

GOOD DEALS IN CANADA

AIR CANADA

If you are over 60, you and a travel mate are eligible for a 10 percent reduction on all fares, including sale fares, for Air Canada flights within Canada and from Canada to more than 150 international destinations in Europe and Asia. The discount also applies to trips from the U.S. to the U.K. However, it has been discontinued on flights between the U.S. and Canada. Air Canada, the largest carrier between the two countries, operates about 500 nonstop flights daily between 59 U.S. and 8 Canadian cities.

Air Canada has just introduced Tango, its low-fare, no-frills service offering nonstop flights between major Canadian cities and to Fort Lauderdale and Orlando.
For information: 888-247-2262; www.aircanada.ca.

GOOD DEALS ON FOREIGN AIRLINES

Always inquire about special senior discounts when you book your flights. Many foreign airlines offer a 10 percent discount to passengers at age 60 or 62 on transatlantic flights originating in the U.S., although a younger companion may not always be entitled to the same deal. Many foreign carriers will also give you a break on domestic flights within a nation's borders or to other nearby countries. Remember that seasonal promotional fares that are available to travelers of all ages may be lower than the senior fare, so be sure to do your homework before committing yourself.

AEROLINEAS ARGENTINAS

On this airline, passengers over the age of 62 and a companion of any age are offered a 10 percent discount on posted fares for flights originating in the U.S. to its South American destinations.
For information: 800-333-0276; www.aeroargentinas.com.

AEROMEXICO

Mexico's largest airline, Aeromexico flies to 80 destinations in the U.S. and Canada, six countries in Europe and South America, and 43 cities in Mexico. It gives passengers 62-plus and a younger traveling companion a 10 percent discount off all fares (except discounted and promotional fares) on all of its international routes. On most flights within Mexico, you and a younger companion can get the same deal at age 60.

For information: 800-237-6639; www.aeromexico.com.

AIR JAMAICA

Fly to Jamaica or about 15 other Caribbean destinations from the U.S., and take advantage of Air Jamaica's 10 percent discount for passengers 60 and over and a companion at least 18 years old. The discount applies to all classes and published fares except for discounted sale fares.

For information: 800-523-5585; www.airjamaica.com.

AUSTRIAN AIRLINES

The Austrian Airlines Group, which includes Austrian Airlines, Tyrolean Airways, and Lauda Air, serves 195 destinations worldwide. On its daily two-class, nonstop service to Vienna and 30 onward cities in Central and Eastern Europe from its gateway cities, New York, Montreal, Toronto, and Washington, D.C., it offers a 10 percent discount to passengers 62 and over—and a travel companion of any age—on all but promotional sale fares on flights across the Atlantic.

In addition, on domestic flights within Austria, passengers age 60 or over can get special senior fares that vary throughout the year.

Austrian Airlines has one more offer to make—Star Alliance European Airpass travel coupons that are sold together with round-trip tickets from the U.S. or Canada to Vienna. The coupons offer deep discounts on economy-class travel to 41 countries within Europe, Russia, and the Russian Federation.

For information: 800-843-0002 in the U.S.; 888-817-4444 in Canada; www.austrianair.com.

BWIA WEST INDIES AIRWAYS

If you are at least 62 years old, a 10 percent discount is yours on most fares from the U.S. and Canada. The same discount applies to a younger companion.

For information: 800-538-2942; www.bwee.com.

CATHAY PACIFIC AIRWAYS

This airline's senior-friendly "Worry Free" fares are a very good deal if you have turned 55. For you and a travel companion, they take about 15 percent off the regular fare on economy-class transpacific flights through Hong Kong to one of nine Southeast Asian destinations. But just as important, Cathay Pacific, unlike other airlines, allows you to change your date of travel at any time, free of charge, and to cancel your reservation with a full refund.

Tickets must be purchased online and can be made in as little as four days in advance of travel. The 55-plus fares apply to flights from Los Angeles, San Francisco, and New York, as well as New York to Vancouver, B.C.

The offer doesn't end there. When you travel on a Worry Free Fare, you can also take advantage of special hotel rates that will save you about 50 percent off regular rates at five Regal Hotels International in Hong Kong.

Cathay Pacific, by the way, is a Hong Kong–based airline that flies to 30 countries and territories around the world.

For information: 800-233-2742; www.cathay-usa.com/55 plus. For Regal Hotels International, call 800-222-8888.

CAYMAN AIRWAYS

This small airline that flies from Miami, Tampa, or Houston to the Cayman Islands will take 10 percent off some fares for you and a younger travel mate too if you are 62.
For information: 800-422-9626; www.caymanairways.com.

EL AL ISRAEL AIRLINES

El Al, Israel's national airline, flies four times more weekly nonstop flights to Israel from the U.S. than any other airline. It offers passengers over 60 and their spouses over 55 special senior fares that represent a 15 percent discount off the regular or super apex fares between the two countries.

Look into El Al's Israel Milk and Honey Vacation packages and others, available only with a transatlantic ticket from the U.S.
For information: 800-223-6700; www.elal.com. For El Al packages, call 800-EL-AL-SUN (352-5786).

FINNAIR

On flights between Finnair's U.S. and Canadian gateway cities and Helsinki, you and a companion of any age get a discount of 10 percent on most transatlantic fares if you are 62 or older. You'll get an even better discount—a whopping 75 percent or thereabouts—off the cost of flights within Finland, but you must be 65 for this privilege and pay for your tickets within three days of booking your flight.
For information: 800-950-5000; www.finnair.com.

IBERIA AIRLINES OF SPAIN

If you are 62 years old, Iberia gives you and a companion 10 percent off most published nonsale fares for round-trip transatlantic flights originating in North America and within Europe if your travel originates here.
For information: 800-772-4642; www.iberia.com.

LUFTHANSA GERMAN AIRLINES

Once you've turned 60, Lufthansa offers you and a travel mate over the age of 18 a discount of 10 percent off most fares across the Atlantic to Germany or its other European destinations. The same discount applies to domestic travel as well if it is booked at the same time as your international flights.
For information: 800-645-3880; www.lufthansa-usa.com.

MARTINAIR HOLLAND

On Martinair's flights from Orlando and Miami to Amsterdam, travelers over the age of 60 and their younger companions pay 10 percent less for all fares except for already discounted promotional sales. On flights from Florida to Costa Rica, those 55 and older get the same deal. The discount also applies to Canadian passengers, again at age 60, and their younger travel mates when they fly to Amsterdam from Vancouver, Toronto, Calgary, or Edmonton.
For information: 800-MARTINAIR (627-8462); www.martinairusa.com.

MEXICANA AIRLINES

On international flights between the U.S. or Canada and Mexico, Mexicana takes 10 percent off most published fares for passengers who are at least 62 and travel companions. It

does the same for domestic flights within Mexico that are reserved in the U.S. at the same time.
For information: 800-531-7921; www.mexicana.com.

OLYMPIC AIRWAYS

The national airline of Greece, Olympic Airways gives passengers over the age of 65 and an accompanying travel companion of any age a 10 percent discount on most nonsale fares on flights from New York to Athens.
For information: 800-223-1226; www.olympic-airways.gr.

SCANDINAVIAN AIRLINES SYSTEM (SAS)

On flights across the Atlantic from gateway cities in the U.S. to Scandinavian countries or other international destinations, SAS passengers age 62 and older (but no companions) get a 10 percent discount on most fares.

On domestic flights within Denmark and Sweden, SAS offers special senior fares too, depending on the route, but this time for those 65 or older.
For information: 800-221-2350; www.scandinavian.net.

SWISS

This brand-new airline offers a 10 percent discount to passengers who are 62 or more and a travel companion of any age. The discount is applied to nonsale fares on transatlantic flights from the U.S. to its many European destinations.
For information: 877-FLY-SWISS (359-7947); www.swiss.com.

TAP AIR PORTUGAL

TAP, Portugal's national airline that serves 30 cities worldwide, gives travelers over the age of 62 a 10 percent discount on most nonpromotional transatlantic fares originating in the U.S. The same discount applies for one traveling companion, any age.

For information: 800-221-7370; www.tapairportugal.pt.

VIRGIN ATLANTIC AIRWAYS

Turn 60 and Virgin Atlantic gives you and a companion of any age a 10 percent discount on all published nonsale fares for flights between the U.S. and London.

If you belong to AARP you may save more—10 to 25 percent, depending on the season—on all advance-purchase fares or higher economy fares from the U.S. to London. On sale fares, the discount is 5 percent. Present your membership card when you check in for your flight.

In addition, as an AARP member, you and a companion can save $25 to $50 on air-inclusive packages and $75 on a transatlantic voyage on the *Queen Elizabeth 2*.

For information: 800-862-8621; www.virgin.com/atlantic. For vacation packages, 888-YES-Virgin (937-8474); www.virgin.com.vacations.

4

Hotels and Motels: Get Your Over-50 Markdowns

Now that you're over 50, you'll never have to pay full price for a hotel room again. Across the U.S. and Canada and often in the rest of the world today, virtually all lodging chains and most individual establishments go out of their way to give you a break on room rates.

You don't even have to wait until you're eligible for Social Security to cash in on your maturity because most hotels, inns, and motels offer discounts to you at age 50, usually requiring only proof of age or membership in a senior organization. Often the best discounts, sometimes as high as 50 percent, however, are reserved at some hotel chains for members of their own senior travel clubs. Some cost little or nothing to join; others charge a yearly fee.

What all this means is that you should *never* make a lodging reservation without making sure you are getting a special rate—a senior discount of at least 10 percent or an even better deal, such as a promotional sale rate or a corporate or weekend rate that is lower. Always inquire about a senior discount, whether or not one is posted or mentioned in the hotel's literature, and then ask if a better rate is available.

The only bad news is that some senior hotel discounts aren't as generous as they were a few years ago. Even so, dozens of hotel chains and thousands of individual hotels continue to use price incentives to attract mature travelers. It makes excellent sense to take advantage of them whenever you can.

But, first, keep in mind:

If you want to use the privileges coming to you because of your age, you must do some advance research and planning with your travel agent or on your own.

- In this rapidly changing world, rates and policies can be altered in a flash, so an update is always advisable.
- Information about discounts is seldom volunteered. In most cases, you must arrange for them when you make your reservations and confirm them when you check in. Do not wait until you're settling your bill because then it might be too late. Some hotels and motels require that you make advance reservations to get their discounts. "Advance" may mean a considerable period of time such as three weeks, but it may also mean only a week, a day, or even a few hours. Check it out before making your plans.

- Although many senior discounts are available every day of the year, some are subject to "space availability." This means it may be hard to get them when you want to travel because only a limited number of rooms may be reserved for special rates. If these are already booked (or are expected to be booked), you won't get your discount. And some hotels have "blackout" dates during special events or holiday periods when the discount is not available. So always book early, ask for your discount privileges, and try to be flexible on your dates in order to take advantage of them. Your best bets for space are usually weekends in large cities, weekdays at resorts, and nonholiday seasons.
- It's quite possible that a special promotional rate, especially off-peak or on weekends, might save you more money than your senior discount. Many hotels, particularly in big cities and warm climates, cut their prices drastically in the summer, for example. Others that cater mostly to businesspeople during the week try to encourage weekend traffic by offering bargain rates if you stay over a Saturday night. Resorts are often eager to fill their rooms on weekdays. So always investigate all the possibilities before you get too enthusiastic about using your hard-earned senior discount, and always ask for the *lowest available rate.*
- When you travel in other countries, remember that your senior discount is valid at participating foreign locations of many major American hotel chains, such as Best Western, Choice Hotels International, Hilton Hotels, Holiday Inn, Marriott, Radisson, and Sheraton.

- Several chains of no-frills budget motels might not offer discounts or too much in the way of amenities but do charge very low room rates and tend to be located along the most-traveled routes.
- If you are traveling with children or grandchildren, remember that at many hotels, children under a specified age, usually 16 or 18, may stay in your room for free. And at some big chains, they may eat free, too.
- In some cases, not every hotel or inn in a chain will offer the discount. Those that do are called "participating" hotels or motels. Make sure the one you are planning to visit is participating in the senior plan.
- In addition to the chains, many independent hotels and inns are eager for your business and offer special reduced rates. Always *ask* before making a reservation. Your travel agent should be able to help you with this.
- Some hotel restaurants will give you a discount, too, whether or not you are a registered guest.
- By the way, your discount usually applies only to the regular rates and, in most cases, will not be given on top of other special discounts. One discount is usually all you get.

AMERIHOST INN

These new-construction economy hotels across the country, all with indoor swimming pools, give a discount of 10 to 30 percent off the room rates to members of AARP, CARP and all other guests age 60 or over. Continental breakfast is included.

For information: 800-434-5800; www.amerihost.com.

AMERISUITES

All of these all-suite hotels with indoor pools throughout the U.S. give members of AARP and CARP a discount of 15 percent on the regular room rates every day of the year. Buffet breakfast is included.

For information: 800-833-1516; www.amerisuites.com.

ASTON HAWAII

At properties that range from economy hotels to luxury condominium resorts located on four of Hawaii's major islands, Aston Hawaii gives a savings or up to 25 percent off the regular room rates to guests who are 50 or over. To qualify for the 50+ Rates program, at least one guest per room must be the specified age. An additional privilege is a seventh night free at many participating properties.

For information: 800-922-7866; www.astonhotels.com.

BAYMONT INNS & SUITES

Baymont Inns & Suites operates more than 190 affordable properties throughout the Midwest, South, and eastern parts of the country, most of them located near shopping areas, restaurants, and entertainment. Guests who are over 55 get a 10 percent discount, and AARP members get the same privilege at age 50. A free breakfast buffet is included.

For information: 877-BAYMONT (229-6668); www.baymontinns.com.

BEST INNS & SUITES

At these economy inns scattered across the country, the Best Guest Silver Edition Program gives guests over 50 a discount

of 10 percent on the regular rates. Join the Best Traveler Program too and you'll get a tenth night free after staying at any Best Inn for nine nights.
For information: 800-237-8466; www.bestinn.com.

BEST WESTERN INTERNATIONAL

If you're 55 (50 in Australia) or you belong to AARP or CARP, you get a discount of at least 10 percent off the regular rates any day of the year at all 2,400 Best Westerns in North America and many of the 1,700 elsewhere in the world. You may even be offered other special privileges such as late checkout, complimentary upgrades, and continental breakfast.
For information: 800-WESTERN (937-8376); www.bestwestern.com.

BUDGET HOST INNS

A network of about 180 mostly family-owned economy inns in the U.S. and Canada, almost all Budget Host Inns offer senior discounts—usually 10 percent off the regular rates—that vary by location. Call the toll-free reservation number and you will be transferred directly to the front desk of the inn, where you can ask about the accommodations, facilities, rates, discounts, and directions to the property.
For information: 800-283-4678; www.budgethost.com.

CAMBERLEY HOTELS

These three historic luxury hotels in elegantly restored landmark buildings are located in Atlanta, Louisville, and Abingdon, Virginia. They offer special packages sure to intrigue

AMERICAN EXPRESS SENIOR CARD

The major benefit of the American Express Senior Member Card, designed specifically for people 62 or over, is a reduction in the yearly fee—$35 for a standard card or $55 for a Gold Senior Member Card—along with the usual charge privileges and customer services. Other benefits are a quarterly newsletter; savings on travel, shopping, and dining; and a 24-hour global hotline for emergency assistance on passports and visas, sources of cash, and legal or medical problems.

For information: 800-THE-CARD (843-2273); www.americanexpress.com/senior.

older travelers and a 10 percent discount off the standard rates to AARP members.

For information: 800-555-8000; www.camberleyhotels.com.

CANDLEWOOD SUITES

Grandparents get a novel deal with the Grandparents Stay Free program at all 103 locations of Candlewood Suites, midscale all-suite hotels scattered around the country. It's a two-night stay at half price. If you stay the night before or after a major holiday—Easter, Mother's Day, Father's Day, Memorial Day, Independence Day, Labor Day, Grandparent's Day, Thanksgiving, Christmas, or New Year's Day—you may stay the holiday night for free. Or on your first visit to a Candlewood Suites hotel, you can stay one night and get the next night free. Just be prepared to show a picture of your grandchildren.

No grandchildren? Just announce that you're over 50 and you'll get a 10 percent discount.

For information: 888-CANDLEWOOD (226-3539); www.candlewoodsuites.com.

CASTLE RESORTS & HOTELS

Castle's 18 hotels and resort condominiums in Hawaii, Saipan, and New Zealand offer guests 50 and over a discount of up to 25 percent off the regular rates every day of the year as well as special rates on rental cars.

For information: 800-367-5004; www.castleresorts.com.

CHOICE HOTELS INTERNATIONAL

Among the better deals at major hotels are those offered by Choice Hotels, an international group of about 4,500 locations in 47 countries with brand names that include MainStay Suites, Sleep Inn, Comfort Suites, Comfort Inn, Quality Inn, Suites and Hotels, Clarion Hotel, Econo Lodge, and Rodeway Inn. All of them take catering to older travelers very seriously, and most give you a choice of three options.

The Sixty-Plus Rate entitles you to savings of 20 to 30 percent when you book your room in advance and request the rate at a participating hotel anywhere in the world. Call their toll-free number to make reservations.

The Fifty-Plus Rate is available every day of the year, with advance reservations or not, in all hotels if the Sixty-Plus Rate is not available at your chosen hotel or you are over 50. It takes 10 percent off the room rate.

AARP members are eligible for a 15 percent discount at all eight brands of Choice Hotels. Just ask for it and be prepared to show your membership card at check-in.

Most of the hotels include complimentary continental breakfast and two brands, Econo Lodge and Rodeway Inns, have designed special senior rooms.
For information: 800-4-CHOICE (424-6423); www.choice hotels.com.

CITADINES APARTMENT HOTELS

If you belong to AARP and make advance reservations, you'll save at least 10 percent on the regular rates when you choose one of these studio or one- or two-bedroom apartments throughout France, and in several other European countries, all with kitchens, linens, and weekly maid service.
For information: 800-755-8266 or 212-688-9467; www .apartmenthotels.com.

CLARION HOTELS, SUITES & RESORTS

See Choice Hotels International. These moderately priced full-service hotels, 150 of them in 15 countries, have special rooms for business travelers and others designed for families. Almost all have swimming pool and/or exercise facilities as well as restaurants and room service.
For information: 800-4-CHOICE (424-6423); www.choice hotels.com.

COMFORT INNS & COMFORT SUITES

See Choice Hotels International. You can find Comforts all over the world, all of them offering reasonable rates and comfortable lodgings. Most provide complimentary continental breakfast, swimming pools, or exercise facilities. Comfort Suites feature separate living and sleeping areas with sleeper sofa and oversize baths.

For information: 800-4-CHOICE (434-6423); www.choice hotels.com.

CONRAD HOTELS

See Hilton Hotels. A subsidiary of Hilton Hotels, many Conrad Hotels in Europe, Australia, Hong Kong, Egypt, Singapore, Turkey, Uruguay, and the Caribbean participate in Hilton's Senior HHonors Worldwide program for over-60s. Members are entitled to up to 50 percent off the regular room rates and 20 percent off the bill for dinner for two.
For information: 800-HILTONS (445-8667); www.hilton .com.

COUNTRY HEARTH INNS

Most of these deluxe economy motels in the South and Mid-west take 10 percent off the room rates for visitors over 50.
For information: 800-848-5767; www.countryhearth.com.

COUNTRY INNS & SUITES BY CARLSON

With more than 300 locations worldwide, mostly in the U.S. Southeast and Midwest, these inns with traditional architecture are designed to have the ambience of a bed-and-breakfast. At all of them you will get at least 10 percent off the regular rates if you are at least 50. A complimentary breakfast is included.
For information: 800-456-4000; www.countryinns.com.

COURTYARD BY MARRIOTT

If you're 62 or older, you'll get 15 percent off the regular room rates every day of the year at participating locations of these moderately priced hotels, most of which feature swimming pools and exercise facilities. Advance reservations are recommended.

For information: 800-321-2211; www.courtyard.com.

CROSS COUNTRY INNS

If you check in at one of these inns located in Ohio, Kentucky, and Michigan, you will get a discount of 25 percent on the regular room rates every day of the year, but you must be at least 60.

For information: 800-621-1429; www.crosscountryinns.com.

CROWNE PLAZA HOTELS & RESORTS

Any day of the year, Crowne Plaza offers members of AARP a 15 percent discount off the regular room rates at participating locations, subject to space availability. A collection of approximately 180 upscale accommodations that are located in 40 countries around the world, these hotels and resorts are designed to cater especially to business travelers, providing business centers, fitness rooms, along with meeting rooms.

For information: 800-227-6963; www.crowneplaza.com.

DAYS INNS WORLDWIDE

Join the September Days Club, free to travelers at age 50 and their spouses or companions, and you'll get discounts of 15 to 50 percent off the regular room rates at all 1,930 of the moderately priced Days Inns all over the world. Other benefits include special offers on car rentals, tours, cruises, and airline tickets. A quarterly newsletter keeps you up to date.

If you aren't a member of the September Days Club but are 60-plus or belong to any senior organization, you're offered a discount of 10 percent on standard room rates.
For information: 800-DAYS-INN (329-7466); www.daysinn.com. For details or to enroll in the September Days Club, call 800-241-5050.

DELTA HOTELS

Delta Hotels, Canada's largest first-class hotel company, with more than 40 properties across the country, is a subsidiary of Fairmont Hotels and Resorts. It offers members of CARP a discount of 10 percent off the best available room rate.
For information: 800-268-1133; www.deltahotels.com.

DOUBLETREE HOTELS & GUEST SUITES

At all Doubletrees, now part of the Hilton Hotels family, ask for the 10 percent discount on the best available room rates for guests 50 and over. It's yours anytime, any day, no advance reservations required. Not only that, but you get the same discount on food and nonalcoholic beverages at participating Doubletree restaurants while you are hotel guests.
For information: 800-222-8733; www.doubletreehotels.com.

DOWNTOWNER INNS

See Red Carpet Inn. 800-874-7798; www.bookroomsnow.com

DRURY INNS

Concentrated in the Midwest and the South, these inexpensive hotels offer about 10 percent off the rates. You must be at least 50 to qualify and have proof of age handy. A free breakfast is included.

For information: 800-DRURYINN (325-8300); www.drury inn.com.

ECONO LODGE

See Choice Hotels International. In addition to three varieties of senior discounts, these affordable hotels feature special accommodations for older travelers. Its "senior rooms" feature bright lighting, large-button telephones and TV remote controls, easy-to-read alarm clocks, and grab bars in the bathroom.

For information: 800-4-CHOICE (424-6423); www.choice hotels.com.

EMBASSY SUITES HOTELS

At participating Embassy Suites Hotels, now part of the Hilton family, guests who are over the age of 50 will receive a 10 percent discount off the regular rates on their two-room suites. Embassy offers amenities such as a free cooked-to-order breakfast each morning and guests can enjoy a Manager's Reception with hors d'oeuvres and beverages every evening.

For information: 800-EMBASSY (362-2779); www.embassy -suites.com.

EXEL INNS

A small group of budget motels in the Midwest, most Exel Inns offer a 10 percent discount to guests who are 55 and over.

For information: 800-356-8013; www.exelinns.com.

FAIRFIELD INN BY MARRIOTT

At Marriott's midprice lodging chain, you will get 15 percent off the regular room rate if you are 62 or older. A continental breakfast is included.

For information: 800-322-4000; www.fairfieldinn.com.

FAIRMONT HOTELS & RESORTS

These grand hotels and resorts, 37 of them including the elegant Canadian Pacific Hotels, are located throughout Canada, the U.S., Bermuda, Mexico, Dubai, and Barbados and give 50-plus travelers a fairly substantial break. AARP members will receive a 25 percent discount off the sell rate of the day. Members of CARP are entitled to a 20 percent discount off of Fairmont's regular bed-and-breakfast rates of the day.

Many of these luxury hotels also design off-peak, three-night almost-all-inclusive packages for older travelers. Recent offerings at Fairmont Jasper Park Lodge, for example, have included the Senior Fall Getaway, the Seniors Christmas Festival, and the Seniors Spring Fling.

For information: 800-441-1414; www.fairmont.com.

FOUR POINTS HOTELS BY SHERATON

At any Four Points, full-service hotels with affordable prices in 15 countries, members of AARP can get a discount of up to 50 percent off the regular rates when they make a nonrefundable reservation for a stay that includes a Thursday, Friday, or Saturday arrival. Without an advance purchase, the discount is 15 to 20 percent off.

For information: 800-325-3535; www.fourpoints.com.

HAMPTON INN & SUITES

These moderately priced hotels and suites, now part of the Hilton family of hotels, have more than a thousand locations in the U.S., Canada, and Latin America. When you make a reservation, ask for the AARP discount that gives you 10 percent off the best rate available. A breakfast buffet is included, and many of the hotels have swimming pools and exercise facilities.

For information: 800-HAMPTON (426-7866); www.hampton-inn.com.

HAWAIIAN HOTELS & RESORTS

There's good news for travelers over the age of 50 at three full-service oceanfront resorts in Hawaii. At both the Royal Lahaina Beach Resort on Maui and the Kauai Coconut Beach Resort on Kauai, the deal is a 50 percent discount on rooms. The Royal Kona Resort on the Big Island offers special discounted rooms with a partial ocean view that includes breakfast. Ask for the 50-plus specials when you make reservations.

For information: 800-22-ALOHA (222-5642); www.hawaiihotels.com.

HAWTHORN SUITES HOTELS

Although there is no official senior discount at these upscale suites-hotels designed for extended stays, many properties do offer a 10 percent savings to older travelers. So ask when you are making a reservation. Each suite includes kitchen facilities and offers a hot buffet breakfast daily.

For information: 800-527-1133; www.hawthorn.com.

HILTON GARDEN INN

These smaller, more intimate and affordable Hiltons located in small cities, major suburban areas, or convenient to airports, all have swimming pools, restaurants, complimentary breakfast, business centers, and free parking. And they all offer the Senior HHonors Club (see Hilton Hotels) that gives its members up to 50 percent off the regular room rate and 20 percent off the bill for dinner for two. You may join at age 60.

Guests without membership get a 10 to 15 percent discount at age 50 just by asking for it.

For information: 800-HILTONS (445-8667); www.hiltongardeninn.com.

HILTON HOTELS

If you're over 60 and do a lot of traveling, an outstanding deal is waiting for you at Hilton Hotels. If you join Senior HHonors, Hilton's travel club, you'll get up to half off the regular rates at more than 450 participating Hiltons and Conrad Hotels in 55 countries worldwide. The cost for annual membership for you and a spouse or other companion, is $55 in the U.S., $75 elsewhere for the first year. Renewal will then become $40 a year in this country and $60 elsewhere.

Other privileges come with membership in the club. You may reserve a second room for family and friends at the same discounted rate when they travel with you. Eat in participating hotel restaurants and 20 percent will come off the bill for dinner for two, whether you are a guest of the hotel or merely dropping in. And you will have free access to the health club facilities.

As a member of the club, you're automatically enrolled in Hilton HHonors, a frequent-stay program, and earn points and miles when you stay in Hiltons, Conrads, and the other brands that belong to this family of hotels: Doubletree, Embassy Suites Hotels, Hampton Inn, and Homewood Suites.

If you don't join the club but are over the age of 50, you'll get a discount of 10 to 15 percent off the regular rates at participating hotels just by asking for it.

For information: 800-HILTONS (445-8667); www.hilton.com. To enroll in Hilton Senior HHonors Worldwide, call 800-548-8690.

HISTORIC HOTELS OF AMERICA

All of these landmark hotels are independently owned and differ on their policies on discounts for seniors, but most give visitors over the age of 50 a 10 percent discount and some offer even more.

Historic Hotels of America is a program of the National Trust for Historic Preservation that has identified 185 hotels that have maintained their historic integrity, architecture, and ambience. They must be at least 50 years old, listed in or eligible for the National Register of Historic Places, or recognized locally as having historic significance. A directory of members can be purchased for $4.00 by sending a check to the address that follows.

For information: Call each hotel directly. Or contact National Trust Historic Hotels of America, 1785 Massachusetts Ave. NW, Washington, DC 20036; 800-678-8946 or www.historichotels.org.

HOLIDAY INN HOTELS & RESORTS

At all 1,500-or-so participating Holiday Inns around the world, and 1,350 Holiday Inn Express locations, members of AARP get 10 percent off nondiscounted room rates every day of the year. The privilege is subject, of course, to space availability. Kids under 12 stay and eat free at all locations in the U.S. and Canada.

For information: 800-HOLIDAY (465-4329); www.holiday-inn.com.

HOMEWOOD SUITES BY HILTON

At participating Homewood Suites by Hilton throughout the U.S., guests age 50 or over get up to 10 percent discount off the regular room rates. Accommodations are one- or two-bedroom suites with fully equipped kitchens. Among the amenities are a free breakfast every day and an evening Manager's Reception with hors d'oeuvres and beverages Monday through Thursday.

For information: 800-CALL HOME (225-5466); www.homewood-suites.com.

HOWARD JOHNSON INTERNATIONAL

At participating Howard Johnson lodging locations in the U.S. and Canada, guests who are over the age of 55 are offered a 15 percent discount on the room rates, while for members of AARP and CARP it's a discount of 15 to 30 percent. The privileges are available at Howard Johnson Inns, Express Inns, and Hotels, as well as at Plaza Hotels.

For information: 800-I-GO-HOJO (446-4656); www.howardjohnson.com.

HYATT HOTELS & RESORTS

A collection of upscale hotels in the U.S., Canada, and the Caribbean, Hyatt offers guests over the age of 62 a special senior rate that varies from property to property. Remember to ask for it when you make a reservation.

For information: 800-233-1234; www.hyatt.com.

INNS OF AMERICA

This lodging chain, with 20 motels located near major highways in California and Florida, gives a small discount off the room rates to members of AARP. Just ask for it.

For information: Call 800-826-0778.

INTER-CONTINENTAL HOTELS & RESORTS

Recently acquired by the Six Continents Hotels lodging family, most of the 135 or so upscale Inter-Continentals offer a 10 percent discount off the regular room rates to AARP members. Present your membership card and ask for it.

For information: 800-327-0200; www.intercontinental.com.

KIMPTON BOUTIQUE HOTELS

A unique collection of European-style hotels with top-notch restaurants in San Francisco and many other big cities across the U.S. and Canada, Kimpton Boutique Hotels cater to older travelers by offering senior rates and special packages to guests who are at least 55 or belong to AARP. Some recent specials included the Senior Summer Package at the Monticello Inn in San Francisco, the Fountain of Youth Package at the Hotel Monaco Chicago, and the Pay the Year You Were Born Rate at the Galleria Park Hotel in San Francisco.

For information: 800-KIMPTON (546-7866) or www.kimptongroup.com.

KNIGHTS INNS

Clean, comfortable, and inexpensive, the Knights Inn properties across the U.S. and Canada give a 10 to 30 percent discount on the room rates to members of AARP and CARP and all other guests who are 50 or older.
For information: 800-843-5644; www.knightsinn.com.

LA QUINTA INNS

With more than 300 locations in 33 states, these inns are inexpensive and become even more so when you ask for your 10 percent discount. You'll get it, except during special events, if you are a member of AARP or a similar organization or if you are 55 and can prove it. Continental breakfast and free local calls are included. Check the website for seasonal senior specials.
For information: 800-531-5900; www.laquinta.com.

LOEWS HOTELS

This group of 14 hotels located in major cities in the U.S. and Canada has a senior rate for guests 62-plus that takes 10 percent off all rates. Its Generation G program, offered all year, is a choice of packages created for grandparents and grandchildren on vacation together. One package is designed for teenagers and features suite accommodations, sports and cultural tours, spa treatments, and tickets to events. Another is targeted for adventurous kids age 10 or older, and the third is suitable for all ages and lets you customize your own itinerary. Because each of the hotels is located in a city with its

own unique attractions, the packages vary but always include activities appropriate for both generations. At several of the hotels, a second room may be reserved at reduced rates.
For information: 800-23-LOEWS (235-6397); www.loews hotels.com.

MAINSTAY SUITES

See Choice Hotels International. MainStay Suites offer studio and one-bedroom accommodations designed for extended stays with kitchens, dining, and living areas. Most locations have swimming pools and exercise rooms. Complimentary breakfast is served weekday mornings.
For information: 800-4-CHOICE (424-6423); www.choice hotels.com.

MARC RESORTS

At age 50, a 35 percent discount is yours, subject to availability, at Marc Resorts. This small group of affordable lodgings ranges from luxury condominium resorts to boutique hotels and has 15 locations throughout the Hawaiian islands.
For information: 800-535-0085; www.marcresorts.com.

MARRIOTT HOTELS, RESORTS & SUITES

Marriott's new program for seniors is a simple 15 percent savings on room rates seven days a week for anybody age 62 or older. These properties include Marriott Hotels, Resorts, and Suites; JW Marriott Hotels and Resorts; Renaissance Hotels; Courtyard; Fairfield Inn; Residence Inn; TownePlace Suites; and SpringHill Suites Hotels.
For information: 800-228-9290; www.marriott.com.

MASTER HOSTS INNS & RESORTS

See Red Carpet Inn. 800-874-7798; www.bookroomsnow.com.

MCINTOSH MOTOR INNS

At many of these economy inns in New Jersey, Pennsylvania, and Delaware, guests who are over 50 are offered a 10 percent discount off the regular rates. Continental breakfast is included.

For information: 800-444-2775; www.mcintoshinns.com.

MICROTEL INN & SUITES

At these newly constructed economy hotels, all virtually identical, there is no official senior program, although some of its 270 or so properties offer a small discount to travelers over 50. Special features include interior corridors and a complimentary breakfast every morning.

For information: 888-771-7171; www.microtelinn.com.

MOTEL 6

Take advantage of a 10 percent discount off the room rates at any of these more than 850 pet-friendly economy budget motels in the U.S. and Canada by showing your AARP or CARP card. Save more by going online for periodical bargains.

For information: 800-4-MOTEL6 (466-8356); www.motel6.com.

NOVOTEL HOTELS

Occasionally, these six hotels in the U.S. and Canada feature special senior rates for guests 65 or over that vary with the season and the location.

For information: 800-NOVOTEL (668-6835); www.accorhotels.com.

OCCIDENTAL-ALLEGRO HOTELS & RESORTS

The largest all-inclusive resort company, the Occidental-Allegro group includes Royal Hideaways, Allegro Resorts, Caribbean Villages, Jack Tar Villages, and Occidental Hotels, properties that range from luxury resorts to budget. Located in Costa Rica, Mexico, Dominican Republic, and the Caribbean, all 26 give a 10 to 15 percent discount all year to guests who are 60 years of age or older.
For information: Occidental-Allegro Resorts, 800-858-2258; www.occidental-hoteles.com.

OHANA HOTELS OF HAWAII

Most of these moderately priced hotels and resorts are located in Waikiki with a couple on the Big Island and Maui. They all offer a straightforward 30 percent off the published rates for anybody 55 and over, plus an additional 5 percent for members of AARP. The two properties in Guam give those 55+ a 20 percent discount with AARP members again getting another 5 percent.
For information: 800-462-6262; www.ohanahotels.com.

OMNI HOTELS

Omni Hotels offers luxury accommodations with a wide range of amenities at more than 40 hotels and resorts through the U.S., Canada, and Mexico. All of its locations offer a 10 percent discount off the published room rates every day of the week to guests who are 50 or more.

For information: 800-THE OMNI (843-6664); www.omni hotels.com.

OUTRIGGER HOTELS & RESORTS

Travelers who are 50 and over get a nice discount on the regular room rates at all Outrigger locations. At the company's hotels and resort condominiums in Hawaii, it's 20 to 30 percent off the regular rates with an additional 5 percent for members of AARP and CARP.

At its Pacific properties in the Marshall Islands, Fiji, and Guam, the discount is again 20 percent for anybody at age 50 although AARP members get the extra 5 percent. And finally, in Australia, those same members receive 20 percent off the regular rates.

For information: 800-OUTRIGGER (688-7444); www.outrigger.com.

PARADORES OF SPAIN

See Spain, Chapter 8.

PARK INN & PARK PLAZA HOTELS

These small hotels in the U.S. and Canada give a discount of up to 25 percent to members of AARP.

For information: 800-670-7275; www.parkhtls.com.

PASSPORT INN

See Red Carpet Inn. 800-874-7798; www.bookroomsnow.com.

POUSADAS DE PORTUGAL

See Portugal, Chapter 8.

QUALITY INNS, HOTELS & SUITES

See Choice Hotels International. This group of about 780 lodging options all over the world offers a full range of amenities in addition to the usual Choice Hotels discount. A hot buffet breakfast is one of them, now available in many locations.

For information: 800-4-CHOICE (424-6423); www.choice hotels.com.

RADISSON HOTELS & RESORTS

At Radisson's more than 430 locations in 59 countries, be sure to take advantage of Senior Breaks, a program that gives you a discount of 25 to 40 percent off the standard rates at age 50 in the U.S. and Canada and 65 in Europe and Australia. You'll get the discount year-round, seven days a week, based on space availability except during peak travel periods. There's no club to join—just be sure to carry proof of your age.

In addition, many Radissons all over the world offer you and your party a senior discount on meals in hotel restaurants usually only at off-peak dining hours, whether or not you are guests of the hotel. All you need is proof of your age.

For information: 800-333-3333; www.radisson.com.

RAMADA LIMITED, INN, AND PLAZA HOTELS

Ramada offers several special options to its older guests at participating locations, subject to availability. First, anybody over the age of 60 gets a discount of 15 percent. Second, if guests over 60 are members of Club Ramada, a loyalty club

GOOD DEALS IN RESTAURANTS

Many restaurants offer special deals to people in their prime, but in most cases you must seek them out yourself by reading the menu, asking at the restaurant, or watching the ads in the local newspapers. At some big chains, such as the International House of Pancakes, Kentucky Fried Chicken, Arby's, Applebee's, TCBY, and Wendy's, there's a recommended corporate policy of senior discounts or special senior menus. The same is true for some smaller regional chains such as Country Kitchen, Max & Erma's, Chili's Grill & Bar, Black-Eyed Pea, and Lyon's.

Sometimes a senior discount is available anytime you decide to dine, but often it's good only during certain hours or as "early bird" specials before 5:00 or 6:00 P.M. The eligible age varies from 50 to 65, and occasionally a restaurant requires that you sign up for its free senior club that issues you a membership card.

In addition, a few hotel chains will give you a break on your meal checks when you eat in their restaurants. For example:

At participating **Hilton Hotels** restaurants in the U.S. and Canada, you're entitled to a 20 percent discount on dinners for two, hotel guests or not, if one of you is a member of Hilton's Senior HHonors Worldwide.

Doubletree Hotels & Guest Suites take 10 percent off the bill for food and nonalcoholic beverages in participating restaurants for 50-plus guests of the hotel.

You and your party will get a senior discount on meals eaten during off-peak hours at participating **Radisson Hotels** restaurants, whether or not you are hotel guests. You qualify for the savings at age 50 in U.S. locations and usually at 65 in Europe.

Stop in at a company-owned **Burger King** before 10:30 A.M. and you'll get free coffee if you're a senior. Check yours out—if it's a participating location, you're in luck. Some McDonald's locations will do the same.

that costs nothing to join, they will receive a bigger reduction—25 percent—off the room rates in addition to earning rewards such as points toward airfares, lodging, and tours. And third, if guests belong to AARP or CARP, most Ramada properties in the U.S. and Canada offer them 15 to 30 percent off.

For information: Call 800-2-RAMADA (272-6232) for reservations; www.ramada.com. To enroll in the Club Ramada, call 800-672-6232.

RAMADA INTERNATIONAL HOTELS

Part of the Marriott family, Ramada International is an affordable group of hotels and resorts found in many countries and territories outside the U.S. Most of them give guests over the age of 60 a 10 to 25 percent discount off the cost of accommodations. Reservations are recommended.

For information: 800-854-7854, www.marriott.com.

RED CARPET INN

Almost all of the independently owned affordable inns in the Hospitality International group give guests over the age of 50 a 10 percent discount on the room rates, subject to availability. Most include a complimentary continental breakfast and parking right in front of your door. Located off major highways throughout the U.S. and Canada, they

include Red Carpet Inn, Passport Inn, Downtowner Inns, Master Host Inns, and Scottish Inns.
For information: 800-874-7798; www.bookroomsnow.com.

RED LION HOTELS & INNS

Most of them located in the western and midwestern states, Red Lion Hotels and Red Lion Inns give a 10 to 20 percent discount to members of AARP. Owned by the WestCoast Family of Hotels, they range from upscale full-service hotels to small inns and all-suites properties.
For information: 800-RED-LION (733-5466); www.red lion.com.

RED ROOF INNS

If you belong to AARP, you will be eligible for a 10 percent discount off the regular rates at all of these pet-friendly budget motels all over the country. You can often save even more money by checking out the "Red Hot Deals" on the website where you can find the current specials in some locations. Also, to accumulate points for free nights, you may want to enroll in this brands Redi-Card Preferred Member program.
For information: 800-RED-ROOF (733-7663); www.red roof.com.

RENAISSANCE HOTELS, RESORTS & SUITES

After your 62nd birthday, you're offered a 15 percent discount off the regular weekday and weekend room rates at any of these upscale lodgings in the U.S. and Canada. Ask for it when you make your reservations.

For information: 800-468-3571; www.renaissancehotels.com.

RESIDENCE INN BY MARRIOTT

These long-stay all-suite accommodations complete with kitchens and separate living areas offer guests age 60 or over a 15 percent discount on regular rates every day of the year at participating locations. Complimentary continental breakfast and evening social hours are usually included.
For information: 800-331-3131; www.residenceinn.com.

RODEWAY INNS

See Choice Hotels International. Rodeway Inn features Senior Rooms with bright lighting, grab bars in the bathroom, and large buttons on telephones, remote controls, and alarm clocks. Complimentary continental breakfast is part of the package.
For information: 800-4-CHOICE (434-6423); www.choicehotels.com.

SANDMAN HOTELS

All located in western Canada, this small group of inns takes 25 percent off the regular room rates for guests age 55 or over. Show proof of age at check-in or, better yet, call the toll-free number below and just ask for a 55 Plus Card. It's free.
For information: 800-726-3626; www.sandman.ca.

SCOTTISH INN

See Red Carpet Inn. 800-874-7798; www.bookroomsnow.com.

SHERATON HOTELS, INNS & RESORTS

All Sheratons all over the world offer you an outstanding break if you are a member of AARP. You'll get a 50 percent discount off the regular room rates if you book a visit that includes a Thursday, Friday, or Saturday night and make a nonrefundable reservation at least 21 days in advance. If you can't plan that far ahead, you can count on 15 to 25 percent off on the room rates.

For information: 800-325-3535; www.sheraton.com.

SHILO INNS

Shilo Inns, most located along major highways in western states, gives a 10 percent discount to AARP members and anybody else who is at least 62.

For information: 800-222-2244; www.shiloinns.com.

SLEEP INN

See Choice Hotels International. At these 400 or so hotels throughout the world, amenities include a complimentary continental breakfast and a discount for guests 50 and over.

For information: 800-4-CHOICE (424-6423); www.choice hotels.com.

SONESTA HOTELS & RESORTS

This collection of 16 upscale hotels, no two the same, are built to reflect the culture and scenery of their unique locations in Boston, New Orleans, and Miami, Egypt, Peru, Italy, Bermuda, and Anguilla. Most of them give members of AARP a discount of 15 percent off the regular rates.

For information: 800-SONESTA (766-3782); www.sonesta .com.

SPRINGHILL SUITES BY MARRIOTT

Make a reservation at one of these all-suite, moderately priced hotels and you'll get a 15 percent discount on the regular room rate if you are at least 62. Included in the package are a complimentary continental breakfast and free local phone calls.

For information: 888-287-9400; www.springhillsuites.com.

STAYBRIDGE SUITES BY HOLIDAY INN

Designed for extended stays by travelers who require lodging for at least five consecutive nights, Staybridge Suites offer studios and one- and two-bedroom accommodations complete with kitchen facilities. If you are a member of AARP, be sure to get your 10 percent discount any day of the year, subject to space availability.

For information: 800-238-8000; www.staybridge.com.

SUMMERFIELD SUITES BY WYNDHAM

A collection of 38 upscale all-suite properties, all of Summerfield's one- or two-bedroom suites have a full kitchen, a separate living room, and a private bathroom per bedroom. Included are a buffet breakfast and a social hour on weekday evenings. If you belong to AARP, ask for your 20 percent discount on the best available rate, subject to availability.

For information: 800-WYNDHAM (996-3426); www.wyndham.com.

SUPER 8 MOTELS

One of the world's largest economy lodging chains, with nearly 2,100 independently owned motels throughout the

U.S. and Canada, Super 8 gives a discount of 10 percent to all guests 50 or older at participating properties. Just ask for it.

For information: 800-800-8000; www.super8.com.

TOWNEPLACE SUITES BY MARRIOTT

Moderately priced all-suites hotels, TownePlace Suites caters to guests who plan extended stays. It offers townhouse exteriors, full kitchens, an outdoor pool, a 24-hour exercise room, and a welcome to your pet. And to guests 62 and older, a 15-percent discount at participating locations.

For information: 800-257-3000; www.townehousesuites .com

TRAVELODGE HOTELS

All Travelodge brands—Thriftlodge Hotels, Travelodge Inns, Travelodge Hotels, Travelodge Suites, and Travelodge World Resorts, almost 600 locations ranging from budget to full-service—have a nice, straightforward plan for older travelers. Members of AARP or CARP will receive 15 to 30 percent off any time, any night, with advanced reservations made through the toll-free number. Or, 10 percent off when space is available for everyone over 50 who arrives with or without reservations.

For information: 800-578-7878; www.travelodge.com.

VILLAGER LODGES

Designed for extended stays, the amenities offered by the Villager chain—Villager Lodge, Villager Premier, and Hearthside by Villager—range from rooms with minikitchenettes to oversized suites with fully equipped kitchens and separate living and sleeping areas. These affordable, independently owned lodgings are found in about 100 locations in the U.S., Canada, and Mexico and give a discount of 10 to 30 percent to members of AARP and CARP as well as all other guests age 50 or older.

For information: 800-328-7829; www.villager.com.

W HOTELS

A group of intimate, upscale downtown hotels with living-room lounges, state-of-the-art technology for business travelers, and elegant restaurants, W Hotels has 19 locations in major cities, 5 of them in New York. To be eligible for a 50 percent discount on the regular room rates, you must belong to AARP and make a nonrefundable reservation for a stay that includes a Thursday, Friday, or Saturday arrival. Otherwise, you get 15 to 25 percent off the rates.

WELLESLEY INN & SUITES

This midpriced group of about 75 hotels, many designed for extended stays, gives a 15 percent discount on room rates to members of AARP and CARP. Concentrated in Florida, Texas, Arizona, and the Northeast, they include a complimentary continental breakfast.

For information: 800-444-8888; www.wellesleyinnandsuites.com.

WESTCOAST HOTELS

At these upscale WestCoast Hotels in the western and midwestern states as well as Alaska, members of AARP get a dis-

count of 10 to 20 percent off the best rate of the day. Many located on waterfront property, each of these full-service hotels and resorts is unique.
For information: 800-325-4000; www.westcoasthotels.com.

WESTIN HOTELS

Part of the Starwood family, Westins can be found in 25 countries. All of them stand ready to give you up to 50 percent off the regular room rates if you belong to AARP and make a nonrefundable reservation at least 21 days in advance. Without an advance purchase, you can count on 15 to 25 percent off.
For information: 800-WESTIN-1 (937-8461); www.westin.com.

WINGATE INN

Wingate Inns are new-construction, moderately priced hotels with sophisticated consumer-based technology that includes free high-speed Internet access in every room and a 24-hour self-service business center. Other amenities include complimentary continental breakfast, whirlpool, and exercise facilities. What's more, they give a 10 to 30 percent discount to members of AARP and CARP and all other guests 60 or more.
For information: 800-228-1000; www.wingateinns.com.

WYNDHAM HOTELS & RESORTS

Wyndham's offer to mature guests is generous and simple. At these upscale, full-service properties throughout the U.S.,

Canada, Mexico, and the Caribbean, AARP members get 20 percent off the lowest available room rate every day of the week with some blackout dates. Rooms at these rates are limited, so always reserve them early.

For information: 800-WYNDHAM (996-3426); www.wyndham.com.

5

Alternative Lodgings for Thrifty Wanderers

If you're willing to be innovative, imaginative, and occasionally fairly spartan, you can travel for a song or thereabouts. Here are some novel lodging options that can save you money and perhaps offer adventures in the bargain. Not all of them are designed exclusively for people over 50, but each reports that the major portion of its clientele consists of free spirits of a certain age who like to travel, appreciate good value for their money, and enjoy getting to know new people from other places.

For more ways to cut travel costs and get smart at the same time, check out the residential/educational programs in Chapter 12.

AFFORDABLE TRAVEL CLUB

Join this bed-and-breakfast club limited to people over 40 and you'll pay a pittance for accommodations, meet interesting people, and see new places. As members, you will act as hosts for fellow members, putting them up in your spare bedroom perhaps a couple of times a year and providing breakfast and a little of your time to acquaint your guests with the area. Visitors pay $15 for a single or $20 for a double per room per night for their stay, and $10 for each additional person. When you travel, you do the same.

There are currently about 2,600 members in this club in 47 states and 30 countries offering accommodations ranging from simple bedrooms to suites and condos. For a membership fee of $60 a year, for U.S. hosts, you receive a newsletter twice a year plus an annual directory from which you choose your own hosts and from which others may choose you. Fees differ for hosts in Canada, Mexico, and overseas and for E-mail delivery. The club also sponsors a group tour at least once a year.

If you have a pet, you may want to take advantage of the club's house-sitting and pet-sitting service—members move into your house and care for your house and/or pets while you're on vacation, meanwhile enjoying a visit to your neighborhood in exchange and no money changes hands. ***For information:*** Affordable Travel Club, 6556 Snug Harbor Ln., Gig Harbor, WA 98335; 253-858-2172; www.affordable travelclub.net.

COOPER COMMUNITIES

Cooper's three adult villages in Arkansas, Tennessee, and West Virginia, offer low-cost, two-night visits for people over 50 who are considering moving to an adult community. Lodging is in a furnished townhouse. You'll spend your time touring the grounds, the golf courses, the clubhouses, and

other facilities and visiting with homeowners to get a flavor of the lifestyle there. Cost per couple for a two-night stay is $89, plus an hour or two spent with a salesperson.
For information: 800-228-7328; www.cooper-land.com.

DEL WEBB'S SUN CITIES

The largest builder of active adult communities, Del Webb offers its Vacation Getaways program at many of its properties, with the details differing with place and season. These are low-cost, short vacation stays so you can sample the lifestyle to see whether you'd like to move in. Reservations are required. You'll stay in your own guest house for a few days, spend time with the residents, try out the facilities, play a round of golf perhaps, explore the clubhouses, tour the model homes. At this writing, the rates range from about $199 for four nights to about $675 for a seven-day package in peak season.

The requirements are that one partner in a visiting couple must be at least 55 years old, no one in the group may be younger than 19, guests may stay no more than twice at the same location, and they must agree to meet with a sales representative during the stay.
For information: Del Webb's Sun Cities, 6001 N. 24th St., Phoenix, AZ 85016; 800-433-5932; www.suncity.com.

EVERGREEN BED AND BREAKFAST CLUB

This bed-and-breakfast club, exclusively for people over the age of 50, was founded in 1982 and now has about 3,500 member families and 1,800 host locations in the U.S. and Canada as well as many in other countries. Whether a host home is elegant or simple, members pay only $10 for a sin-

ELDER TRAVELERS.COM

If you're sociable, adventurous, 50 or more, and love making new friends, check out ElderTravelers.com, a website that helps match up potential guests with hospitable hosts all over the U.S., Canada, and several foreign countries. Travelers are hosted at no cost when they share their hosts' homes for short visits. Hosts enjoy the company of their guests from other places while showing them the local sights.

When you join the service (free at this writing), you may post information about yourselves, your home, hometown, interests, and accommodations, perhaps including photographs. You may then contact one another by E-mail and together make plans for a visit. The database can be searched by country, state, or city.

For information: ElderTravelers.com, 1615 Smelter Ave., Black Eagle, MT 59414; www.eldertravelers.com.

gle or $15 per couple (add $5 for all locations outside of the continental U.S.) for each overnight stay and bountiful breakfast. In return, they welcome members of the club into their own homes as often as they wish.

Twice a year the club publishes directories of members with relevant information about all of the host families and the special attractions of their areas. You then make your own arrangements for visits and pay the gratuities directly to the hosts. A quarterly newsletter provides the latest information. Annual club dues are $60 for a single and $75 per couple.

An important aspect of this hospitality club is the opportunity for members to make new friends and perhaps travel together, as many members do.

For information: Evergreen Bed and Breakfast Club, 201 W. Broad St., Ste. 181, Falls Church, VA 22046; 800-962-2392 or 815-456-3111; www.evergreenclub.com.

JENSEN'S RESIDENTIAL COMMUNITIES

If you are prospective buyers, you may stay free of charge for a couple of nights in your own fully furnished guest house at one of Jensen's three communities for adults over the age of 55. You'll have access to the clubhouse, the swimming pool, and all organized activities and have plenty of time to talk to the residents at the villages that are located in North and South Carolina.

For information: 800-458-6832; www.jensencommunities.com.

NEW PALTZ SUMMER LIVING

Think about spending a couple of summer months in the mountains, about 75 miles north of New York City. Every year, while the usual student occupants are on vacation, 140 furnished garden apartments are reserved for seniors in the village of New Paltz, near Mohonk Mountain and home of a branch of the State University of New York. The rents at this writing for the entire summer (from early June until late August) range from $1,500 to $3,300, depending on the size of the apartment. Living right in town next to the campus, you may audit college courses for free, attend lectures and cultural events, and take part in planned activities in the clubhouse. A heated pool and tennis court are in the complex. Buses travel to New York City frequently for those who want to go to the theater, and there are frequent day trips to places of interest.

For information: New Paltz Summer Living, 4 Southside Ave., New Paltz, NY 12561; 800-431-4143 or 845-255-7205.

ROBSON COMMUNITIES

The Preferred Guest Program at Robson's four villages for "active adults" in Arizona offers prospective homeowners a three-night stay for two in your own house, with free rounds of golf, use of the recreational amenities, and a complimentary dinner with homeowners. You may use the clubhouse, swimming pools, tennis courts, spas, and golf courses. Of course, visitors must also spend a few hours talking with a salesperson.

The requirements for a visit are that one person in your party must be at least 40 and no one may be under 19. Current cost ranges from $99 to $329 for the package, depending on the time of year.

For information: Robson Communities, 9532 E. Riggs Rd., Sun Lakes, AZ 85248; 800-732-9949; www.robson.com.

SENIORS ABROAD

Seniors Abroad, celebrating its 20th anniversary, is a cultural exchange program for adventurous people over the age of 50. It pairs American travelers with host families for three-to-four-week homestays in Japan or New Zealand and Australia. There, singly or as couples, visitors spend five or six days in the homes of several different families during the trip. In the U.S., host families do the same for foreign visitors from those same countries. Hosts are volunteers, and guests pay only for transportation, tours, hotels between stays, and other such expenses.

For information: Seniors Abroad, 12533 Pacato Circle North, San Diego, CA 92128; 858-485-1696; E-mail: haev @pacbell.net.

U.S. SERVAS

Servas, the oldest free hospitality organization in the world, is an international cooperative system of peace activists who offer free lodging as a way to promote friendship and understanding across national and cultural boundaries. With more than 15,000 hosts in 135 countries who welcome other members into their homes for a day or two without charge, its yearly fee for travelers is $65 (U.S.) or $50 (Canadian). This nonprofit, interracial, interfaith organization is open to travelers of all ages who must provide two letters of reference and an interview. Hosts in the U.S. are asked for a donation of $35 a year to cover administrative costs.
For information: Send a #10 self-addressed, stamped envelope to US Servas, 11 John St., Room 505, New York, NY 10038; 212-267-0252; usservas.org.

WCI COMMUNITIES

The Preferred Guest Getaways offered at this developer's 33 locations for adults in Florida, including the Sun City Centers in Tampa and Fort Meyers, are designed for potential homebuyers so they can see what they're getting. They offer special discounted rates at nearby hotels, passes for the community's facilities and restaurants, and discounted golf fees. Hotel rates current start at $70 per night, depending on location and time of year.
For information: 800-924-2290; www.wcicommunities .com.

HOME EXCHANGE FOR 50-PLUS

One way to go on vacation without seriously depleting your funds is to exchange homes with other adult travelers who live in a place you'd like to visit and who want to spend time in your house. No money changes hands, and you can save plenty on the cost of hotel rooms and perhaps even car rentals if you swap cars.

Although many exchange programs are ready to serve as house-swapping matchmakers, we know of only one that deals exclusively with people over the age of 50. Seniors Home Exchange provides listings of about 800 houses or apartments in the U.S. and Canada and 31 other countries around the world that may be traded for yours for a period of time to be mutually agreed upon. Even motor homes and caravans are traded. The catch is that you must have access to the Internet, possess an E-mail address, and pay $60 ($90 Canadian) for a three-year membership or $100 ($150 Canadian) for a lifetime membership. Members of AARP and CARP pay only $30 for a two-year membership.

Any arrangement that suits both parties is encouraged—you may trade abodes simultaneously or exchange hospitality by visiting them at one time while they visit you at another. The trades need not come out even, including length of visits, size of homes, or amenities.

For information: Seniors Home Exchange, www.seniorshome exchange.com.

WOMEN WELCOME WOMEN WORLD WIDE (WWWWW)

A hospitality club, 5W has more than 3,000 members in 70 countries who may stay in one another's homes without cost. Dedicated to furthering friendships among women from different cultures, it asks its members for a donation of $35 in return for a membership list and three newsletters a year. Members, the majority of whom are over 50, correspond with potential hostesses who have offered to share their homes. Together they arrange their visits at a time convenient to both. The newsletters include notices of 5W gatherings all over the world and a list of women seeking travel companions.

For information: 203-454-1609; www.womenwelcomewomen.org.uk.

6

Beating the Costs of Car Rentals

Never rent a car without getting a discount or a special promotional rate. Almost all car-rental agencies in the U.S. and Canada give breaks to all manner of customers, including those who belong to over-50 organizations (see Chapter 19) or have reached a certain birthday. The discount that's coming to you as a senior member of society can save you some money, although short-term sales will almost always save you more. Refer to the membership material sent by the group to which you belong for information about your discount privileges.

It's almost impossible to sort out the confusing choices of rates, discounts, and add-on fees from the rental companies. To save money, you must shop around, compare costs, and make many decisions that can raise or lower your bill. In general, the best rates are to be found online. When applicable, add the senior discount for renters over 50. It may not amount to much, but it will help a little.

But, first, keep in mind:

- Car-rental agents might not always volunteer information about senior discounts or special sales, so always ask about them when you reserve your car.
- Don't settle for a senior discount or senior rate too hastily without investigating the possibility of an even better deal. Shop around yourself or ask your travel agent to find the *lowest available rate or package* at the time you are going to travel. Ask for the total price that includes all extra charges such as airport fees, taxes, and drop-off fees. Senior discounts are usually given on the full published rental rate. So special promotional rates—in other words, sales—or even weekend rates are almost always better, sometimes much better. On the other hand, if you can get the senior discount *on top of the lowest posted rate*, regular or promotional, that's the deal you want.
- Book your car as far in advance as you can, especially if you are traveling during a holiday season. Generally, the later you book the more expensive it will be and the less likely you are to get the car you want. If closer to departure you find a better rate that suits your needs, you can rebook it.
- Remember that weekly and weekend rates are less expensive than daily rates.
- Read newspapers and magazines—especially those targeting over-50s. Look for ads for seasonal sales and clip out "value-added coupons" for additional discounts, cash

savings, or upgrades. Sometimes you'll also get coupons in the mail from clubs, associations, frequent-flyer programs, and credit-card companies. Your travel agent might have some to offer too. But read the details carefully. Many of these specials cannot be combined with other promotional offers, such as senior discounts. And some may apply only to specific car sizes.

- Most of the major car-rental companies offer weekly specials linked to those of the major domestic airlines. Remember to check them out if you are flying to the city where you will pick up your car.
- Be especially cautious if you are planning a one-way rental because rates can be outrageously high for picking up a car in one city and returning it in another.
- If you have access to the Internet, check the rental agencies' websites for special deals and last-minute offers. Most car-rental companies give a discount for booking online.
- Before driving away in your rented car, inspect it for dents, scratches, or other damage. If you find any, ask the agent to sign a statement on the condition of the car and attach it to your rental agreement. That way, you won't be in danger of being charged for the damage upon your return.
- Ask if there is an additional-driver fee, and don't sign up for it if you don't need it or rent from a company that doesn't charge for additional drivers. If your spouse will be a second driver, rent from a company that allows both a husband and wife to drive at no extra cost.
- When you reserve a car, always ask for a confirmation number. When you pick up your car, verify the discount

or special rate *before* signing the agreement and ask if a better rate has become available since you booked.

- When you call to ask about rates or reservations, always be armed with your organization's ID number and your own membership card for reference. Present them again at the rental counter when you pick up your car, and be sure to confirm your rate before signing the agreement.
- Special savings might not be available at every location, so remember to check them out every time you make a reservation.
- Don't purchase insurance you don't need. Review your personal auto insurance coverage and credit-card policy to determine if you require the optional loss/damage coverage offered by the rental companies. Your homeowners policy may cover your personal belongings on the road.
- In the U.S., there is no maximum age for renting a car, but there are restrictions in other countries that vary by country and agency. One agency, for example, denies rentals to people over 65 in Greece and Northern Ireland or over 75 in Ireland and Israel. Another restricts drivers over 60 in Malaysia or the Philippines. In the United Kingdom and Ireland, most agencies will not rent a car to a driver over 75. So make your age clear when you make your reservation. Shop around, and also consider leasing a car, in which case age may not be an issue.
- If you are traveling outside the U.S., don't wait until you arrive at your destination to arrange a rental. Book it here before you go because renting abroad is much more expensive. Remember to request your senior discount. Consult with your insurance carrier and credit-card companies to be sure you are covered overseas. Most per-

sonal automobile insurance covers you only for driving in the U.S., and coverage may not include certain types of vehicles.

- If you can drive a stick shift, you can cut the cost of a rental significantly. In other countries, automatic transmissions are not readily available and when they are, they are much more expensive.

ADVANTAGE RENT-A-CAR

Independently owned and managed, Advantage maintains locations in nine western states. It gives AARP members a discount of 10 percent off the regular rates every day of the year, charges no additional fee for a second driver, and provides roadside assistance. If you join the Advantage Frequent Rental club, you'll earn a free day when you've rented four times. Do it online and you need only two rentals for a free day.

For information: 800-777-5500; www.advantagerentacar.com.

ALAMO RENT A CAR

Alamo's offer to seniors who want to take to the road is very simple—it's a discount of up to 10 percent, depending on the season and location, off the weekly or daily rates to anybody over the age of 50.

For information: 800-GO-ALAMO (462-5266); www.alamo.com.

AUTO EUROPE

If you rent a car from Auto Europe—a company that services more than 4,000 car-rental locations worldwide—you are guaranteed the lowest rates based on those of comparable car-rental companies. And, if you are 50 or over, you will also get a discount of 5 percent, sometimes even on promotional rates, on all rentals including chauffeur drives and prestige sports cars.

Short-term leases are also available from Auto Europe, which has partnered with Peugeot to lease factory-new cars from Peugeot for periods of more than 17 days. All short-term leases include unlimited mileage; insurance; 24-hour, English-speaking roadside assistance; and taxes. And, very important to many travelers, unlike car rentals that may be limited to drivers between the ages of 25 and 70, they have no maximum age requirement.

For information: 800-223-5555; www.autoeurope.com.

AVIS RENT A CAR

If you are a member of AARP or CARP, you'll get a discount of 5 to 20 percent on the lowest available rate from Avis, a company with more than 4,700 locations in 145 countries. All rates include enhanced insurance coverage, unlimited free mileage at participating locations, and no charge for second drivers who are spouses.

For information: 800-331-1800; www.avis.com.

BUDGET RENT A CAR

Budget's offer to everyone over the age of 50 is 10 percent off the regular rates. That's great, but if you visit the website, you might find that you can take advantage of an even better deal—one of the company's periodically posted Senior Savings specials for 50-plus renters. But first, check out the Hot Deals pages where specials for all ages are listed.

For information: 800-527-0700; www.budget.com.

DOLLAR RENT A CAR

Join the free Silver Dollar Club if you are over 50 and you'll get a discount of up to 10 percent on most rentals, with unlimited mileage and no charge for additional drivers. You must make an advance reservation, request the special rate, and mention the customer discount number SR2000. If you want to be notified about special promotions and sales, sign up for the club's E-mail newsletter.

For information: 800-800-4000; www.dollar.com. You may join the club online or by writing to Dollar Rent a Car, CIMS #7070, 5330 E. 31 St., Tulsa, OK 74135.

ENTERPRISE RENT-A-CAR

Enterprise specializes in renting vehicles in neighborhoods "where people live and work," and that means its 5,000 or so branches in five countries are located in big cities and small towns as well as at major airports in the U.S. It offers a discount of 5 percent off the regular rental rates to members of AARP.

For information: 800-RENT-A-CAR (736-8222); www.enterprise.com.

EUROPCAR

Car renters who are 50-plus can save up to 15 percent on applicable rates when they rent from Europcar, a subsidiary of the Volkswagon Group. You get unlimited mileage and no charge for an additional driver at its approximately 2,600 locations in 100 worldwide locations that include Europe, Africa, Mexico, the Caribbean, India, China, the Middle East, and Australia. Simply ask for the Topaz USA rate for people over 50.

For information: 877-940-6900; www.europcaramericas .com.

HERTZ CAR RENTAL

Members of AARP and NARFE are eligible for savings at 7,000 Hertz locations in 150 countries all over the world. They can get a discount of up to 15 percent off the rates with unlimited mileage and enhanced insurance coverage.
For information: 800-654-2200; www.hertz.com.

KEMWEL

This car-rental broker, with multiple suppliers, offers a discount of 5 percent off any rentals to anybody over the age of 50 at any of its locations in 25 European countries. Ask for it when you make your booking whether by telephone or online. Kemwel also offers short-term leases valid for a minimum of 17 days and a maximum of 264 days on brand-new Peugeots, complete with nondeductible, fully comprehensive insurance; 24-hour roadside assistance; and unlimited mileage. Best of all, there is no maximum age limit for drivers.
For information: 800-678-0678; www.kemwel.com.

NATIONAL CAR RENTAL

If you belong to AARP or CARP, you will get a discount of 5 to 30 percent off the daily and weekly rates at all locations in the U.S., Canada, and Europe. And if you don't belong but are over 50, you'll still get a discount if you produce proof of your age.
For information: 800-CAR-RENT (227-7368); www.nation alcar.com.

PAYLESS CAR RENTAL

The free Nifty Fifty Program from Payless gives travelers 50 and over a straightforward 5 percent discount on the lowest applicable rate. Simply state your age when you make your reservations for a car from 150 locations worldwide.
For information: 800-PAYLESS (729-5377); www.payless carrental.com.

RENAULT EURODRIVE

As an alternative to car rentals, Renault Eurodrive offers short-term leases valid to drive in more than 30 countries for a minimum of 17 days and a maximum of 6 months. Designed for leisure travelers who reside outside of Europe, the program gives you a brand-new car with unlimited mileage; insurance coverage with no deductible or VAT, an extensive service network; and 24-hour, English-speaking road assistance. The 35 pick-up and drop-off sites are located in nine countries.

Leasing may be cheaper than car rentals, but, even more important to many travelers, it has no maximum age requirement whereas car rentals are often limited to drivers between the ages of 25 and 70.
For information: 800-221-1052 or 212-532-1221; www .renaultusa.com.

RENT-A-WRECK

This company, whose cars are not wrecks but three to five years old, claims to be 15 to 20 percent cheaper than the major car-rental agencies. Because all of its 500 locations across the country are independently owned, it is up to each one of them to set its own senior discount, but most give

renters who are at least 50 or 55 years old a 5 to 10 percent discount off the regular rates. Cars are rented round-trip only and must be returned to their home locations.
For information: 800-535-1391; www.rent-a-wreck.com.

THRIFTY CAR RENTAL

Now here's a really good deal. If you are over 55, Thrifty guarantees you a 10 percent discount on most standard rentals, at all of its locations throughout the world. To get it, you must make an advance reservation using the toll-free number. Before going for it, make sure there are no better promotional rates available.
For information: 800-THRIFTY (847-4389); www.thrifty.com.

U-SAVE AUTO RENTAL OF AMERICA

U-Save Auto Rental, with about 1,400 locations in the U.S. and Canada—all independent franchises—caters to the off-airport or neighborhood market and provides rental cars directly to consumers or local businesses. Many of its locations offer discounts of 5 to 10 percent to drivers over 50, so ask when you call for a car. Ask, too, about special seasonal sales that may save you even more.
For information: 800-272-8728; www.usave.net.

7

Saving a Bundle on Trains, Buses, and Boats in North America

Getting around town, especially in a city where driving is not a practical option, probably means depending on public transportation to get you from hither to yon. Remember that once you reach a particular birthday—in most cases, your 60th or 65th—you can take advantage of some good senior markdowns on trains, buses, subways, and, in some places, even taxis. All you need in most cases is a Medicare card, a Senior ID card, or your driver's license to play this game, which usually reduces fares by half. Although you may find it uncomfortable at first to pull out that card and flash it at the bus driver or ticket agent, it soon becomes very easy. Do it and you'll realize some nice savings.

And don't fail to take advantage of the bargains available to seniors on long-distance rail, bus, and boat travel as well.

RIDING THE RAILS

Just about every commuter railroad in the U.S. and Canada gives older passengers a break in fares, although you may have to do your traveling during off-peak periods when the trains are not filled with go-getters rushing to and from their offices. New York's Metro North, for example, charges anyone over 65 only half the regular fare for all trains except those arriving in Manhattan during weekday morning peak hours. And on the New York subways and buses, too, you pay only half whether you pay in cash, tokens, or with Reduced Fare MetroCard. In Washington, D.C., passengers who are 65 or more pay only 50 cents to ride the buses and half fare on Metrorail trains.

As for serious long-distance journeys, many mature travelers are addicted to the railroads, finding riding the rails a leisurely, relaxed, romantic, comfortable, economical, and satisfying way to make miles while enjoying the scenery.

So many passes and discounts on railroads are available to travelers heading for other parts of the country that sorting them out becomes confusing. But, once you do, they will help stretch your dollars while you cover a lot of ground.

See Chapter 8 for the best deals on transportation in foreign countries for travelers of a certain age.

ALASKA RAILROAD

Passengers over 65 are entitled to a reduction of about 20 percent in weekend fares during the winter months—late September through early May—between Anchorage and Fairbanks and anywhere in between. You're encouraged to

take food and drink with you because there's limited food service on the train for this 12-hour journey.
For information: 800-544-0552; www.alaskarailroad.com.

AMTRAK

To accommodate the increasing numbers of senior travelers who love to travel by train, Amtrak offers a 15 percent discount on the lowest available coach fares, including Explore America Fares, in the U.S. and on some Canadian routes, every day of the week to anyone over 62. The discount is also available on the Metroliner Service on Saturdays and Sundays but does not apply to the Auto Train or sleeping accommodations.

Amtrak and Via Rail Canada have teamed up to offer the North America Rail Pass. It lets you travel to more than 900 destinations with unlimited stopovers on the 28,000-mile rail system in the U.S. and Canada, for 30 consecutive days after purchase. If you're at least 60, you are entitled to 10 percent off the regular adult fare. Buy the pass that's good during peak and off-peak seasons from either the company or a travel agent. You'll need advance reservations, and you'll travel coach although you may upgrade to sleeping accommodations or other higher classes of travel for an additional charge.
For information: 800-USA-RAIL (872-7245); www.amtrak.com.

ONTARIO NORTHLAND

This passenger railroad serving northeastern Ontario gives travelers over the age of 60 a 10 percent fare reduction any day of the year on the Northlander train running between Toronto and Cochrane. The same discount applies to the Polar Bear Express, a summer excursion line between Cochrane and Moosonee. The Little Bear Train runs three times a week from Cochrane to Moosonee, returning the following day, and offers a 20 percent discount for travelers over 60.

For information: 800-461-8558 or 705-472-4500; www.ontc.on.ca.

VIA RAIL CANADA

The government-owned Canadian railroad that provides coast-to-coast passenger service, gives seniors 60 and over a 10 percent discount off any fare every day of the year, even on top of other special fares. For example, add this discount to a 25 percent reduction on off-peak travel, available to all ages and good every day of the week. You'll end up with a 35 percent savings.

The Senior Companion Fare is another perk. This one allows adults over 60 to buy an economy ticket at the regular senior fare and take along a companion of any age for free, except during the winter holiday period and on trips starting on Fridays or Sundays on the Quebec City–Windsor corridor. If you'd like more onboard service, you can also get a discount (with some restrictions) on premium travel by buying one first-class ticket for yourself and a second ticket for a companion at 75 percent off.

At 60 you are also eligible to buy three rail passes at a 10 percent discount. The first is the Canrailpass, available for peak or off-peak travel and valid for 12 days within a 30-day period anywhere on VIA Rail's transcontinental system. You may get on and off the train as many times as you wish, stopping wherever you like along the way after reserving your space for all segments.

The second pass to offer a senior discount is the Corridorpass. Sold year-round for first-class or economy-class seating, it gives you ten days of unlimited train travel within the Quebec City–Windsor corridor.

And last, the North America Rail Pass, a cooperative venture with Amtrak, allows you to explore North America by train, giving access to all Via Rail trains in Canada and almost all Amtrak trains in the U.S. It gives you 30 consecutive days of unlimited travel (no more than four one-way trips on any given route or segment) to more than 900 destinations in the U.S. and Canada. You get as many stopovers as you like, but reservations are required for all portions of your journey.

TRAVEL TIPS FOR A HEALTHY TRIP

The U.S. Department of State offers a long list of tips for older travelers to help you plan a safe and healthy trip to other countries. You can get this useful advice as a brochure by calling 202-512-1800 or by sending a check for $1.50 to Superintendent of Documents, PO Box 371954, Pittsburgh, Pennsylvania 15250. You may also read it online at www.travel.state.gov/olderamericans. Among the issues discussed: reviewing your health insurance policies and, if necessary, buying supplemental insurance; considering trip insurance in case you must postpone, cancel, or interrupt your trip; carrying extra copies of prescriptions; getting the appropriate immunizations; finding medical assistance; and dealing with medical emergencies abroad.

For information: 888-VIA-RAIL (842-7245); www.via rail.ca.

GOING BY BUS

Never, never board a bus without asking the driver whether there's a senior discount, because even the smallest bus lines in the tiniest communities (and the largest—New York City, for example) in the U.S., Canada, and abroad give seniors a break, usually 50 percent off at age 60 or 65. In Europe, your senior rail pass is often valid on major motorcoach lines as well, so always be sure to inquire.

COACH CANADA

This bus line, which serves southwest Ontario and the Niagara Peninsula and runs between Toronto and Montreal, offers discounts of 10 to 25 percent to passengers over the age of 60. In cooperation with Greyhound Lines (U.S.), it also offers through service to Boston; New York; Washington, D.C.; and Chicago.
For information: Coach Canada, PO Box 1017, Peterborough, ON K9J 7A5; 800-461-7661 or 705-748-6411.

GRAY LINE WORLDWIDE

Gray Line is an association of 150 independent sightseeing tour companies serving about 200 destinations on five continents. Participating locations give members of AARP a discount of 10 percent on fares for half- or full-day sight-seeing tours. You must purchase tickets at a Gray Line terminal and present a valid membership card. Some Gray

CITYPASS: SEE THE SIGHTS FOR LESS

Visitors to Boston, New York City, Chicago, Hollywood, Philadelphia, San Francisco, or Seattle who take in several of the city's main attractions during their stay can save time and money with CityPass. It is a booklet of admission tickets to six of each city's most popular cultural attractions, cutting your cost by at least half the price of box office prices if you use them all. An added benefit is immediate admission without standing in ticket lines.

Tickets may be purchased at any of the CityPass attractions in each city or at city visitor centers and are available in advance at the website or through a travel agent. The booklets have no expiration date but are good only for nine days (30 days in Hollywood) after you've used the first ticket. ***For information:*** 800-330-5008 or 707-256-0490; www.citypass.com.

Line companies also give discounts to nonmembers if they are 55 or 60, so inquire before signing up for a tour. ***For information:*** Call the Gray Line Worldwide office in your area or the corporate headquarters at 303-394-6920; www.grayline.com.

GREYHOUND CANADA

Here you'll get 10 percent off all regular fares, any day of the week, all year round, if you are a traveler over 62 with a valid ID. What's more, if you're accompanied by a companion and buy your tickets three days in advance, the companion travels for free. On the family fare, you get 10 percent off and an accompanying child under 16 goes free.

The 10 percent discount also applies to the Canada Pass, good for unlimited travel, with as many stopovers within the country as you like for specified numbers of days; and to the CanAm Discovery Pass, which gives you the same privileges on all routes wherever Greyhound and participating carriers go within the U.S. and Canada.

But hold on. If you are planning to travel long distances within Canada and the U.S., Greyhound Canada offers an even better deal than you'll get using your senior discount. That's the Go Anywhere Fare that with a 7- or 14-day advance purchase lets you take the bus between any two destinations serviced by Greyhound Canada in Canada and the U.S.—no matter how far—for only $125 to $149 one way, $200 to $298 round trip (Canadian). No stopovers with this fare, however, and no additional senior discount. ***For information:*** 800-661-8747 or 403-265-9111; www.greyhound.ca.

GREYHOUND LINES

Greyhound Seniors Club, exclusively for passengers over 62, gives its members a 10 percent discount on any unrestricted fare. Plus, you'll receive 10 percent off food at Greyhound-operated restaurants, 10 percent off charter services for groups, and 25 percent off on prepaid personal Greyhound Package Express shipments. Join the club for an annual fee of $5 at any Greyhound terminal. If you don't join, you're offered a 5 percent discount on the regular fares if you are over 62 and can show proof of age.

But before you make reservations, check out a couple of special fares that can help you save money. First, Greyhound's Friendly Fares allow you to travel from 501 miles to more than 3,000 miles between any two destinations with no stopovers at fares starting at $49 one way or $98 round trip. A seven-day advance purchase is required, and you get no senior discount on this fare. The Companion Fare that's available in most parts of the country, on the other hand, gives you the senior discount on a three-day advance purchase round trip and lets you take a companion with you absolutely free.

The 62-plus traveler can also take advantage of a 10 percent discount on the North America Discovery Pass that gives you unlimited travel for varying numbers of days (from 7 to 60) to any U.S. destination with as many stopovers as you like. The pass comes in several versions. The Ameripass covers travel in the U.S., the Canada Pass covers Canada, and the CanAm Pass allows for travel in both countries. You'll get your senior discount on all of them.

For information: Call your local Greyhound reservation office or 800-231-2222; www.greyhound.com.

ONTARIO NORTHLAND

On all Ontario Northland's scheduled intercity bus lines in northeastern Ontario (with connections to Toronto), passengers over the age of 60 are offered a 10 percent discount on the regular fare every day of the week.

For information: Ontario Northland, 555 Oak St. East, North Bay, ON P1B 8L3; 800-268-9281 or 705-472-4500; www.ontc.on.ca.

PETER PAN BUS LINES

All passengers 62 or over can get a 5 percent discount on all journeys aboard Peter Pan buses, but if they pay $5 for a

Senior Saver Card, valid for a year and available at ticket counters, the discount goes up to 10 percent. Peter Pan is concentrated mainly in the New England states.
For information: 800-343-9999; www.peterpanbus.com.

VOYAGEUR BUS LINES

Voyageur's Club 60 gives passengers who are 60 or more a 25 percent discount on all journeys at all times on all bus fares on its intercity service in Ontario and Quebec. Simply present proof of your age when you buy your tickets, but first make sure the "Same Day Return" specials don't give you an even better deal.
For information: www.voyageur.com.

GOING BY BOAT

ALASKA MARINE HIGHWAY

Traveling on the Alaska Marine Highway, also known as the Alaska Ferry, in the off-season is a bargain for foot passengers 65 and older. Between October and April, you sail for half the regular adult fare within Alaskan waters. The discount does not apply to vehicle or cabin space or a round trip on the same sailing to the Aleutian Islands. Sometimes in the summer, too, there are half fares for seniors on several of the smaller vessels. The message is always ask if a senior rate is available.
For information: 800-642-0066; www.alaska.gov/ferry.

8

Cutting Your Costs Abroad

The most enthusiastic voyagers of all age groups, Americans over 50—one out of three adults and more than a quarter of the total population—spend more time and money on travel than anybody else, especially when it comes to going to foreign destinations. It's been estimated that more than four out of every ten passport holders are at least 55 years old. And there's hardly a country in the world today that doesn't actively encourage mature travelers to come for a visit.

Because you are now being avidly pursued, you can take advantage of many good deals in other lands. Airlines, for example, often offer you fare reductions on domestic flights within the country or the continent. Railroad and bus systems in most European countries give seniors deep discounts that are especially valuable if you plan an extended stay in one place. Even ferries and cruise ships are often ready to make you a deal. This chapter gives you a rundown on these and other ways to cut your overseas holiday costs, especially if you are planning your trip on your own. For the U.S. and Canada, see Chapter 7.

But, first, keep in mind:

- Always ask about senior savings when you travel on planes, trains, buses, or boats anywhere in the world. Do the same when you buy tickets for movies, theaters, museums, tours, sight-seeing tours, historic buildings, and attractions. Don't assume, simply because you haven't heard about them or the ticket agent hasn't mentioned them, that they don't exist. Senior discounts are becoming more and more common everywhere, and you'll be amazed how much money you can save.
- Some countries require that you purchase a senior card to take advantage of senior discounts, but most require only proof of age, usually in the form of a passport.
- Always have the necessary identification with you and be ready to show it. Occasionally you may need an extra passport photograph.
- For specifics on a country's senior discounts, call its national tourist office here before you go.
- Call Rail Europe, 800-4-EURAIL (438-7245), which represents most European railways, for information about train passes.
- Your passport may be required along with your rail pass while you are in transit, so keep it with you.
- If you plan to use a rail pass in Europe, you must usually buy it at least 15 days before you leave the U.S. or Canada. Any travel agency can do it for you or contact

Rail Europe, CIT North America, or DER marketing agencies that specialize in European rail passes. However, some national passes that are good only within one country's borders are not available on this side of the Atlantic and must be purchased there, usually at major railroad stations or airports. Have your passport handy. Best to check out all your options before you make your plans.

- Although there are many European rail-pass plans, only a few of them offer senior discounts to travelers age 60 or over. Details to come in this chapter.
- Major U.S. hotel chains, such as Radisson, Marriott, Hilton, Choice, and Best Western, offer senior discounts that almost always apply at their participating properties in other countries.
- Travel passes for sight-seeing trips are available in confusing profusion, and, because many overlap and some must be purchased before you leave home, it's wise to check them out before you go. Contact the national tourist offices of the countries you plan to visit.
- Ask about rail pass insurance when you buy your pass, just in case it is lost or stolen during your trip. You might want to seriously consider overall travel insurance as well.
- Be sure your rail pass is validated at a railway ticket office the first time you use it, before boarding the train.
- Tourist passes usually cost older travelers the same as everyone else, but in most cases they are definitely worth buying. Among the best buys everywhere are the inexpensive, easy-to-use "city cards" available for many major European cities. Usually good for one to four days, they give you free public transportation plus admission to the most important tourist sites. Many also offer discounts

on tours, meals, theater tickets, cultural attractions, and shopping.

EUROPE BY RAIL

Rail passes make the going cheaper in Europe, especially if you travel with a companion or a group, and it's easier to use the passes than to buy tickets as you go. It can also make your life simpler if you get them before you leave home. Besides, some of them offer senior discounts. It's not a simple matter to sort them all out, however. Some are multinational, good for travel in more than one country. Others are valid only within the borders of one country but can be useful to tourists who plan a long stay or considerable travel in that country.

Most passes are available in two different versions: a flexipass that permits travel for a specified number of days within a certain time period, and a consecutive-day pass that is valid on any day within a certain period. Many are not available overseas and must be purchased on this side of the Atlantic before you go. Others may only be purchased in the country that issues them. Be sure to get your rail pass validated at a railway station ticket office the first time you use it—before you board the train.

Rail Europe, the official North American representative for 60 European railroads, offers passes that cover single countries, regions of two or more countries, much of continental Europe, and Britain and Ireland. Since many passes must be purchased here before you travel and are not available over there, it is worth giving Rail Europe or your travel agent a call to explore the possibilities and decide whether

FINDING A DOCTOR OVERSEAS

Before you leave on a trip to foreign lands, it would be wise to send for the **International Association for Medical Assistance to Traveller's** (IAMAT) list of physicians all over the world who speak English; have had medical training in Great Britain, the U.S., or Canada; and have agreed to reasonable preset fees. When you join the free, nonprofit IAMAT, you will get a membership card entitling you to its prearranged rates, a directory of English-speaking physicians in 125 countries and territories, a clinical record to take along with you, and advice on immunizations and preventive measures for many diseases including malaria. A packet of information about climate, food, water, clothing suggestions, and sanitary conditions in 1,450 cities is given to members who donate $25 or more.

For information: IAMAT, 417 Center St., Lewiston, NY 14092; 716-754-4883; www.iamat.org.

a pass is what you need. And always ask whether there is a senior discount. Some passes give seniors a break, others don't.

EURAILPASS, EURAIL SELECTPASS, AND EUROPASS

The Eurailpass gives you free, unlimited first-class train travel on all the major railways of Hungary and 17 western European countries. There is no senior discount on this pass, but it is worth considering if you plan to cover many miles across many borders. On the other hand, if you are visiting just one country, you'd probably do better with that nation's senior discounts or national pass.

Available for various numbers of days up to three months, the Eurailpass also entitles you to free or discounted travel on many buses, ferries, steamers, and suburban trains. If you are traveling with at least one other person, you can get a Eurailpass Saver or Eurailpass Saver Flexi which are even better deals.

Or choose the Eurail Selectpass that allows you to travel in your choice of four or five adjacent European countries out of the participating 17 European nations for five, six, eight, or ten days within a two-month period. This one too is discounted when two or more people travel together using the Eurail Selectpass Saver.

None of these passes is sold in Europe—each must be purchased before you leave home. And none gives seniors a special break.

For information: Rail Europe, 44 S. Broadway, White Plains, NY 10601; 800-4-EURAIL (438-7245); www.raileurope.com.

BALKAN FLEXIPASS

Buy it here, and use it there for travel in Bulgaria, Greece, Macedonia, Romania, Turkey, and Yugoslavia (including Serbia and Montenegro). If you are 60 or more, you may buy a first-class pass, good for 5, 10, or 15 days within one month, for a 20 percent discount off the regular adult price.

For information: Rail Europe, 800-4-EURAIL (438-7245); www.raileurope.com.

EUROSTAR

The Channel Tunnel train, connecting Paris or Brussels with London, offers many round trips a day beneath the English

Channel. The senior fares—you're eligible if you're over 60—are about 25 percent cheaper than the regular adult fares on first-class tickets. They are also unrestricted and refundable.
For information: Rail Europe, 800-EUROSTAR (387-6782) or 800-4-EURAIL (438-7245); www.raileurope.com.

SCANRAIL SENIOR PASS

Sold only on this side of the Atlantic, the Scanrail Pass provides unlimited travel in Denmark, Finland, Norway, and Sweden. If you're over 60, buy the Scanrail Senior Pass. It offers you the same privileges on second-class travel but for about 10 percent less than younger adults pay. For more, see Scandinavia later in this chapter.
For information: Rail Europe, 800-4-EURAIL (438-7245); www.raileurope.com.

THALYS TRAIN

Thalys, the European high-speed rail network, with trains that connect Paris with more than 25 cities in four countries, gives a discount of over 30 percent on the cost of first- and second-class tickets to travelers 60 and older. Tickets may be booked three months in advance.
For information: Rail Europe, 800-4-EURAIL (438-7245); www.raileurope.com.

COUNTRY-BY-COUNTRY TRAVEL DEALS

AUSTRIA

Women who are at least 60 and men at least 65 can purchase an official Senior Citizen Railway card for about $30 and travel around Austria at half fare on trains and buses run by the federal government. That makes it a good deal for those planning many trips. You can get it at major rail stations in Austria.

On its daily nonstop service across the Atlantic to Vienna, Austrian Airlines gives a discount of 10 percent to passengers over 62 and a younger companion on all fares except for seasonal sales. On domestic flights within Austria, anyone 60 or over is offered special senior fares that vary throughout the year. And more: this airline's Star Alliance European Airpass travel coupons, sold together with round-trip tickets from the U.S., can save you significant money on flights between Austria and 41 countries. See Chapter 3 for more.

The Vienna Card and similar city cards in other Austrian cities and provinces including Salzburg, Linz, and Innsbruck, are very good deals. Sold for varied numbers of days, they give you unlimited travel on all public transportation—no more fumbling for the proper change—as well as free or reduced admission to museums, shops, attractions, and historic sites.

For information: Austrian National Tourist Office, PO Box 1142, New York, NY 10108; 212-944-6880; www.austria-tourism.at.

BELGIUM

If you're planning to explore Belgium and you're a senior traveler (60 and over), then you should consider buying a Golden Passport that allows you to purchase six first-class tickets on the Belgian Railways, valid for a year, for about $41 (U.S.), a 50 percent savings over the regular adult pass.

The pass is valid for travel on weekdays, Monday through Friday, after 9 A.M., and on Saturdays, Sundays and major holidays throughout the day. In addition, it may be passed along to other seniors over 60. Buy it before you leave.

Something else to remember is that most hotels in Brussels offer a 50 percent reduction on room rates on weekends and during the months of July and August, when the staffs of many international organizations leave town for home.

For information: Belgian National Tourist Office, 780 Third Ave., New York, NY 10017; 212-758-8130; visit www.belgium.com.

BERMUDA

February is Golden Rendezvous Month in Bermuda, when visitors over the age of 50 are treated to special events and free activities every day. For example, there are complimentary bus tours around the island and talks on the traditions, culture, history, flowers, and wildlife. Plus, there are bridge tournaments, ballroom dancing, and visits to museums. Many hotels offer special packages and rates, while the Visitors' Service Bureau distributes two free ferry/bus tokens per person as well as discount coupon books to use at retail stores and sight-seeing attractions.

For information: Bermuda Department of Tourism, 800-BERMUDA (237-6832); www.bermudatourism.com.

BRITAIN

Bargains abound in the U.K., undoubtedly the most popular foreign destination for Americans. Senior rates and special privileges are offered almost everywhere, from railroads and bus lines to museums, theaters, swimming pools, and historic sites. Visitors over 60, for example, get 25 percent off the cost of admission to Windsor Castle and Hampton Court; 50 percent off at Westminster Abbey; and up to 40 percent at other castles, stately homes, galleries, and gardens. So wherever you go be sure to ask if there is a senior rate, for which you'll usually qualify at age 60 or 65. Carry proof of your age with you. Most national museums and galleries have recently done away with admission fees altogether.

Theatergoers in London can buy tickets at half price or sometimes less at most major theaters simply by arriving at the box office after 6 P.M. for evening performances and about an hour before the curtain rises for matinees. Have your IDs in hand and ask for "Senior Standbys."

Several hotel chains in Britain give discounts to guests over 50. Among them are Comfort, Quality, and Clarion Hotels, marketed as Choice Hotels Europe (800-654-6200 or www.choicehotelseurope.com), and they will give you 10 percent off the room rate. Many Best Western Hotels in the U.K. give the same discount to members of AARP and other travelers who are at least 55 (800-937-8376 or www.best western.com). Not to be outdone, four Red Carnation Hotels in London (800-424-2862 or www.redcarnationhotels.com) offer a substantial dining credit to 50+ travelers.

For information: British Tourist Authority, 551 Fifth Ave., New York, NY 10176; 877-899-8391; www.travelbritain.org or www.maturebritain.org. Ask for the free guide, *Time to Travel*, for mature travelers.

Traveling by train. In Britain, where virtually every town may be reached by train, it pays to consider a rail pass, especially because travelers over 60 get discounts of about 15 percent off the regular adult prices on first-class tickets. The passes are not sold in the U.K. but must be purchased here before you go. They are not accepted in Ireland or on special excursion trains, but they do include service between London and its two international airports, Heathrow and Gatwick. You may get on and off the trains along the way as often as you like.

If you buy the BritRail Senior Flexipass, you may choose any 4, 8, or 15 days of unlimited first-class travel within a two-month period in England, Scotland, and Wales. The days need not be consecutive. The BritRail Classic Senior Pass, another option, gives you 8, 15, 22 days, or one month of unlimited first-class travel that must be on consecutive days.

One child age 5 through 15 can travel free with each senior (or adult) pass holder. Additional children 5 through 15 travel at half fare. Children under 5 are free.

For information: BritRail, 877-677-1066; www.britrail.net. Rail Europe, 800-4-EURAIL (438-7245); www.raileurope.com.

Traveling by bus. Starting at age 50, you'll get a break of about 25 percent on the Tourist Trail Pass that provides unlimited travel for varying numbers of days on National Express coaches in England and Wales and to and from Scotland from either of them. It includes transportation to and from all major international airports. You can buy it here before you go or at any major bus station in Britain.

For information: National Express, 540-298-1395; www.britbus.com.

Another option designed for visitors age 50 or more is the Advantage 50 Discount Coach Card that costs about $13.50 for one year. With it, you will get discounts of up to 30 percent on point-to-point travel on all National Express coaches in England and Wales as well as to and from Scotland. Buy it online using a credit card or at any major bus station in Britain.
For information: www.gobycoach.com or National Express bus terminals in the U.K.

Travelers over 55 are eligible for a discount of $60 per person on all escorted bus tours over seven days by Prestige Tours of Scotland. The leisurely itineraries take you around the country from Edinburgh to the Highlands and the Isle of Skye with everything included, even gratuities.
For information: Prestige Tours, PO Box 77, Thompson Ridge, NY 10985; 800-890-7375; www.prestigetours.com.

Travel passes. Several passes will let you see the sights for less in Britain. The Great British Heritage Pass, for example, available to non-U.K. residents only, gives you unlimited free entry to nearly 600 historic houses, castles, and gardens in England, Scotland, Wales, and Northern Ireland. Buy it from your travel agent, BritRail, or Rail Europe before you leave home or from Tourist Information Centers in Britain. A 7-day pass (you may also buy it for 15 days or a month) currently costs about $54.

The London Visitor Travelcard, which must be purchased outside of Britain, gives you unlimited travel for three, four, or seven consecutive days, in all zones or in the central zone only, on London's buses and subways as well as many trains. The all-zones card includes transfer via underground from Heathrow Airport to central London.

On all BritRail packages from the U.S. to the U.K. that include air and hotels, travelers who are at least 60 years of age are entitled to a 5 percent discount.

And then there's the London Pass that may be purchased for one, three, or six days. Use it for free admission to more than 60 attractions and unlimited travel on buses, subways, and trains in London's Transport Zones 1 to 6. Buy it from Rail Europe, at Tourist Information Centers in London, or online at www.londonpass.com. Sorry, no senior discount on this pass.

For information: BritRail, 866-BRITRAIL (274-8724); www.britrail.net. Rail Europe, 800-4-EURAIL (438-7245); www.raileurope.com.

HEALTH COVERAGE ABROAD

The standard Medicare plan, with a few exceptions, does not cover medical care outside the U.S. Some Medicare HMOs do cover emergency procedures abroad but not routine care, and many of the available Medigap policies provide 80 percent, after a deductible, of the cost of emergency care incurred in the first two months of a trip outside the country. If you do not carry your own private health insurance that will pay the expenses incurred overseas, talk to your travel agent about temporary health insurance that will cover you for the length of your trip.

For information: Call 800-MEDICARE (633-4227); www.medicare.gov.

A Scottish Explorer Ticket gives unlimited access to about 60 of Scotland's historic sites such as castles, abbeys, and distilleries. Buy it at a Tourist Information Center or a Historic Scotland property and be sure to ask for the senior discount that will save you about a third off the regular adult cost.

The Welsh Historic Monuments (CADW) Explorer Pass, good for unlimited entry to all Welsh Heritage Properties, are also available at Tourist Information Centers, without a senior discount, however.

DENMARK

When you buy tickets for the Danish State Railway system at any train station in Denmark, be sure to ask for the discount for passengers 65 and older. You get a 50 percent reduction on tickets every day, except Friday and Sunday and some holidays when the discount drops to 25 percent. For information about the Scanrail Senior Pass to be used on the railroads of Denmark, Finland, Norway, and Sweden, see Scandinavia later in this chapter.

When traveling by air, remember that SAS offers passengers over the age of 62 a 10 percent discount on most fares for flights from North America to Scandinavia and other destinations in Europe. For domestic travel within Denmark, the 65-year-old traveler gets a special senior fare. See Chapter 3 for more details.

Don't forget to buy the Copenhagen Card. Available for 24, 48, or 72 hours, it provides free unlimited travel by bus and train throughout the metropolitan region; free admission to more than 70 museums and historic sites; and discounts on car rentals, canal rides, and ferry crossings. City cards are also sold for Odense and Aalborg.

For information: Danish Tourist Board, 355 Third Ave., New York, NY 10017; 212-885-9700; www.visitdenmark.com.

FINLAND

Travel within Finland is discounted, sometimes steeply, for people over 65. Simply show proof of your age—your passport—at the ticket office, and you will pay half fare on all trains and receive a 30 percent reduction on motorcoach journeys of at least 80 kilometers in length.

In addition, Finnair, the national airline, offers you at 62 and a companion 10 percent off most transatlantic fares and at age 65 a discount up to 75 percent on domestic flights. See Chapter 3 for more details.

Although the Helsinki Card is not discounted by age, it offers substantial savings on a city tour and admission to museums, exhibitions, attractions, buses, trams, and metro and commuter trains within the city limits. Available at the airport, many hotels, and tourist offices, it is sold for periods of one, two, or three days. For information about the Scanrail Senior Pass for railroad travel in Denmark, Finland, Norway, and Sweden, see Scandinavia later in this chapter.

For information: Finnish Tourist Board, PO Box 4649, Grand Central Sta., New York, NY 10163; 212-885-9700; www.gofinland.org.

FRANCE

Wherever you go in France, from museums to historic sites, the movies and theaters to concerts, always ask whether there is a senior discount and you will be amazed how often you'll get one. Most Paris municipal museums, by the way, are free to everyone.

The privileges that come with age are especially good, however, when it comes to transportation. You are offered several choices. For example, simply by showing proof that you are 60 or more when you buy a ticket at a railway station, you will get the Decouverte Senior rate that gives you 25 percent off on all TGV rail services (except overnight accommodations) throughout the entire country, except on trips entirely within the Paris Transport Region. You will get the same reduction on non-TGV mainline and regional rail services for travel during off-peak periods.

If you plan extensive travel in France, you may prefer a Carte Senior. Valid for a year, again at age 60, it allows unlimited travel in first or second class at a 50 percent discount on some journeys in non-rush hours and a 25 percent discount on others, plus 25 percent off on some rail travel in 27 other European countries. This pass currently costs about $35 and requires a passport photo when you buy it at a major train station.

Finally, there is the France Seniorpass that costs you a little percent less at 60-plus than it does other adult travelers and must be purchased over here. It gives you any four days of unlimited first-class travel within a month and the option of buying up to six additional days.

For getting around in Paris, the Paris Visite Card, available for varying numbers of days, allows you to travel for free on public transportation. That includes the metro, buses (including shuttle buses to central Paris from the airports), the RER (fast trains between main stations), the tramway, the Montmartre Funicular, and all SNCF trains in the greater Paris region. You may buy it here or in Paris at metro or SNCF stations and tourist offices.

And here's something else to remember. Seniors are invited, along with the disabled and families with small children, to ride the elevator to the top of the Arc de Triomphe for a panoramic view of the city.

For information: French Government Tourist Office, 444 Madison Ave., New York, NY 10022; 212-838-7800; www.franceguide.com. For the France Seniorpass: Rail Europe; 800-4-EURAIL (438-7245); www.raileurope.com.

GERMANY

Many restaurants in Germany have a *Seniorenteller*, a special menu that offers lighter fare in smaller portions at a lower cost for older guests. Ask to see it and also ask if there are discounts for seniors wherever you go. You'll find they are available in places such as department stores, hair salons, museums, historic sites, and other attractions such as day cruises on the Rhine. Even some hotels and spa resorts have them, especially in off-peak seasons.

If you plan to travel by train and are over 60, you may buy a BahnCard Senior for about 70 euro second class or 140 euro first class at any railway station (have your passport with you). The card gives you 50 percent off on tickets wherever you go in Germany on the Deutsche Bahn. For a small additional fee, you can get a card that takes 25 percent off all train tickets in 25 European countries. If you are traveling with children between the ages of 6 and 11, a family Bahncard may be an even better deal. It gives you 50 percent off on your tickets plus a reduction of 25 percent on the children's.

Although there is no senior discount on the German Rail Pass, you can lower the cost by 25 percent for two people traveling together by using the German Rail Twin Pass, available here and in Germany.

For those who would rather travel by motorcoach, Deutsche Touring, a long-distance bus line that will transport you in comfort almost anywhere in Germany as well as to most other European countries, takes 10 percent off the price of all tickets for all passengers 60 or older. You can buy tickets through a travel agent or at railroad stations.

And another good deal awaits travelers who are 60 or more, this time from the KD Cruise Line that takes you along the Rhine River, past castles and vineyards, small villages, spectacular scenery and big cities, with more than 40 places to get on or off as you like. You'll get half-price tickets on sailings Monday through Friday.

There is a 10 percent discount on most fares across the Atlantic Ocean to European destinations on Lufthansa for people 60 and older and companions over the age of 18. The same discount applies to domestic flights in Europe. See Chapter 3.

Finally, check out the city cards, now available at local tourist offices, railway stations, and hotels in most major cities for savings on transportation, tours, and admissions. ***For information:*** German National Tourist Office, 122 E. 42nd St., New York, NY 10168; 212-661-7200; www.visits-to-germany.com.

HONG KONG

In this bustling city, there are several ways to save money on transportation, assuming you are at least 65. The *Star Ferry* will take you free of charge on the eight-minute crossing from central Hong Kong to Kowloon, giving you a fabulous view of Victoria Harbor. You pay half fare on the Mass Transit Railway, the HYF Ferry to outlying islands, the Light Rail (LR), and the Kowloon-to-Canton Railway (KCR). And on the famous Peak Tram, you are offered a discount of about 60 percent off the regular adult fare. Always be prepared with ID, such as your passport.

Several museums, too, give seniors a break on admissions, charging only half the regular entrance fee.

The Meet the People program in Hong Kong costs nothing, requires no reservations, and schedules events every day of the week to introduce visitors to English-speaking specialists who share their knowledge of local traditions. Among the topics are tai chi, the rituals of tea, Chinese antiques, Cantonese opera, pearl appreciation, and even a ride on a Chinese junk. Pick up the weekly schedule at a Visitor Information Centre.

For information: Hong Kong Tourist Association, 800-282-4582 or 212-421-3382; www.discoverhongkong.com.

JAPAN

To get around Japan on its fast and spotless railroads, there is no better deal than the JR rail pass, although it offers no special senior privileges. It is available only to visitors to the country and allows unlimited travel on almost all Japan Railway trains and its affiliated bus and ferry lines for 7 or 21 days. You may also buy passes good for travel in limited parts of the country. You must buy your pass here before you go, getting an exchange order, then trading it for the pass in Japan.

Three special programs—not just for seniors but for all visitors to Japan—are designed to make your trip more enjoyable. Welcome Cards, for example, are available in many cities or areas of the country, giving you discounts and special services at art galleries, museums, sight-seeing attractions, shops, restaurants, and transportation. Pick them up at tourist offices.

The Good Will Guide System (SGG) connects foreign travelers with local volunteers in 58 cities or towns who offer free guided tours and help with any problems you may encounter during your visit to their country. Brochures with details about the program are available at the Japan National Tourist Office or on its website.

The Home Visit System, another volunteer organization, offers you a chance to spend a few hours as a guest in a Japanese home in your choice of 14 cities. For these visits, applications and appointments are required and are not available from abroad. You can get information at local visitor centers in Japan.

For information: Japan National Tourist Organization, 1 Rockefeller Plaza, New York, NY 10020; 212-757-5641; www.jnto.go.jp.

NETHERLANDS

Whenever you go to museums, attractions, theaters, concerts, and cultural and historic sites or on tours in the Netherlands, always ask if there is a senior discount, because people over 65 are usually given a significant break on admission fees. Remember to have your passport handy to prove your age.

For extensive travel in the country, it may make sense to buy a Holland Railpass-Senior purchased at railroad stations in the Netherlands or from Rail Europe or your travel agent.

At age 65, you are eligible to buy a *strippenkaart* at railroad stations or post offices in the Netherlands. It allows you to ride buses, metros, and trams throughout the country for about 40 percent off the usual fare.

And consider the Amsterdam Pass, which provides vouchers for free or discounted admission to museums, cruises, tours, and more.

For information: Netherlands Board of Tourism, 355 Lexington Ave., New York, NY 10017; 888-GO-HOLLAND (464-6552); www.holland.com.

NEW ZEALAND

Travelers over the age of 60 qualify for a 30 percent savings off the standard fares on Tranz Scenic Trains any time of the year. Tickets must be reserved in New Zealand at Tranz Scenic travel centers in Auckland, Wellington, or Christchurch.

The same 30 percent savings is offered for tickets aboard the ferries operated by the same company to 60+ travelers who use the Inter-Island Line sailing between the North and South Islands as well as the Lynx Line. Again, bookings must be made in New Zealand through the Inter-Island Line's reservation center or accredited travel agents.

For information: www.tranzrail.co.nz or www.interisland line.co.nz. Also Tourism New Zealand, 501 Santa Monica Blvd., Santa Monica, CA 90401; 866-639-9325; www .purenz.com.

NORWAY

In this beautiful country, you're entitled to half fare on buses and trains, any time, any place. For this break, however, you must be at least 67 and ready to prove your age with a proper ID.

At age 60, you can buy a Norway Rail Pass Senior and save about 20 percent over what younger adult travelers pay for the same unlimited first- or second-class rail travel on trains operated by the Norwegian State Railways (NSB), plus a 30 percent reduction on the Flam Railway, for three, four, or five days within one month. It must be purchased in the U.S. or Canada through your travel agent, or Rail Europe, as it is not available in Norway.

At age 67, you become eligible for a discount of up to $220 on Norwegian Coastal Voyages (when you sail off peak) that sail up the coast past myriad fjords to the Arctic Circle and back. What's more, if you belong to AARP, you may add another discount on top of that one—you'll get a reduction of $70 to $150 per cabin on all sailings year-round. See Chapter 9.

SAS, the Scandinavian airline, offers travelers 62 or over a 10 percent discount on most flights to Scandinavia and its other international destinations.

For information about the Scanrail Senior Pass to be used on railroads in Denmark, Finland, Norway, and Sweden, see Scandinavia later in this chapter.

As for hotels, there are discounts for all of Scandinavia (discussed later in this chapter). In addition, check out the Norway Fjord Pass (www.fjordpass.com). It costs about $10 and offers discounts on rooms from May through September in hotels, guest houses, apartments, and holiday cottages.

As you should everywhere, ask if there is a senior discount wherever you go and consider purchasing city cards for Oslo and Bergen. They will provide free public transportation plus free or discounted admission at most museums, historic sites, and cultural attractions.

For information: Norwegian Tourist Board, 655 Third Ave., New York, NY 10017; 212-885-9700; www.visitnorway.com.

PORTUGAL

If you're over 65, there's hardly anywhere you can go in Portugal without being offered a senior discount of 30 to 50 percent off the regular price. So make a point of asking for it when you take a train or a bus and when you go to a museum, a national monument, a theater, a movie, and anyplace else that charges admission.

If you're a mere 60, you can take advantage of a very good deal called the Golden Age Program which gives you a 40 percent discount on the regular rates for accommodations and breakfast for two at all but two of Portugal's famous pousadas. These are the historic government-run inns scattered around the country, many of them in former castles, monasteries, or palaces. The discount applies on Sunday through Thursday nights, with some exceptions, from April through October and sometimes other times of the year, too. The catch is that rooms with the senior discount are limited, so book them far in advance.

There's also a Tourist Pass available for all ages, which offers free unlimited travel on Lisbon's transportation system. Sold at the airport and tourist information offices, a four-day pass costs about $10.

The Lisbon Card gives you the same access to the underground, buses, trams, and lifts, plus free entry into 26 museums, monuments, and other sites. It also provides discounts on sight-seeing tours, river cruises, and theatrical events. Porto, Portugal's second-largest city, offers the Passe Porto with similar benefits.

And don't forget that TAP Air Portugal, the national airline, will give you at age 62 and a younger companion a 10 percent discount on transatlantic flights. See Chapter 3 for more details.

For information: Portuguese National Tourist Office, 590 Fifth Ave., New York, NY 10036; 212-354-4403; www.portugal.org. For pousadas: Petrabax, 800-634-1188; www.petrabaxusa.com. Or Marketing Ahead, 800-223-1356; www.marketingahead.com.

SCANDINAVIA

Scandinavia—which includes Denmark, Finland, Norway, and Sweden—has many good deals for mature travelers. Here are some that are valid in all four countries. (Those that are unique to the individual countries are described under their own headings throughout this chapter.)

The Scanrail Senior Pass costs tourists over 60 about 10 percent less than what others pay for unlimited rail travel in Sweden, Norway, Denmark, and Finland. You may travel first or second class anywhere within the four countries for 5 or 10 days within two months, or for 21 consecutive days.

Among the added bonuses: half fare on many bus lines and reduced fares on some ferries and cruise ships. Reservations are occasionally required and always recommended.

For information: Rail Europe, 2100 Central Ave., Boulder, CO 80301; 800-4-EURAIL (438-7245); www.raileurope.com.

You and other travelers can also save money in the Scandinavian countries by using hotel passes. The Nordic Hotel Pass, for example, that costs about $12, gives you discounts of up to 50 percent off the regular room rates at more than 120 first-class hotels that are part of Choice Hotels International. The Scan+ Hotel Pass (www.scanplus.no) provides vouchers for discounted rates at about 200 other participating hotels throughout Scandinavia and is valid May through September.

SAS, the Scandinavian airline, gives passengers 62 and over a 10 percent discount on most fares between the U.S. and Scandinavia and its other international destinations. In Sweden and Denmark, it gives special fares for passengers who are 65 or older. See Chapter 3.

Finnair also takes 10 percent off most transatlantic fares for you at age 62 and your companion at any age. But on domestic flights within Finland, you'll get a spectacular discount—up to 75 percent off—at age 65, whether you buy your tickets here or in Finland. You must pay for your tickets within three days of booking. See Chapter 3.

And, finally, you should seriously consider buying city cards for free public transportation plus free or discounted entry to museums, historic sites, and cultural attractions.

They can be purchased ahead of time in the U.S. or at tourist information offices, train stations, airports, and hotels in Scandinavia. The cities include Copenhagen, Odense, and Aalborg in Denmark; Helsinki in Finland; Oslo and Bergen in Norway; and Stockholm, Gothenburg, and Malmo in Sweden.
For information: Scandinavian National Tourist Offices, 655 Third Ave., New York, NY 10017; 212-885-9700; www.goscandinavia.com.

SINGAPORE

When you send for the Tourism Board's free brochure, "Mature Travelers Guide," for visitors over 55, you will also receive an extensive list of senior discounts, some as high as 50 percent, on admission fees and prices for many of this small island country's attractions, museums, harbor/river cruises, spas, and sight-seeing tours.
For information: Singapore Tourism Board, 590 Fifth Ave., New York, NY 10036; 212-302-4861; www.tourism-singapore.com.

SPAIN

In addition to discounts for mature travelers at just about every museum, cultural event, and historic site in Spain, there is another good deal for visitors over 60. The Golden Days Promotion offers a 35 percent discount on the cost of a room and a buffet breakfast at most of the country's famous paradores. These are government-owned inns, 87 in all, and many of them are former palaces, castles, convents, or monasteries located in the Spanish countryside. The special rates apply all year except in July, August, September, and Easter and Christmas weeks. Some paradores are available every day of the week; others only from Sunday to Thursday; and still others only on Friday, Saturday, and Sunday. There are limited numbers of rooms at the special rate so make your plans far ahead.

For information: Tourist Office of Spain, 666 Fifth Ave., New York, NY 10103; 212-265-8822; www.okspain.org. For paradores: Petrabax, 800-634-1188; www.petrabaxusa.com. Or, Marketing Ahead, 800-223-1356; www.marketingahead.com.

SWEDEN

Travel by bus in Sweden is inexpensive and hassle-free. Besides, seniors get substantial discounts. Hop on a local bus in Sweden, and, if you're 65, you'll pay about 40 percent less than the regular fare. Travel on the express buses operated by Swebus Express, the country's largest long-distance bus operator with 180 destinations in Sweden plus Oslo (Norway) and Copenhagen (Denmark), you are offered a 20 percent discount.

For seeing the sights in the greater Stockholm area, consider buying the SL Tourist Card sold at tourist offices and kiosks. It's half price for seniors (about $9 for three days). With this card, you get free transportation on buses, local trains, subways, and ferry tours.

For information about the Scanrail Senior Pass for travel in Denmark, Finland, Norway, and Sweden, see Scandinavia earlier in this chapter.

SAS, the Scandinavian airline, takes 10 percent off the regular fares for passengers over 62 flying from this side of the Atlantic to SAS destinations worldwide. On flights within Sweden, the airline offers special senior fares, depending on the route, to passengers 65 and older. See Chapter 3.

And don't forget the city cards—the Stockholm Card, Gothenburg Card, and Malmo Card. These very good deals give you free or discounted transportation and admission to places you'll want to visit.

For information: Swedish Travel and Tourism Council, 655 Third Ave., New York, NY 10017; 212-885-9700; www.visitsweden.com.

SWITZERLAND

The Swiss Hotel Association will provide, for the asking, a list of about 400 hotels in 160 cities and towns that participate in a program called "Season for Seniors." This program gives reduced room rates—sometimes discounted as much as 50 percent—to women over 62 and to men over 65. If two people are traveling together, just one must be the required age. The only catch is that in most cases the reduced rates do not apply during peak travel periods, including the summer months.

The Swiss Museum Passport is good for a month of unlimited visits to about 180 museums. If you are a woman over 62 or a man over 65, you may buy it at a discount at participating museums and tourist offices in Switzerland.

Switzerland's new airline, SWISS, gives passengers 62 and over and a travel companion of any age a 10 percent discount on nonsale fares on flights from the U.S. to Europe. See Chapter 3.

For information: Switzerland Tourism, 608 Fifth Ave., New York, NY 10020; 877-794-8037 or 212-757-5944; www.myswitzerland.com.

9

Trips and Tours for the Mature Traveler

Many enterprising organizations, tour operators, and travel agencies now cater exclusively to the mature traveler. They choose destinations designed to appeal to those who might have already "been there and done that," arrange trips that are leisurely and unhassled, give you congenial contemporaries to travel with and group hosts to smooth the way, and provide many special services you never got before. They also give you a choice between strenuous action-filled tours and those that are more relaxed. In fact, most of the agencies offer so many choices that the biggest problem is making a decision about where to go.

Options range from cruises in the Caribbean or the Greek Isles to grand tours of the Orient, sight-seeing excursions in the U.S., trips to the Canadian Rockies, theater tours of London, safaris in Africa, and snorkeling vacations on the Great Barrier Reef off Australia. There's just no place in the world where mature travelers won't go.

Among the newer and most popular trends are apartment/hotel complexes in American and European resort areas, as well as apartments in major cities. Here you can stay put for as long as you like, using the apartment or hotel as a home base for short-range roaming and exploring with the guidance of on-site hosts.

There are many choices, too, for the growing number of intrepid, energetic, and courageous members of the 50-plus population who prefer travel that is adventurous and unusual, perhaps even exotic. Many are described in this chapter along with the more traditional variety. Because they are planned specifically for the seasoned traveler, they usually offer some measure of comfort and convenience even in the wilderness, plus a leisurely pace that allows time for relaxation and independent exploration. Most important, they offer clean, comfortable accommodations, though sometimes rustic or spartan, and, almost always, a private bathroom.

ADVENTURE SOUTH

If you're looking for action, consider Midlife Adventures, a 13-day itinerary for those who are "too young to be called old, and too old to be called young." Offered by Adventure South in New Zealand, it is a tour of both North and South Islands with soft adventure activities including sailing, sea kayaking, walking, visits to volcanoes and glaciers, scenic flights, and visits with New Zealanders in their own homes. This company also plans bike tours and walking vacations.

For information: The Best of New Zealand, 2811 Wiltshire Blvd, Ste. 950, Santa Monica, CA 90403; 800-528-6129; www.advsouth.co.nz.

AFC TOURS & CRUISES

Specializing in escorted tours designed for mature travelers, AFC schedules trips to all the most popular destinations in the U.S. and Canada and some in other countries. Not only that, but if you live in southern California, where AFC is based, you will be transported free between your home and the airport. Many of the most popular tours are "unpack once," which means you stay in one hotel and take day trips from there. Domestic tours take you to such places as the national parks, Branson, Charleston, New York City, Savannah, the Pacific Northwest, and Washington, D.C. International adventures cover all of Europe. Other choices include: cruises, steamboating, train tours, holiday tours, and grandparent trips. In other words, almost anything you want. Special for singles: if you sign up four months in advance and a roommate cannot be found to share your room, you need not pay a single supplement.

For information about AFC's new women-only tours, see Wander Women in Chapter 11.

For information: AFC Tours and Cruises, 11772 Sorrento Valley Rd., San Diego, CA 92121; 800-369-3693 or 858-481-8188; www.afctours.com.

BACK-ROADS TOURING CO.

The tours planned for adults only by Back-Roads Touring Co. take groups of no more than 11 participants on explorations of the U.K. and other European countries, along the

back roads to out-of-the-way places. You'll travel by minicoach with a trained guide for one or two weeks and lodge in country inns, guest houses, and small family-owned properties. These are leisurely tours with plenty of time to explore. You'll stay several nights in the same location and spend time with local residents. You may even help plan the itinerary. Add-on stays in London are available, too, and so are four-day "country breaks" and day trips out of London.
For information: Back-Roads Touring Co., International Travel Marketing, 1047 W. 6th St., Corona, CA 92882; 800-830-1083; www.smallgrouptouring.com.

CIE TOURS INTERNATIONAL

An agency specializing in escorted vacations in Ireland, Northern Ireland, Scotland, Wales, and England, CIE offers motorcoach tours and fly/drive vacations, some of which come with a "55 and Smiling Discount." This means that on selected tours you get $55 off the cost of the trip if you are 55 or older and are among the first 15 people to book the tour.
For information: CIE Tours International, 100 Hanover Ave., PO Box 501, Cedar Knolls, NJ 07927; 800-243-8687 or 973-292-3438; www.cietours.com.

COLLETTE VACATIONS

Collette Vacations has been around for more than 80 years, offering worry-free worldwide vacations to the mature traveler. Its escorted tours move at a relaxed pace, put you up in good hotels, and provide experienced tour guides to see that all goes well. But this agency offers other kinds of vacations too. For example, its "hub and spoke" programs feature multiple nights in one place—city stays, resort stays, castle stays—so you can settle down for a while without constantly climbing on buses and unpacking your bags at the next destination. Meanwhile, day excursions take you to see the sights.

Collette's independent travel packages, land-only or air-inclusive, let you customize your own trip in North America or Europe. You have hotel options at each destination, optional activities, and rental cars or train transportation if you want them.

And remember that members of AARP can save up to $100 per person on escorted tours and up to $50 on some independent packages.

For information: Collette Vacations, 162 Middle St., Pawtucket, RI 02860; 888-344-5578; www.collettevacations.com.

ELDERHOSTEL

The educational tours from Elderhostel number in the thousands, all of them bargains for adults over the age of 55 (and younger travel mates). See Chapter 12.

For information: Elderhostel, 11 Avenue de Lafayette, Boston, MA 02111; 877-426-8056 or 617-426-7788; www.elderhostel.com.

ELDERTREKS

This Canadian-based adventure travel company specializes in active, small-group, off-the-beaten-path, all-inclusive land journeys to exotic places in more than 50 countries, from Argentina to Mongolia. All of them are offered exclusively to people 50 and over (and their companions of any age). It stresses cultural interaction, nature exploration, and physical activity, for which you should be in good condition. Itineraries, however, are chosen with older trekkers in mind and groups are limited to 16 participants. Trips are rated for difficulty and housing conditions (huts to hotels).

Accommodations for the city portions of the tours are in clean, comfortable, tourist-class hotels and guest houses chosen for charm and location. Accommodations on the adventure portions may be on the floor of a nomadic tent or under a canopy of trees in the jungle, but you can always count on an air mattress. Guides, cooks, meals, and porters are part of the package. Recent destinations have included Bhutan, Borneo, Vietnam, Laos, Sumatra, Java, Bali, Tibet, Nepal, Ecuador, Bolivia, Peru, Madagasgar, Patagonia, Yemen, Belize, Lapland, Guatemala, and Honduras.

By the way, if you are traveling alone and are willing to share, you can avoid a single-supplement charge.

For information: ElderTreks, 597 Markham St., Toronto, ON M6G 2L7; 800-741-7956 or 416-588-5000; www.eldertreks.com.

FANCY-FREE HOLIDAYS

Geared for senior travelers, this agency's domestic escorted motorcoach tours, all originating in Chicago, include the usual favorite destinations such as Branson, New England, Alaska, Williamsburg, Asheville, New Orleans, and Washington, D.C. Its fully escorted overseas tours by air, motorcoach, or cruise ship include Ireland, England, Scotland, and Wales.

For information: Fancy-Free Holidays, 24 W. 500 Maple Ave., Naperville, IL 60540; 800-421-3330 or 630-778-7010; www.fancyfreeholidays.com.

50PLUS EXPEDITIONS

This company plans adventure travel exclusively for travelers over 50 and specializes in exotic trips all over the world. Consider these: exploring the Ecuadorean rainforest and the Amazon jungle; cycling along the Danube; ballooning over the Serengeti; hiking in the Canadian Rockies; searching for tigers in India; sailing on a small ship to Antarctica.

These are small group tours composed of 2 to 16 people who are escorted by experienced local guides. All trips are graded for difficulty from easy to demanding, depending on the level of physical activity, elevation, climate, and so forth, and most allow for optional extensions.

For information: 50plus Expeditions, 415 Oakdale Rd., Toronto, ON M3N 1W7; 866-318-5050 or 426-749-5150; www.50plusexpeditions.com.

GLOBUS & COSMOS TOURS

This affiliated pair of escorted tour companies, together the largest in the world, offers everything from the traditional escorted tours everywhere in the world to more leisurely vacations that give you a few days in each city on your itinerary. All of the tours are designed to appeal to over-50 travelers who comprise the vast majority of their clients. The upscale escorted tours from Globus will take you to all seven continents of the world including Antarctica. Additionally, they provide guest accommodations in three- and four-star hotels.

A Globus specialty is a choice of Tour & Cruise Vacations that combine land tours and cruises. One trip, for example, takes you to Vienna for four nights and then on a Danube River cruise to Budapest and Bratislava.

The company's LeisureStyle Vacations feature two- or three-night stays per city and activities such as cooking classes, golfing, and wine tasting. The Independent City Stays, here and abroad, offer a chance to independently explore with advice and assistance from a professional on-site host.

Cosmos specializes in vacations for cost-conscious travelers and offers traditional escorted motorcoach tours all over the world. By the way, if you are traveling alone and are willing to share a room, you'll get a roommate and pay no single supplement. Members of AARP can save $50 on any Globus or Cosmos Vacation.

For information: Globus & Cosmos Tours, 5301 S. Federal Circle, Littleton, CO 80123; 800-241-9853 or 303-797-2800; www.globusandcosmos.com.

GO AHEAD VACATIONS

Go Ahead Vacations is a division of EF Education, a company that has focused for many years on intercultural exchange and educational travel. This tour operator caters to the 50-plus traveler and offers traditional escorted tours that include airfare, accommodations, transfers, breakfast, guided sightseeing, and a full-time bilingual tour director.

In addition, it features walking tours, combination land and cruise tours, and independent city-stay vacations. Benefits include pre- and post-tour extension options, credits for repeat travelers, and free travel opportunities for organizers of groups.

For information: Go Ahead Vacations, 1 Education St., Cambridge MA 02141; 800-242-4686; www.goaheadvacations.com.

GOLDEN AGE FESTIVE HOLIDAYS

Another agency that caters to the 50-plus crowd, this one offers tours to everywhere from Wildwood (New Jersey), Myrtle Beach, Nashville, Maine, and New York to the national parks, Las Vegas, Europe, Greece, China, and Australia—plus plenty of cruises. All packages are escorted and include accommodations, meals, and just about everything else.

In addition, Golden Age offers an innovation—"drive-to tours" for individual travelers, allowing them to take advantage of group discounts that make the trips remarkably inexpensive. On these, all on the East Coast, you drive yourself to your destination—for example, Wildwood, Ocean City, Myrtle Beach, Newport and Mystic Seaport, Hilton Head, Williamsburg—and join others traveling on their own for meals, entertainment, and tours.

For information: Golden Age Festive Holidays, 5501 New Jersey Ave., Wildwood Crest, NJ 08260; 800-257-8920 or 609-522-6316; www.goldenagefestival.com.

GOLDEN AGE TRAVELLERS CLUB

This over-50 club specializes in discounted cruises on major lines everywhere in the world, but it also offers land tours from well-known tour operators. When you join the club ($10 single or $15 per couple a year), you receive a newsletter with listings of upcoming sailings. Other inducements are tour escorts and bonus points. Single travelers may choose to be enrolled in the Roommates Wanted list to help them find companions to share cabins and costs. For members in the San Francisco and Sacramento areas, there are one-day travel shows where you may meet fellow travelers and share a snack.

Especially intriguing to mature travelers are the agency's long-stay trips. On these, you stay put—for example, in Spain, Portugal, Guatemala, Australia, Costa Rica, or Argentina—at the same hotel for two or three weeks and, if you wish, take short side trips. The packages include air, hotel, and sometimes meals.

For information: Golden Age Travellers Club, Pier 27, The Embarcadero, San Francisco, CA 94111; 800-258-8880 or 415-296-0151; www.gatclub.com.

GRAND CIRCLE TRAVEL

Grand Circle Travel, the first U.S. company to market senior travel, caters to people over 50 and plans all of its trips exclusively for them. That means the trips are easygoing with longer stays, unhurried itineraries, and plenty of time to relax. Grand Circle specializes in four varieties of travel. Its classic escorted tours take groups of mature travelers all over the world, accompanied by experienced guides who take care of everything. All you have to do is show up and keep your eyes open. Its extended vacations allow you to travel in a group but, at the same time, be an independent traveler. You stay up to two weeks in one, two, or three destinations such as the Costa del Sol, Sicily, or Thailand. You live in hotels or apartments, with meals, social activities, tours, and a program director included.

River cruises are another option, taking you on leisurely voyages throughout Europe aboard the company's own fleet of private river boats. And finally, the ocean cruise tours that combine sailing the major seas with land-based stays for in-depth explorations of the ports of call.

If you are a solo traveler, you may ask to be matched with an appropriate roommate to avoid the single supplement or choose an occasional trip when the supplement is waived. ***For information:*** Grand Circle Travel, 347 Congress St., Boston, MA 02210; 800-248-3737 or 617-350-7500; www.gct.com.

HORIZON HOLIDAYS

This Canadian tour operator offers "worry-free" escorted holidays exclusively to travelers 55 and older. Its groups are small, never more than 39 and often much smaller, and the cost includes everything from tipping to luggage handling except for a few lunches. With no optional sight-seeing trips, you can go everywhere without an extra charge. Leisure time is built into the holidays and multinight stopovers allow a relaxed pace. Horizon specializes in extensive tours of Canada but includes destinations to about every place else in the world in addition to a roster of cruises. ***For information:*** Horizon Holidays, 160 John St., Toronto, ON M5V 2X8; 800-387-2977 (in the U.S. and Canada); 416-585-9911; www.horizon-holidays.com.

HOSTELLING INTERNATIONAL (USA)

This international organization, formerly known as American Youth Hostels, offers low-cost lodging all over the globe to people of all ages. Membership for adults costs $25 a year, but if you are 55 or older, you pay only $15. You get a membership card, a free guide to hostels in the U.S., and a free map of U.S. hostels. For an added fee, you may order a guidebook listing more than 4,000 hostels in more than 60 countries including about 115 in the U.S. In addition, you are entitled to hundreds of discounts on transportation, car rentals, restaurants, admissions, festivals, ski lifts, and more.

Lodgings are dormitory-style, women in one room, men in another, although some hostels also have private rooms for families, couples, and groups which may be reserved in advance. These include the Gateway City Hostels in eight of the country's major cities—New York City, Los Angeles, San Francisco, Miami Beach, Washington, D.C., Chicago, Seattle, and San Diego. All are centrally located and have program directors who arrange special activities—such as walking tours and cultural events—for their guests. Although most hostels are located in basic structures, some are in castles, former dude ranches, convents, lighthouses, base camps, or other exotic locations.

You can book your space directly by phone, mail, or fax; or, for more than 300 destinations throughout the world, you can reserve a prepaid bed by using HI's computerized international booking network via telephone or website.

A new benefit for members of Hostelling International is an eKit card that gives you access to an all-in-one communication service that includes low-cost long-distance calling within the U.S. and abroad, free voice-mail system, fax service, and E-mail service.

For information: Hostelling International-USA, 733 15th St. NW, Washington, DC 20005; 202-783-6161; www.hiayh.org.

HOSTELLING INTERNATIONAL–CANADA

A network of hostels throughout the Canadian provinces, HI-Canada offers members of all ages an inexpensive night's sleep in a wide variety of places ranging from modern facilities to historic homes, and refurbished jails to log cabins in the Rockies. Located in all major gateway cities and also in remote locations, your accommodations—private or shared—cost an average of $15 (Canadian) a night. Membership for Canadian residents over 18 costs $35 (Canadian) per year and allows you to use any HI facility worldwide. No senior discount here but at these rates, who needs it?

For information: Hostelling International–Canada, 205 Catherine St., Ste. 400, Ottawa, ON K2P 1C3; 800-663-5777 (Canada only); www.hihostels.ca.

IMMERSIA TRAVEL

Immersia specializes in unique and exotic adventure travel for ages 50 and up, taking small groups of intrepid travelers to hidden places to experience the scenery, culture, and people of faraway lands. It divides its adventures into two groups. Its "in-depth" tours are "culturally intensive" with parts of the excursions spent in villages living the local lifestyle and overnighting in local homes, cottages, tents, or other basic accommodations. They are rated "moderate" and "vigorous" and range from 9 to 21 days. Most meals are family style. At the moment, destinations include Bali, Thailand, Saluwesi in Indonesia, Kenya, Nepal, New Guinea, and other exotic places.

Most of Immersia's "in-focus" tours, on the other hand, are rated "easy" and range from 7 to 14 days. They too introduce their participants to indigenous people and their culture but offer a more leisurely pace and more luxurious accommodations such as boutique hotels, villas, inns and guesthouses. Among the current destinations are Japan,

India, Italy, France, Greece, Costa Rica, Russia, Finland, Ecuador, Mexico, and Brazil.
For information: Immersia Travel, PO Box 2218, Middleburg, VA 20118; 800-207-5454 or 540-687-8555.

MATURE TOURS

Mature Tours organizes trips for "youthful spirits" over the age of 50 who wish to roam the world with other travelers in their own age group. A division of Solo Flights, which has a long history of catering to single voyagers of all ages, it welcomes both solo seniors and couples on its trips. Regular destinations include Costa Rica, Ireland, Spain, and New York City. Also frequently on its schedule are cruises to Alaska and on the Mississippi River.
For information: Mature Tours, 10 Tait's Mill Rd., Trumbull, CT 06611; 800-266-1566 or 203-445-0107; E-mail soloflights@aol.com.

MAYFLOWER TOURS

Most of Mayflower's travelers are "55 or better," so the pace of its tours is leisurely and rest stops are scheduled every couple of hours. You travel by motorcoach, stay in good hotels or motels, and eat many of your meals together. The trips are fully escorted by tour directors who make sure all goes well. If you are a single traveler and request a roommate at least 30 days before departure, you'll get one or a room to yourself with no single supplement to pay. Tours go almost everywhere in the U.S., Canada, and the rest of the world, especially Europe, Asia, the South Pacific, and South Africa.

For information: Mayflower Tours, 1225 Warren Ave., Downers Grove, IL 60515; 800-323-7604 or 630-435-8500; www.mayflowertours.com.

OUTWARD BOUND

Outward Bound is famous for its rugged wilderness survival trips for young people and is aimed at building self-confidence, self-esteem, and the ability to work as a team. But it also offers short adventure courses specifically designed for adults, some for those over the age of 40 or 50, who seek to examine their goals or gain personal insights. Among the recent courses for these mature adventurers: sailing in the Florida Keys or along the coast of Maine and whitewater canoeing down the Rio Grande.

For information: Outward Bound, 100 Mystery Point Rd., Garrison, NY 10524; 888-882-6863; www.outwardbound.org.

OVERSEAS ADVENTURE TRAVEL (OAT)

OAT's soft adventures, exclusively for travelers over 50, combine creature comforts with off-the-beaten-path experiences in exotic places all over the world, from the rain forests of Borneo to Botswana or the Galapagos Islands. Groups are small, with no more than 16 participants. The trips—rated from "easy" to "demanding"—move at a leisurely pace and offer many optional side adventures. You'll travel by minivan and lodge in accommodations ranging from five-star hotels to jungle lodges or spacious tents and sometimes use unconventional modes of transportation such as dugout canoes, camels, yachts, or your own two feet.

Among recent tours, always including round-trip air, from this affiliate of Grand Circle Travel are excursions to such places as the Amazon, Peru, Morocco, Nepal, China, Tibet, Borneo, and Tanzania.

Solo travelers are not charged a single supplement if they are willing to share accommodations, even if a roommate is not available.

For information: Overseas Adventure Travel, 1 Broadway, Ste. 602, Cambridge, MA 02142; 800-955-1925; www.oattravel.com.

PETRABAX VACATIONS

An agency that specializes in affordable escorted tours to Spain, Portugal, and Morocco for mature travelers, Petrabax offers up to a $500 discount for travel companions from November through March (except during the holiday season) on the cost of the land portion of escorted tour packages. For those who want to spend more time at resorts on the Costa del Sol or the Algarve, known for mild winter weather, additional weeks are available at low cost.

If you choose one of this company's self-drive vacation packages in Spain and Portugal (these include airfare, accommodations, and rental car) and wish to stay in the government-owned inns called paradores or pousadas, your rates will reflect the Golden Days program. That means if you are over the age of 60, you can get a 35 or 40 percent discount on the room rates at certain times of the year and sometimes certain days of the week. See Portugal and Spain in Chapter 8.

For information: 800-634-1188; www.petrabax.com and www.petrabaxusa.com.

PLEASANT HOLIDAYS

Many of Pleasant Holiday's discounted vacation packages to resorts in many countries include airfare, hotel or condo room, and sometimes a rental car. The Makua Club for people over 55 gives you free room and car-rental upgrades and a gift certificate for activities and events. When you make a booking, mention your age and ask for your privileges. ***For information:*** Pleasant Holidays, 2404 Townsgate Rd., Westlake, CA 91361; 800-242-9244 or 818-991-3390; www.pleasantholidays.com.

RIVER ODYSSEYS WEST (ROW)

ROW reserves a couple of whitewater river trips each summer exclusively for adventurous people over 50 who like to travel with others their own age. These Prime Time trips take you down Idaho's Salmon River or the Snake River on the Oregon border for five days, passing through four spectacular volcanic canyons. You travel in rubber rafts by day and sleep in tents at the edge of the river by night.

Mature travelers may also choose one of ROW's raft-supported walking trips in Hells Canyon or the Salmon River in Idaho. See Chapter 13 for details.

For its canoe trips on Montana's scenic upper Missouri River, ROW schedules a few five-day float trips for older adventurers. Following the trail of Lewis and Clark, you travel in comfortable 34-foot voyageur canoes carrying up to 14 passengers plus 2 guides. You'll float down the river, stopping to explore many historic sites along the way. At the end of the day, you'll stop at luxury campsites with tents set up in advance, eat five-course meals, try your luck at fishing, and tell stories around the campfire.

For information: River Odysseys West, PO Box 579-UD, Coeur d'Alene, ID 83816; 800-451-6034 or 208-765-0841; www.rowinc.com.

SENIOR AUSTRALIA TOURS

These luxury tours to Australia and New Zealand cater to older travelers who want a leisurely pace, lots of free time, plenty of service, and a plethora of individual attention. You can travel with a group, always limited to only 20 people, or take an independent journey planned just for you, choosing from a variety of itineraries in one or both of these South Pacific countries. Tour directors, who travel with you all the way from North America until you're home again, take care of all the details. Most meals are included and a visit with a local family is usually part of your adventure. This company, founded by former missionaries, also offers tours for women only, grandparents and grandchildren, and wheelchair-bound travelers.

For information: 11134 Town Hall Rd., Phillips, WI 54555; 800-713-4851 or 715-339-6634; www.seniorluxurytravel.com.

SOPHISTICATED VOYAGES

A sister company to Grandtravel, Sophisticated Voyages operates one or two upscale tours a year for older travelers who want a relaxed itinerary rich in cultural activities, outstanding meals, fine hotels, and plenty of free time. What they don't want are hassles, large groups, all-day bus rides, hurried breakfasts, and many events crammed into the day. Recent trips have included a ten-day Britain tour that combines five nights in London with three nights at Thornbury

Castle in County Avon; and a two-week safari in Kenya where you are put up in elegant hotels, lodges, and tented camps.

For information: Sophisticated Voyages, 6900 Wisconsin Ave., Chevy Chase, MD 20815; 800-247-7651 or 301-986-0790; www.grandtrvl.com.

TRAFALGAR TOURS

After 50 years of taking Americans on tours all over the world, Trafalgar has now added a first-class tour program in the U.S. and Canada with more than a dozen regional itineraries. Catering to older travelers who want to see the sights without worrying about logistics and details, these escorted motorcoach tours include luxury coaches, first-class hotels or lodges, guided sight-seeing tours, gratuities, and most meals. Trafalgar also continues its overseas tours, both first-class and budget, to Europe, Britain, Australia, New Zealand, China, and South Africa. Traveling alone? You'll be matched with an appropriate roommate and won't be charged the single supplement.

For information: Trafalgar Tours USA, 29-76 Northern Blvd., Long Island City, NY 11101; 800-854-0103 or 718-685-3000; www.trafalgartours.com.

VALUE WORLD TOURS

An agency that specializes in river cruises, Value World Tours takes 10 to 20 percent off the cost of some sailings on off-peak departure dates for travelers over the age of 55. Cruises are mainly on inland waterways in Russia, Ukraine, central Europe, Egypt, and China, while hosted or escorted motorcoach tours go to many destinations in the same parts

of the world. The two-week programs may be extended before or after the trips.
For information: Value World Tours, 17220 Newhope St., Fountain Valley, CA 92708; 800-795-1633 or 714-556-8258; www.vwtours.com.

VANTAGE DELUXE WORLD TRAVEL

Vantage features upscale, fully escorted group travel packages for mature travelers. These all-inclusive vacations include land tours, train trips, and both river and ocean cruises. Accommodations are always deluxe and explorations are leisurely and relaxed, so there is plenty of time to savor the sights. All trips are led by tour directors who see to it that everything—from ticketing and baggage handling to check-ins, meals, and tips—is taken care of for you. Among Vantage's most popular tours are a Danube River cruise, a trip through the Panama Canal, a visit to China and the Yangtze River, an exploration of Ireland, and a tour through the countries of Eastern Europe. There are also longer, more exotic trips including a deluxe around-the-world tour.

If you are traveling alone and want a roommate, a compatible companion will be found or you'll pay only half the single supplement on land programs.
For information: Vantage Deluxe World Travel, 90 Canal St., Boston, MA 02114; 800-322-6677; www.vantagetravel.com.

VIRGIN VACATIONS

Choose one of Virgin's many air-inclusive package vacations, ranging from a few days in London and its countryside to lengthy excursions everywhere in Europe, and you will get a discount of $25 to $50 per person if you belong to

AARP. On the ten-day transatlantic packages on the *Queen Elizabeth 2*, it's $75 per person.
For information: 888-937-8474; www.virgin.com/vaca tions.

VISTA TOURS

Another agency providing escorted tours almost exclusively for the mature set, Vista Tours plans leisurely trips with plenty of stops and ample time to enjoy the points of interest and relax too. You travel on comfortable motorcoaches with escorts who deal with the reservations, transfers, luggage, meal arrangements, and all other potentially problematic situations. Destinations, although mainly in the mainland U.S., also include Canada, Europe, and Hawaii. A highlight every year is a five-day trip over the New Year's holiday to California for the Pasadena Rose Parade and a New Year's Eve party with a big band and a celebrity show. If you're a woman who doesn't have a dancing partner or wants a better one, you may take your turn whirling around the floor with one of the gentleman hosts who accompany the group.
For information: Vista Tours, 1923 N. Carson St., Ste. 105, Carson City, NV 89701; 800-647-0800 or 775-882-2100; www.frontiertours.com.

WARNER HISTORIC HOTELS

Reserved exclusively for guests over the age of 50, the all-inclusive holiday stays in the U.K. offered by the U.S. division of Warner Holidays are designed to give you a relaxed vacation without the distractions of children or business travelers.

Choose a three-night weekend or four-night midweek package at a historic hotel in the British countryside. The group of hotels includes castles and country mansions with gardens, parklands, restaurants, spas, indoor pools, and game facilities.

Breakfasts and dinners, leisure activities, and nightly entertainment are part of the package.

If you book a holiday and belong to AARP, you will receive 20 percent off the spa and wellness treatments at the hotels plus a free 670-page travel guide to Great Britain.

For information: Warner Historic Hotels, 75 Fleetwood Dr., Rockaway, NJ 07866; 866-850-5452; www.warnervacations.com.

WARREN RIVER EXPEDITIONS

Warren River Expeditions offers many whitewater raft trips limited to adventurers over 50, plus two expeditions a year for grandparents and their grandchildren. All the trips take you down Idaho's Salmon River, the longest undammed river in the country—fast and wild in the spring, tame and gentle in late summer. You'll float through unique ecosystems, down the deep Salmon River Canyon, and through the Frank Church Wilderness Area, where you'll view the lush scenery and abundant wildlife. Planned as soft adventure trips for people who are not enthusiastic about camping out, the six-day senior trips, limited to 16 guests, put you up each night in comfortable rustic backcountry lodges. There's a 10 percent discount on all trips for those over 55 or under 16.

For information: Warren River Expeditions, PO Box 1375, Salmon, ID 83467-1375; 800-765-0421 or 208-756-6387; www.raftidaho.com.

WEST COAST RAIL TOURS

If you love to ride the rails, check out the tours run by West Coast Railway Association, a nonprofit society dedicated to the preservation of Canada's railway heritage. The association restores, preserves, and maintains vintage railcars. Its unique excursions, one to nine days long are escorted by experienced rail buffs and treat you to rail adventures in scenic and historic areas of Canada. On some tours, you eat and sleep on board; on others, you stop for meals and lodging along the way. Seniors, usually starting at age 60, get a price break on almost all of them.

For information: West Coast Rail Tours, PO Box 2790 Stn. Main, Vancouver BC V6B 3X2; 800-722-1233 or 604-524-1011; www.wcra.org/tours.

CRUISING THE OCEANS, RIVERS, AND SEAS

Cruises have always appealed to the mature crowd. In fact, the majority of passengers on most sailings are over the age of 50, if not 60. So you are sure to find suitable companionship.

Whatever your age, never book a cruise without shopping around. Cruise rates have always been heavily discounted, but today anybody who pays the full sticker price (also called the brochure rate) should also be offered a chance to bid on the Brooklyn Bridge. Usually the best bargains come from travel agents who specialize in sea voyages or from cruise brokers who buy blocks of cabins and sell them at a discount. But the cruise lines offer special rates, too, on advance-purchase or last-minute bookings, introductory or off-season sailings, repositioning cruises, group

TIPS FOR FRUGAL TRAVELERS

A lively bimonthly 12-page newsletter packed with ways to stretch your travel dollars, ***ThriftyTraveling.Com*** includes tips, resources, tours, travel news, and a special section for readers over the age of 50. You have your choice of receiving it by mail or online.

For information: ThriftyTraveling.com, PO Box 8168, Clearwater, FL 33758; 800-532-5731; www.thriftytraveling.com.

bookings, and two-for-one deals. Occasionally, they will have special senior rates too. All of this means you must do your homework before signing up for a cruise.

In the meantime, here are some opportunities specifically for you.

CARNIVAL CRUISE LINES

Carnival's periodic Senior Citizen Rates can save you as much as 70 percent on the published brochure rates and are available on certain ships and voyages if you are at least 55 years of age. To inquire about them, call your travel agent or their toll-free number and mention the code CPSE or FPSE.

If you belong to AARP, you can save $100 per stateroom on most seven-day or longer voyages; or $50 per stateroom on shorter trips to the Bahamas, Mexico, the Caribbean, or Alaska. Singles save half that much. If you are traveling alone, you may request a roommate and pay no single supplement if none is available.

For information: 800-CARNIVAL (227-6482); www.carnival.com.

COSTA CRUISES

Make an early booking for a Costa Cruise using the advance-purchase Andiamo rate and, if you are 60 or more, you will save $50 to $200 per stateroom. So will friends or families traveling together, while children 17 and under sharing a stateroom with two adults cruise for $199 to $299.

The major cruise line in Europe, Italy-based Costa has an international fleet that sails the Caribbean and the Mediterranean as well as in northern Europe, South America, and across the Atlantic.

For information: 800-33-COSTA (332-6782).

CRUISE WEST

Cruise West's small ships that take only about 100 passengers give you an up-close look at the shoreline, hidden coves, narrow waterways, and little ports on voyages to Alaska; British Columbia; the California wine country; Baja, Mexico; or Costa Rica and Panama. Members of AARP who are making new bookings can get onboard credits of $25 to $200 per person, depending on the length of the cruise.

For information: 800-296-8307; www.cruisewest.com.

ELDERHOSTEL'S ADVENTURES AFLOAT

One of Elderhostel's most popular categories of learning vacations for its 55-plus members is its selection of cruises on the world's most spectacular waterways. Your education will take place aboard river barges, yachts, cruise ships, or even the *QE2*. Choices can be made from dozens of voyages all over the world, from the Mississippi River to Scandinavia, the Aegean Sea, the Yangtze River, the Texas Gulf Coast, the

Danube River, the Mediterranean, and across the Atlantic Ocean. International programs include airfare, and all trips include tuition, field trips, meals, and accommodations. For more about Elderhostel, see Chapter 12.
For information: Elderhostel, 11 Avenue de Lafayette, Boston, MA 02111; 877-426-8056 or 617-426-7788; www.elderhostel.org.

eWATERWAYS

Choose a cruise on a deluxe floating hotel on the canals and rivers of Europe and you will get a discount of 5 percent if you belong to AARP even on the two-for-one specials published 45 days before departure on www.bargespecials.com. Boating holidays are fully crewed and all-inclusive.
For information: 800-999-3636; www.ewaterways.com.

HOLLAND AMERICA LINE

If you are a member of AARP and book an outside cabin on a Holland America cruise or Alaska cruise tour of seven days or longer, you can save $100 per stateroom, except on Grand Voyages, and $50 per stateroom on shorter trips. Single travelers save half those amounts.
For information: 800-887-3529; www.hollandamerica.com.

KD RIVER CRUISES OF EUROPE

Here you're in luck if you are celebrating a big anniversary. This company, the oldest and biggest river cruise line in Europe, takes 20 percent off of the bill for couples celebrating their 25th, 40th, 50th, or 60th anniversaries on most of its sailings on the Rhine, the Danube, or the Elbe Rivers in central Europe. The anniversary needn't coincide with the

cruise departure date—it just has to take place some time in the same year. A marriage certificate or other proof of the wedding date is required.
For information: 800-346-6525 or 914-696-3600; www.rivercruises.com.

MSC ITALIAN CRUISES

Staffed by Italian crews, these cruise ships sail the Caribbean and South America in the winter and the Mediterranean the rest of the year. If you belong to AARP, you can save $200 per cabin except on suites. Single passengers can save $100 per cabin.
For information: 800-666-9333; www.msccruises.com.

NORWEGIAN COASTAL VOYAGE

The 11-ship Norwegian Coastal Voyage fleet sails daily year round along Norway's 1,250-mile west coast, passing myriad fjords and calling at 34 ports between Bergen and Kirkenes above the Arctic Circle. The voyage is a combination of a first-class cruise ship and a working ship that carries local passengers and cargo between remote coastal towns and villages with shore excursions by foot, bus, or snowmobile.

Passengers age 67 or older get a nice break on the rates, a reduction of $95 to $220 per person, one way or round trip, depending on the date and length of the trip, any time of the year except between June 1 and August 15. There is no single supplement in 10 categories of outside cabins on off-peak sailings.

Any time of year, however, AARP members receive discounts of $70 per person on one-way journeys and $100 on round-trip sailings, and on air-inclusive independent or escorted vacations, the amount deducted increases to $100 and $150 respectively. These discounts may be added to the off-peak discounts for 67-plus passengers.

For information: Norwegian Coastal Voyage, 800-323-7436 or 212-319-1300; www.coastalvoyage.com.

NORWEGIAN CRUISE LINE

NCL offers senior-only fares periodically throughout the year, all of them listed on the "specials" page of its website. Check them out when you get the urge to sail.

For information: 800-327-7030; www.ncl.com.

ROYAL CARIBBEAN INTERNATIONAL (RCI)

Check with your travel agent or on the website to find out when this cruise line will be offering one of its special promotions for seniors, because it offers periodic specials for passengers 55+ and their cabin mates on all of its ships at various times, depending on the availability of space. And, so you know what you're getting into, each shore excursion on RCI voyages is rated "mild" or "strenuous."

For information: 800-327-6700; www.royalcaribbean.com.

SAGA HOLIDAYS

The voyages of the *Saga Rose* and *Saga Pearl* are planned exclusively for travelers over the age of 50 (and spouses who must be at least 40). Both cruise ships are owned by Saga Holidays, a British tour company that caters to mature travelers, and sail from England. The *Saga Rose*, a 587-passenger ship with large public rooms and lots of open deck space, travels to the Mediterranean, making stops in France, Portugal, and Spain. Its other itineraries take you to Bergen, Norway, then up the coast into spectacular fjords; or to the Baltic Sea with ports of call in Sweden, Finland, Russia, Estonia, Germany, Denmark, and Norway. The routes of the smaller more intimate 352-passenger *Saga Pearl* include lengthy voyages to Norway and the North Cape; the western Mediterranean, with landings in Portugal, Morocco, Corsica, and Spain; or to Iceland by way of Ireland and Scotland.

For information: Saga International Holidays, 1161 Boylston St., Boston, MA 02215; 800-343-0273; www.saga.co.uk.

WORLD EXPLORER CRUISES

When the S.S. *Universe Explorer* is not serving as a floating university campus (see Chapter 12, Semester at Sea), it cruises to Alaska, the Caribbean, and Central America with university professors speaking on the history, wildlife, and culture of each of the ports visited. Members of AARP get a 20 percent discount off published rates for certain cabin categories and 10 percent on others. No single supplement is charged in some categories.

By the way, this ship features a computer lab with instructors from SeniorNet (see Chapter 12) who teach passengers everything from basic word processing to the Internet. The classes are free to SeniorNet members who pay the annual membership fee.

For information: 800-854-3835 or 415-393-1565; www.wecruise.com.

GENTLEMEN HOSTS

Many cruise lines take a few gentlemen hosts along on their voyages to dance, dine, and go ashore on excursions with women passengers who haven't brought partners with them. The hosts are carefully chosen, unattached older men who have polished social skills and the ability to be charming no matter what. Especially important, they must be accomplished dancers in everything from the rumba and the waltz to the foxtrot, cha-cha, and swing. The screening procedure for hosts is stringent, and since there are many more applicants than positions, don't be surprised if you are not encouraged to apply. Hosts usually pay a small fee for every day at sea and sometimes their own airfare to and from the port city. **Celebrity Cruise Line** carries two to four gentleman hosts along on most of its longer voyages.
For information: To Sea With Z, 19195 Mystic Pointe Dr., Aventura, FL 33180; 305-931-1026; www.toseawithz.com.

Crystal Cruises, whose worldwide cruises carry three or four "ambassador hosts" per trip, look for personable social hosts over the age of 65 who are great dancers and enjoy keeping older single women passengers entertained both on board and ashore.
For information: Entertainment Dept., Crystal Cruises, 2049 Century Park East, Ste. 1400, Los Angeles, CA 90067.

Cunard Line's cruises aboard *Queen Elizabeth 2* and the *Caronia* carry along four to ten friendly gentleman hosts between the ages of 45 and 70. Their job is not only to whirl around the dance floor with women who need partners but also to act as friendly diplomats who help passengers get to know one another. A knowledge of foreign languages is a plus.

For information: The Working Vacation, 12544 W. 159th St., Lockport, IL 60441; 708-301-7535; www.theworking vacation.com.

Delta Queen Steamship Co. whose replicas of old-time steamships sail on America's major rivers, takes a couple of hosts on all of its voyages aboard the *American Queen* and the *Mississippi Queen.*
For information: The Working Vacation, 12544 W. 159th St., Lockport, IL 60441; 708-301-7535; www.theworkingvacation .com.

Holland America Line recruits retired professionals with good social skills to act as hosts on its long cruises and big band sailings. Usually two to six hosts go along on each trip.
For information: To Sea With Z, 19195 Mystic Pointe Dr., Aventura, FL 33180; 305-931-1026; www.toseawithz.com.

Norwegian Cruise Line's sailings to many places around the world usually include at least two gentleman hosts on its longer voyages.
For information: To Sea With Z, 19195 Mystic Pointe Dr., Aventura, FL 33180; 305-931-1026; www.toseawithz.com.

Merry Widows Dance Tours offers many cruises and land tours for single, widowed, or divorced women who were born to dance. Accompanying them on the trip are gentleman hosts, one for every four women, who are expert in both Latin and traditional ballroom dancing.
For information: Merry Widows Dance Tours, 1515 N. Westshore Blvd., Tampa, FL 33607; 813-289-5923.

Orient Lines, whose ships, the *Marco Polo* and *The Crown Odyssey*, operate in the Far East, South Pacific, Indian Ocean,

Mediterranean, and Antarctica, take three or four gentleman hosts along on all voyages. The hosts act as dance and dinner partners for the women traveling on their own.
For information: The Working Vacation, 12544 W. 159th St., Lockport, IL 60441; 708-301-7535; www.theworkingvacation.com.

Radisson Seven Seas Cruises includes two male hosts on all voyages of its vessels the *Navigator* and the *Mariner*, and on some sailings of the *Diamond*. Their job is to act as social liaison between the passengers and the staff.
For information: The Working Vacation, 12544 W. 159th St., Lockport, IL 60441; 708-301-7535; www.theworkingvacation.com.

Royal Olympic Cruises takes two professional hosts on some sailings of its longer winter cruises. Their assignment is to socialize and dance with the women who haven't brought partners along.
For information: The Working Vacation, 12544 W. 159th St., Lockport, IL 60441; 708-301-7535; www.theworkingvacation.com.

Silversea Cruises has introduced gentleman hosts aboard all of its ships. The hosts' job is to dance, mingle, and mix, making sure all guests have an enjoyable voyage.
For information: The Working Vacation, 12544 W. 159th St., Lockport, IL 60441; 708-301-7535; www.theworkingvacation.com.

World Explorer Cruises offers *The Universe Explorer*, whose summer ports are in Alaska and winter ports in the Caribbean and Central and South America. A couple of hosts are taken along on some summer and holiday sailings.
For information: The Working Vacation, 12544 W. 159th St., Lockport, IL 60441; 708-301-7535; www.theworkingvacation.com.

10

Intergenerational Adventures

If you'd like to get to know your grandchildren (or children, nieces, nephews, young friends) better, take them on vacation. A trip with the kids or your adult children is a wonderful way to strengthen your relationships, especially for far-flung families who seldom have a chance to spend solid time together. Whether it's a one-day tour of a nearby city or a week on a dude ranch, this is the kind of family togetherness that works. You can plan your own itineraries, maybe visiting places you both want to see, renting a cottage at the beach, or choosing a resort or cruise that offers special activities for the youngsters.

Many grandparents, however, don't want the hassles and anxieties of traveling on their own with kids. If you are among them, do it the easy way by going with a tour company that specializes in intergenerational vacations. These are scheduled in the summer and during winter breaks when the children are out of school. The best of them are fully escorted by counselors, often schoolteachers on holiday. The tours, ranging from a visit to Washington, D.C., to a safari in Kenya, move at a leisurely pace suited to both generations with plenty of stops and time to relax and relate. Some are designed for children in a certain age range, while others accept all youngsters over 7 and up to 17 or 18.

By the way, consider taking a cruise together. Several cruise lines cater to children now, providing activities for all of them, from toddlers to teenagers. Besides, many ships have cabins that accommodate three or four passengers. These extra beds or bunks are often sold at very low rates, especially for children. And sometimes third and fourth passengers, children or otherwise, can go along absolutely free except for port taxes and extras.

Growing in popularity, too, are other multigenerational holidays, such as adventures for mothers and grown daughters, hostelers and adult children, and whole families including children, parents, and grandparents. Here are some of the current choices for a vacation with the family.

AFC TOURS

AFC will take you and your grandchildren over the age of 7 to Washington, D.C., Boston, or San Antonio and sometimes to other destinations for a week of sightseeing together. The supervised programs include activities for both age groups, a tour manager to lead the way, and a swimming pool at every hotel. You and the grandkids will visit the famous sights wherever you go.

For information: AFC Tours, 11555 Sorrento Valley Rd., San Diego, CA 92121; 800-369-3693 or 858-481-8188; www.afctours.com.

COUNTRY COTTAGES

Choose from among more than 10,000 private homes—from cottages to castles—in England, Ireland, Scotland, or Wales, and take the kids along for a week or more. Country Cottages offers its Grandparents' Houseparty package that at certain times of the year costs about $100 a day per person, including round-trip air from New York and a rental car or minivan. In some seasons, it adds a small discount for grandparents and grandchildren. All of the properties are second homes equipped with linens, tableware, and cookware and have accessible caretakers to provide information or assistance.

For information: Country Cottages, Box 810997, Boca Raton, FL 33481; 800-674-8883; www.villacentral.com.

ELDERHOSTEL INTERGENERATIONAL AND FAMILY PROGRAMS

Both of these programs have been designed for adults who want to share a learning adventure with their children, grandchildren, or other younger relatives or friends. The intergenerational programs are for members of two generations—adults and young people—while the family offerings are open to the entire family and may include grandparents, aunts, uncles, adult children, and grandchildren. In either case, there is a limit of one child per adult. Usually the youngsters must be at least nine years old, and sometimes they must be within a specified age range. Many of the activities in the programs are for the entire group while others are limited to the adults or the children.

You may choose programs in the U.S. or in foreign countries such as Bermuda, Costa Rica, Greece, and Ireland.

For information: Elderhostel, 11 Avenue de Lafayette, Boston, MA 02111; 877-426-8056 or 617-426-7788; www.elderhostel.org.

EXPLORATIONS IN TRAVEL

Multigenerational weekend trips for mothers, daughters, granddaughters, aunts, and other female friends or relatives are scheduled several times a year by Explorations in Travel, a company that specializes in action vacations for women over the age of 40 (see Chapter 13). At least two generations should be represented, with one participant over 40 and the other 21 or older. Current offerings include canoeing in Vermont, cruising aboard a 67-foot schooner in Maine's Penobscot Bay, and hiking in remote areas of Georgia and North Carolina.

For information: Explorations in Travel, 2458 River Rd., Guilford, VT 05301; 802-257-0152; www.exploretravel.com.

FAMILYHOSTEL

Sponsored by the University of New Hampshire and a cousin of Interhostel, FamilyHostel specializes in learning vacations for families (grandparents and/or parents and school-age children). A few trips each year are offered exclusively to grandparents or parents over the age of 50 and children 8 to 15 years old. Its ten-day, all-inclusive summer vacations combine travel with an inside look at culture and history in this country and abroad, and its destinations include such places as England, France, Greece, Italy and Costa Rica, as well as Alaska, Hawaii, California, New England, and Oklahoma.

Separately and together, adults and children enjoy workshops, recreation, sight-seeing adventures, and social activities that include visits with local families. The groups of intergenerational travelers, limited to five to ten families, are accompanied by university representatives and teachers from the U.S. and the host countries. Lodging is in three- or four-star hotels, and the cost is moderate for what you get. ***For information:*** FamilyHostel, University of New Hampshire, 6 Garrison Ave., Durham, NH 03824; 800-733-9753 or 603-862-1147; www.learn.unh.edu.

GRANDKIDS AND ME CAMPS

Take your grandchildren to camp for a weekend of fun and togetherness; that is, if you live within range of the twin cities of Minneapolis/St. Paul, Minnesota. Grandkids And Me Camps offers three seasonal three-day weekend camps each year that give you a chance to spend quality time together and enjoy one another's company. Exclusively for grandparents of all ages and children between the ages of 4 and 13, they are scheduled in winter, spring, and fall at Camp Icagawahn near Amery, Wisconsin, or Grand View Lodge near Nisswa, Minnesota, both located a short drive from the Twin Cities. Activities include crafts, canoeing, hiking, dog sledding, ice fishing, snowshoeing, wagon rides, music, dancing, telling stories around the campfire, and old-fashioned hoedowns.

For information: Grandkids And Me Camps, 1764 Hampshire Ave., St. Paul, MN 55116; 651-695-1988; www.grandkidsandme.com.

GRANDTRAVEL

This company pioneered the notion of sending grandparents and their grandchildren off on vacations together. For grandparents of any age and children from 7 to 17, its tours go to many parts of the world, including London, Paris, New York, South America, Scandinavia, Greece, the national parks, the Pacific Northwest, Kenya, Australia, and Italy. If you want to go on your own, the agency will also arrange a special tour just for your family group. You needn't be an authentic grandparent, either—aunts, uncles, cousins, godparents, and other surrogate grandparents are welcome. Its 5- to 15-day tours are deluxe, educational, and limited to groups of 20.

Tours, each designated for certain ages of children, are led by teacher-escorts and always include plenty of rest stops and opportunities for both generations to spend time alone with their own age groups. As part of the package, Grandtravel provides predeparture counseling to help you deal with any special concerns such as what to pack or how to deal with kids who miss their moms.

For information: Grandtravel, The Ticket Counter, 6900 Wisconsin Ave., Chevy Chase, MD 20815; 800-247-7651 or 301-986-0790; www.grandtrvl.com.

RASCALS IN PARADISE

Specializing in family vacations for parents and children, Rascals in Paradise also invites grandparents and grandchildren to go along on its adventure trips to places such as Mexico and the Caribbean, the Bahamas, Europe, New Zealand, Thailand, Australia, the Canadian Rockies, Africa, the Galapagos Islands, Hawaii, Alaska, and ranches in the West. All group trips, three to six families per group, include escorts who plan activities for the older children and arrange baby-sitters for the little ones. This agency will plan independent vacations, too, as well as family reunions and other multigenerational celebrations.

For information: Rascals in Paradise, 1 Daniel Burnham Ct., Ste. 105C, San Francisco, CA 94109; 800-872-7225 or 415-921-7000; www.rascalsinparadise.com.

RIVERBARGE EXCURSIONS

Aboard the 198-passenger riverboat *River Explorer*, the only hotel barge traveling America's inland waterways, you'll chug along on a four- to ten-day excursion exploring the country on its famous rivers. You'll stop along the way to visit nearby towns, eat home-style meals on board, and enjoy regional entertainment. Pricing is all-inclusive, including tips. Even better, you can take your grandchildren on one of the barge's Grand Vacations, scheduled year round, that invite children 12 and under to sail free when sharing your stateroom and older youngsters up to 18 to sail half price when staying in their own rooms.

By the way, if you are a teacher, active or retired, you can travel half price.

For information: RiverBarge Excursions, 201 Opelousas Ave., New Orleans, LA 70114; 888-GOBARGE (462-2743); www.riverbarge.com.

SAGAMORE GRANDS CAMP

Spend a week with the grandkids (no parents allowed) at Grandparent-Grandchild Summer Camp held annually at the Sagamore Conference Center, the Vanderbilt family's former summer retreat in the Adirondacks. Children age four or older are welcome, as are teenagers. This popular program, scheduled for two sessions in July every year, is designed to foster the vital connections between generations and teach stewardship and respect for nature.

Mornings at camp are spent hiking, swimming, canoeing, biking, berry picking, and other activities. Afternoons you may choose swimming, crafts or music, or simply relaxing. In late afternoon, the grandparents meet to discuss their own issues while the children play games. Evenings, there are music shows, a night hike, a square dance, a campfire, and a gala "talent show."

Other intergenerational programs take place at the camp in August in cooperation with Elderhostel.

For information: Great Camp Sagamore, PO Box 40, Raquette Lake, NY 13436; 315-354-5311; www.sagamore.org/grandcamp.htm.

SENIOR AUSTRALIA TOURS

If you take your grandchildren to Australia on one of this company's special tours just for grandparents and kids, you'll have exciting adventures snorkeling on the Great Barrier Reef, viewing marine life from the windows of a semi-submersible, meeting crocodiles up close, and riding a gondola over the rain forest. The luxury trips planned include just about everything including tour directors who act as escorts and take care of all the details. To join a group tour, the children must be 12 years old or more.

For information: Senior Australia Tours, 11134 Town Hall Rd., Phillips, WI 54555; 800-713-4851 or 715-339-6634; www.seniorluxurytravel.com.

SENIOR WOMEN'S TRAVEL

Recently added to the roster of trips for solo women travelers over 50 are grandmother/grandchildren adventures. One, Adventures in Paris, is just for the girls and it takes you and your school-age granddaughters on a one-week trip to Paris, with side trips to Versailles, and Girverny. Others that include grandsons too are planned for Costa Rica or the northern national parks. All are scheduled in the summer.

For information: Senior Women's Travel, 136 E. 56th St., New York, NY 10022; 212-838-4740; www.poshnosh.com.

SIERRA CLUB

Among the famous outings of the Sierra Club, the largest grassroots environmental group in the country, is a remarkably affordable summertime vacation for grandparents and their grandchildren. Long an annual event, it is a six-day stay at the club's rustic lodge in California's Sierra Nevada Mountains. The laid-back holiday is designed for people between the ages of 5 and 95 who may pick and choose among the available activities that include short hikes, fishing, lake swimming, a beach picnic, and a tram ride at Squaw Valley. Lodging and meals are part of the package.

Check the club's website for more intergenerational events. Plans are in the works for more outings. Participants must be members of the club. If you consider yourself a senior, your yearly membership costs only $24, compared to $39 for other adults. Two seniors in the same household may join for $32 a year, compared to $47 for younger adults.
For information: Sierra Club Outing Dept., 85 Second St., San Francisco, CA 94105; 415-977-5522; www.outings.sierraclub.org.

VISTA TOURS

The family tours offered by Vista are designed for children and their relatives, whether grandparents, parents, aunts and uncles, or otherwise. There are several different trips, ranging from 4 to 14 days, such as the Railroads of the Rockies, the Idaho and Oregon Trail, and the California National Parks. Activities are planned for the different generations separately and together.
For information: Vista Tours, 1923 N. Carson St., Ste. 105, Carson City, NV 89701; 800-647-0800 or 775-882-2100; www.frontiertours.com.

WARREN RIVER EXPEDITIONS

Take the grandkids down the Salmon River in Idaho on a raft trip run by Warren River Expeditions. On special summer trips reserved for grandparents and grandchildren, you'll float through canyons and forests, taking time to swim and kayak. You'll sleep in comfortable backcountry

lodges, some quite rustic, along the river's edge and have plenty of exciting adventures on the big rubber rafts powered by expert oarspeople. At least two midsummer departures, with a 10 percent discount for those over 55 or under 16, are reserved each summer for the two generations.
For information: Warren River Expeditions, PO Box 1375, Salmon, ID 83467-1375; 800-765-0421 or 208-756-6387; www.raftidaho.com.

11

Singles on the Road

If you're single, on your own again, have a partner who isn't the traveling kind and couldn't care less about seeing Venice, or simply like to travel independently, you can do it your own way. Many people love to vacation on their own, never having to cater to anyone else's whims or demands about where to go, when to eat, how long to stay at the museum, or what time to go to bed. Others, however, find traveling solo to be a rather lonely business and would prefer not to wander around the world by themselves.

To encourage and accommodate the growing numbers of mature single travelers, an increasing number of tour companies, cruise lines, and clubs now cater to them. Some plan itineraries for the independents while others organize singles group tours or schedule special departure dates specifically for solo travelers. Most mix them with everyone else but try to match you up with a roommate so you can avoid paying a single supplement, the extra charge for the privilege of sole occupancy of a room or cabin. Another way to avoid paying more than paired people is to watch for the special deals when single supplements are waived altogether. These are usually offered on off-peak packages with space that may otherwise go unclaimed.

Going with a group provides ready-made companions and an organized travel plan. But if you don't want to go places by yourself even in a group, consider joining a matchmaker club that helps you find a fellow traveler who is also looking for someone with whom to share adventures and expenses.

Finally, one of the surest ways to enjoy a vacation on your own is to sign up for a trip that features activities that especially intrigue you, because you'll meet people who like the same things you do. Consider, for example, art tours, bike trips, golf schools, gourmet tours, tennis camps, language programs, or volunteer vacations.

MATCHMAKERS AND NEWSLETTERS

TRAVEL COMPANION EXCHANGE (TCE)

TCE specializes in helping singles find compatible vacation partners. Managed by veteran travel expert Jens Jurgen, TCE is the largest, most enduring, and most successful matchmaking service, with close to 3,000 active members whose ages range from 20 to 85.

Members of TCE receive fact-filled bimonthly newsletters packed with travel tips and helpful advice plus long listings of people who are seeking new friends and/or travel partners of the same or opposite sex. For more information about those who seem to be good possibilities, you can send for full profiles and photographs so you may judge their suitability for yourself. You do your own matchmaking. Jurgen suggests you talk by telephone, correspond, meet, and, even better, take a short trip together before setting out on a major adventure.

You may join TCE for a year at an introductory fee of $159, using a credit card if you wish. Membership includes its award-winning newsletter. By the way, you don't have to join TCE to subscribe to the *TravelCompanions.com Newsletter* (without the listings) for $48 per year. It is a gold mine of detailed travel news, tips, and bargains for all enthusiastic travelers, single or not.

For information: Travel Companion Exchange, Inc., PO Box 833, Amityville, NY 11701; 631-454-0880; www.travelcompanions.com. Send for a free brochure or enclose $6 for a sample newsletter. For *Foiling Pickpockets*, a 24-page booklet full of tips on travel safety, send $4.95.

CONNECTING: SOLO TRAVEL NETWORK

A club based in Canada, Connecting is a "solo travel network" that aims to keep its more than 1,500 single members—almost half of them over 50—in touch with each other, advising them on where to go, what to do, and how to enjoy their travel alone or with friends. Members pay a yearly fee of $35 (Canadian) or $25 (U.S.) for an informa-

MERRY WIDOWS DANCE TOURS

Designed for solo women from 50 to 90 who love to dance but don't have partners, **Merry Widows Dance Tours** runs many cruises every year to places such as the Caribbean, Southeast Asia, Alaska, Greece and the Mediterranean, and the Panama Canal. The trips range from 7 days to 18. Sponsored by the AAA Auto Club South, the cruises take along their own gentleman hosts, one professional dancer for every four women. Each woman receives a dance card that rotates her partners every night throughout the cruise, whether she's a beginner or a polished dancer. The men are also rotated at the dinner tables so everyone gets the pleasure of their company. You don't have to be a widow and you don't even have to know the cha-cha or even the waltz to enjoy these trips. If you are traveling alone and wish to avoid paying a single supplement, you will be assigned a roommate. ***For information:*** Merry Widows Dance Tours, 1515 N. Westshore Blvd., Tampa, FL 33607; 800-955-1365 or 813-289-5923.

tive bimonthly newsletter sent by E-mail; or if they prefer to have the newsletter delivered by regular mail, $45 (Canadian) or $35 (U.S.). Both versions offer access to other services, such as a constantly updated Singles-Friendly Travel Directory. The newsletter includes information on upcoming singles trips and cruises, including those reserved for "mature" travelers, unlimited free listings for members looking for compatible travel companions, reader recommendations, travel tips and tales, and a directory of travel companies that offer special accommodations or programs for singles. An added benefit: you may participate in the

Hospitality Program, which recruits volunteers to spend time with visiting members from elsewhere.

For information: Connecting: Solo Travel Network, 689 Park Rd., Gibsons, BC V0N 1V7; 800-557-1757 or 604-886-9099; www.cstn.org.

TOURS FOR SOLO TRAVELERS

Most tour operators and agencies specializing in escorted trips for people in their prime will try to find you a same-sex roommate to share your room or cabin so you do not have to pay a single supplement. And, if they can't manage to find a suitable roommate for you, they will usually reduce the supplement or even cancel it. Some offer singles-only trips, too. In any case, keep in mind that you'll hardly have time or opportunity to be lonely on the typical escorted tour run by these agencies. If you are planning an extended stay in just one location, however, you may have more need for company.

TRAVELING ON YOUR OWN

For those who travel without a companion, here's a website run by a long-time flight attendant and author that offers resources, safety tips, tour information, and other useful advice to help you happily go solo. It posts new solo-travel tips every month, publishes a free monthly newsletter, and provides a place to share opinions and recommendations.

For information: www.travelaloneandloveit.com.; 7210-D Adams St., Willowbrook, IL 60527; 630-654-1156 or editor @travelaloneandloveit.com.

GO SOLO TRAVEL CLUB

This club for "the mature and discriminating traveler without a partner" guarantees private rooms on all trips, domestic and overseas, and no single supplements for those traveling alone. And its guided group tours travel in their own private buses. A newsletter issued three times a year offers travel tips and announcements of upcoming tours that have recently included Ireland, Branson, Paris, San Francisco, Santa Fe, and Alaska. The annual fee of $35 is deducted from the cost of your first trip of the year.

For information: Go Solo Travel Club, Tallyho Travel, 92 E. Main St., Elmsford, NY 10523; 800-354-4484 or 914-592-4316; www.gosolotravelclub.com.

SPECIAL FOR SOLO DINERS

Check out **SoloDining.com** if you eat meals alone for pleasure or business whether in your own hometown or on the road. It publishes a bimonthly newsletter (mailed) and maintains a website (with a new solo travel section). Both of them are full of tips and strategies to increase your options and comfort as a solo diner.

For information: SoloDining.com, PO Box 1025, S. Pasadena, CA 91031; 800-299-1079 or 323-257-0026; www.solodining.com.

GOING SOLO TRAVEL CLUB

A club that caters to solo travelers, singles, or people whose spouses want to stay home, Going Solo costs nothing to join and will send you announcements of upcoming trips as they are scheduled. Members may be any age, but most are between 35 and 70. Located in Calgary, Canada, the club has many U.S. members and welcomes them all on its worldwide escorted tours to places like England, Africa, Guatemala, Belize, Mexico, and Turkey.

You will be matched up with a roommate if you want one and wish to avoid the single supplement fee. Or bring your own roommate and share a room.

For more information: Going Solo Travel Club, 629 11th Ave. SW, Calgary, AB T2R OE1; 888-446-7656 (outside Alberta) or 403-256-7871; www.goingsolotravel.com.

O SOLO MIO SINGLES TOURS

A travel club for singles who like to vacation in groups, O Solo Mio welcomes members of all ages but designs some of its tours specifically for "late 40s-plus" who prefer traveling with other singles their own age. Members who pay a fee of $50 a year receive a quarterly newsletter announcing upcoming plans and may ask to be matched with a roommate to avoid paying a single supplement fee. The many tours vary every year but recent destinations have included Nova Scotia and Prince Edward Island, Italy, China, and the Greek Isles, and trips to Branson and Mexico.

For information: O Solo Mio Singles Tours, 636 Los Altos Rancho, Los Altos, CA 94024; 800-959-8568 or 650-917-0817; www.osolomio.com.

SENIOR WOMEN'S TRAVEL

Solo women travelers over the age of 50 are invited to join the special one-week tours offered by Senior Women's

FOR WOMEN ONLY

Journeywoman.com is an award-winning, free online resource for women travelers. Packed with female-centered travel information, tips, advice, and stories designed to inform and inspire solo travelers of any age, it includes a special section for the "50-plus adventuress." Topics range from female-friendly cities around the world to culturally correct clothing, health concerns, safety advice, money-saving tactics, and much more. The site also allows you to sign up for a free quarterly E-newsletter that is full of travel tips and advice for women.

A sister site is HERmail.net, a free E-mail–based service that allows you to connect with other women all over the world who are ready to offer advice and assistance when you visit their cities or countries.

For information: www.journeywoman.com; 416-929-7654; and www.hermail.net.

Travel. Planned for "women who want it all," the upscale guided tours of no more than ten participants concentrate on food, history, art, music, and literature. They take you to Paris, Venice, Provence, Malta, Bilbao, New York City, or London where you unpack once, settle down, and then set forth to explore the destination in depth.

Grandmother/grandchildren tours are recent additions. Adventures in Paris takes grandmothers and school-age granddaughters on a whirlwind tour of Paris, Versailles, and Giverny during the summer vacation. Others scheduled for the summer take the boys along too, these going to Costa Rica or the northern national parks.

For information: Senior Women's Travel, 136 E. 56th St., New York, NY 10022; 212-838-4740; www.poshnosh .com.

SOLO FLIGHTS

This company established in 1974 makes it its business to know about the best tours, cruises, packages, and groups for single travelers of all ages. It represents major tour operators and cruise lines and also offers its own exclusive trips, some marketed by its affiliate Mature Tours for "youthful spirits" over 50. Regularly featured tours go to Costa Rica four times a year and also to New York City, Ireland, Spain, and Morocco. Get in touch to discuss your best options. You will be matched with a roommate if you want one and perhaps find a travel mate at no charge from the company's clients.

For information: Solo Flights, 10 Taits Mill Rd., Trumbull, CT 06611; 800-266-1566 (outside Connecticut) or 203-445-0107; E-mail soloflights@aol.com.

SOLO'S HOLIDAYS

The U.K.'s largest singles tour operator, Solo's Holidays offers hosted group vacations for unattached people. Although it is based in England, it will happily take Americans and Canadians on tour all over the world, giving them a chance to talk, dine, dance, and share experiences with other lone travelers. All trips are divided into two groups, the first exclusively for ages 28 to 55 and the second for ages 45 to 69, although sometimes the ages are mixed.

For information: Solo's Holidays, 54-58 High St., Edgware, Middlesex HA8 7EJ, England; E-mail travel@soloholidays .co.uk; www.solosholidays.co.uk.

WANDER WOMEN

"On your own but not alone" is the motto of Wander Women, a new travel club exclusively for active women over 50. Affiliated with AFC Tours (see Chapter 9), the club, which charges no membership fees, schedules several women-only trips each year for its 1,200 or so members who receive frequent newsletters announcing new adventures. Recent outings have been a six-day tour of the northern California coast and a seven-day stay in San Antonio, Texas. Members who live in southern California are invited to get-acquainted lunches, teas, travel shows, and seminars. Benefits include the security of traveling with a group and a way to avoid paying single supplements. List yourself and your preferences in the Share Finder program if you're looking for a compatible travel companion.

For information: Wander Women Travel Club, AFC Tours, 11772 Sorrento Valley Rd., San Diego, CA 92121; 800-369-3693 or 858-481-8188; www.wanderwomen.com.

WINDJAMMER BAREFOOT CRUISES

Sign on for Windjammer's mid-summer Silver Singles Cruise for people over the age of 55 and spend almost two weeks cruising the Caribbean aboard the *M.V. Amazing Grace*, a 92-passenger motor vessel, with other mature singles out to have fun. The cruise is all-inclusive, even covering snacks and drinks, and casual. The journey starts in Freeport, in the Bahamas, covers 3,800 nautical miles and 13 islands before pulling into its final port in Trinidad. Plenty of shore adventures during the day and activities every evening.

For information: Windjammer Barefoot Cruises, PO Box 190120, Miami Beach, FL 33139; 800-327-2601; www.windjammer.com.

HOOK-UPS FOR SOLO RVers

RVers who travel alone in their motor homes or vans can hook up with others in the same circumstances when they join one of the groups mentioned on this and the next few pages. All of the clubs provide opportunities to travel together or to meet at campgrounds on the road, making friends with fellow travelers and having a fine time.

FRIENDLY ROAMERS

Founded by former members of Loners on Wheels, Friendly Roamers is open to everyone, couples as well as singles, so friendships and RV activities can be continued despite a change of marital status or travel arrangements. Membership gets you admission to all club events, such as rallies and campouts; a newsletter; and a membership directory. Annual dues are $10 plus a one-time registration fee of $5 for new members. Local chapters hold their own events and join the others as well.

For information: Friendly Roamers, c/o Herbert Ott, PO Box 3153, Paradise, CA 95967; 530-872-8702.

LONERS OF AMERICA (LOA)

LOA is a club for single campers who enjoy traveling together. Established in 1987, it currently has 29 chapters throughout the country and well more than 500 active members from their 40s to their 90s, almost all retired and widowed, divorced, or otherwise single. Many of them live year-round in their motor homes or vans, and others hit the road only occasionally. They camp, rally, and caravan together, often meeting at special campgrounds that cater to solo campers.

A not-for-profit, member-operated organization, the club publishes a biannual membership directory and a lively monthly newsletter that keeps its members in touch and informs them about campouts and rallies all over the country. The chapters organize their own events as well. Currently, dues are $40 a year plus a $5 registration fee for new members.

For information: Loners of America, Rte. 2, PO Box 2495 E, Elsimore, MO 63937; www.lonersofamerica.net.

LONERS ON WHEELS (LOW)

A camping and travel club for mature single men and women, Loners on Wheels is not a lonely hearts club or a matchmaking service, but simply an association of friends and extended family who enjoy traveling, camping, RV caravaning, and camaraderie. With 68 chapters located throughout the U.S., Canada, and Mexico, LOW now has a membership of about 2,400 unpartnered travelers. The chapters schedule hundreds of campouts, rallies, and other events during the year at campgrounds, some of which are remote and cost little.

The club's newly acquired LOW-HI RV Ranch in Deming, New Mexico (which also serves as its headquarters), offers special rates for club members, two rallies a year, dances and games in the clubhouse, and occasional forays into Mexico. A monthly newsletter and an annual directory keep everyone up to date and in touch.

Annual dues at this writing are $45 U.S. and $54 Canadian, plus a one-time enrollment fee of $5.

For information: Loners on Wheels, PO Box 1060-WB, Cape Girardeau, MO 63702; 888-569-4478 or 505-546-4058; www.lonersonwheels.com. Ask for a free sample newsletter.

RVing WOMEN

Women travelers who take to the highways in recreational vehicles can get advice and support from RVing Women, a club with more than 4,000 female members. The group sponsors rallies, caravans, and other events across the U.S., Canada, and Mexico, plus weekend RV maintenance and driving classes in many locations around the country. Members pay an annual fee of $42 and receive a bimonthly magazine that covers topics such as safety, scams on the road, vehicle maintenance, and announcements of upcoming events and includes an annual directory of members.

For information: RVing Women, PO Box 1940, Apache Junction, AZ 85217; 888-55-RVING (557-8464) or 480-671-6226; www.rvingwomen.com.

S*M*A*R*T

A club for retired and active members of the U.S. and Canadian armed forces, Special Military Active-Retired Travel

Club (S*M*A*R*T) provides social and recreational activities for its more than 3,000 members with "an avid interest in recreational vehicles." Through a network of 60 chapters, it provides seminars and workshops, assists military installations with the improvement of their campgrounds, and sponsors annual rallies.

The club offers several caravans a year in many destinations, including Arkansas, Tennessee, and several western states. It also tours Canada, Mexico, and Alaska, often in fully equipped rented RVs. A national muster, packed with activities, entertainment, seminars and fellowship, is held every year.

To join, U.S. residents pay an initiation fee of $10 and then $30 a year per family; Canadian residents pay a $15 initiation fee and $35 dues per family, while associate members (disabled, former POWs, Medal of Honor recipients, surviving spouses of eligible members) pay a $10 initiation fee, then $15 a year.

For information: S*M*A*R*T, Inc., 600 University Office Blvd., Pensacola, FL 32504; 800-354-7681 or 850-478-1986; www.smartrvclub.org.

12

Learning After 50

Have you always wanted to speak Swedish; study African birds; examine Eskimo culture; learn to paddle a canoe or ski down a mountain; or delve into archaeology, international finance, horticulture, the language of whales, or great literature of the 19th century? Now is the time to do it. If you're a typical member of the over-50 generation, you're in good shape, healthy, and alert, with the energy and the time to pursue new interests. So why not go back to school and learn all those things you've always wished you knew? Many of us find it easier and cheaper than ever to go back to school.

You are welcome as a regular student at just about any institution in the U.S. and Canada, especially in the continuing-education programs, but many colleges and universities have set up special programs designed to lure older people back to the classroom. Some offer good reductions in tuition (so good indeed that often you may attend regular classes at half price or even free) and give credits for life experience. Others have designed programs and, sometimes, whole schools specifically for mature scholars. And almost every state college and university in the U.S. is now mandated to permit seniors to audit courses for free.

Going back to class is an excellent way to generate feelings of accomplishment and to exercise the mind—and one of the best ways to make new friends. It doesn't always mean you'll have to turn in term papers or take excruciatingly difficult exams. Sign up for one class a week on flower arranging or Spanish conversation or a once-a-month lecture series on managing your money. Register as a part-time or full-time student in a traditional university program. Or take a learning vacation on a college campus. Do it *your* way.

You don't even have to attend classes to learn on vacation. You can go on archaeological digs, count butterflies, help save turtles from extinction, brush up on your bassoon playing, listen to opera, search for Roman remains in England, study dancing or Belgian cuisine, or go on safari in Africa.

CHAUTAUQUA INSTITUTION

For more than a century people have been traveling up to the shores of Lake Chautauqua, in southwestern New York, to a cultural summer center set in a Victorian village. The 856-acre hilltop complex offers a wide variety of educational programs, including summer weeks and off-season weekends designed for people over the age of 55. The 55-Plus Weekends and the Residential Week for Older Adults are filled up far in advance, so if you are interested, don't waste a moment before signing up.

Each 55-Plus Weekend has a specific focus, such as the U.S. Constitution, natural history, national politics, music appreciation, or trade relations with Japan. They include discussions, workshops, lectures, films, recreational activities, and evening entertainment, all led by professionals. Housing and meals are available in a residence hall with double rooms and shared baths.

The Residential Week for Older Adults is similar but longer and includes lodging and meals as well as admittance to other happenings at the center.

It's all quite cheap. The cost of tuition, room, meals, and planned activities for a Residential Week is currently $500, while a 55-Plus Weekend costs $40 for commuters or $175 with accommodations and meals.

For information: Program Center for Older Adults, Chautauqua, NY 14722; 800-836-2787 or 716-357-6200; www.ciweb.org.

CLOSE UP WASHINGTON

For a behind-the-scenes view of Washington, D.C., and the democratic process, you can attend classes on current events, study the presidents, exchange views with national political leaders, and gain insights on public policy, all in a tightly packed five- or six-night program of on-site seminars organized for older adults by the Close Up Foundation's Lifelong Learning Series. What's more, there's time for relaxation, conversation, social events, and theater in and around the nation's capital.

For your stay in Washington, D.C., your lodging is at a comfortable hotel. All meals, activities, in-town transportation, and a night at the theater are included in the modest fee.

There are two ways to participate. First, you can sign up with Elderhostel for a five-night program by calling 877-426-8056. Or, if you have a group of 35 or more participants, you can arrange for your own Lifelong Learning Series program in the nation's capital by calling the Close Up Foundation.

For information: Close Up Foundation, 44 Canal Center Plaza, Alexandria, VA 22314; 800-CLOSEUP (256-7387); www.closeup.org/lifelong.htm.

THE COLLEGE AT 60

At Fordham University's The College at 60, you're welcome at a mere 50, despite its name. It offers you the option to take classes at leisure or become fully matriculated and pursue a college degree. Meanwhile, you learn in a community of peers.

As an enrolled student, you are entitled to a discount on courses in liberal arts at Fordham's Lincoln Center Campus. You pay half the regular university tuition to take the courses for credit and only half of that to audit. The 13-week courses are taught by university faculty. Included are a lecture series and the use of all college facilities. After taking four courses, you are eligible to enter the Fordham College of Cultural Studies at a 50 percent discount on tuition if you receive Social Security benefits.

For information: The College at 60, Fordham University at Lincoln Center, 113 W. 60th St., Room 301, New York, NY 10023; 212-636-6372; www.fordham.edu/collegeat60.

COLLEGE FOR SENIORS

A membership program for those 50 or older, the College for Seniors is a component of the North Carolina Center for Creative Retirement at the University of North Carolina at Asheville. The courses, most of them taught by peer seniors, range from Chaucer to computers, foreign affairs to opera, and chemistry to tap dancing. The per-term fee is currently $55 to $115, depending on the number of weeks involved. Added benefits include social events, travel programs, wellness clinics, exploration weekends, library privileges, parking decals, and access to the fitness center.

FEDERAL WEBSITE FOR SENIORS

FirstGov for Seniors (www.seniors.gov) is a website created specifically for older adults who are seeking information about government services. Maintained by the Social Security Administration, it helps users access all government sites that provide services for them and also provides links to all federal agencies and all 50 states. Still evolving, this site will eventually assist seniors with helpful services, resources, and information 24 hours a day, allowing them to complete applications and forms on-line and submit them electronically.

Currently the site offers information on consumer protection, education, health, legislation, computers, tax assistance, travel, volunteerism, and more.

For information: College for Seniors, 104 Carmichael Hall, CPO #1660, UNCA, Asheville, NC 28804; 828-251-6384; www.unca.edu/ncccr.

EDUCATION VACATIONS

Formerly known as Senior U, Education Vacations offers three- or four-night learning vacations for older adults in several different locations in the Northeast. The programs include multiple class sessions in a choice of subjects such as art, literature, crafts, music, movies, history, holistic studies, and self-improvement, as well as lodging, three meals a day, use of hotel facilities, and a graduation luncheon. All courses are taught by university professors and local experts.

School's currently in session at the Golden Inn in Avalon, New Jersey, and the Pocmont Resort in Bushkill, Pennsylvania. Soon to come are locations in Baltimore, the Catskills, Atlantic City, and Philadelphia.

For information: Education Vacations, 520 N. Delaware Ave., Riverview Pl., Philadelphia, PA 19123; 215-922-0100; www.educationvacations.net.

ELDERFOLK

Each of Elderfolk's two- to five-week Journeys for Learning, courses in Nepal, India, Tibet, Bhutan, and China, focuses on Himalayan culture, history, natural history, religion, cuisine, and arts and crafts. Exclusively for adventurers over the age of 55, they are offered by the Folkways Institute, a small international school without walls "whose projects are designed to permit cross-cultural understanding," which plans study courses for students and professors.

Some of the courses, combining education and exotic travel, are cultural treks on which you'll be put up at night in roomy tents or lodges. Others are residential or overland trips where you lodge in small hotels or guest houses, such as the Ancient Silk Road trip from Xian to Lahore.

No expertise or training is required but some stamina definitely is.

For information: Elderfolk, Folkways Institute, 14600 SE Aldridge Rd., Portland, OR 97236-6518; 800-225-4666 or 503-658-6600; www.folkwaysinstitute.org.

ELDERHOSTEL

Elderhostel, the vast campus study program of learning vacations for mature Americans that was initiated 25 years ago, offers some of the world's best bargains. Its remarkably affordable and infinitely varied short-term noncredit programs number in the thousands. All are hosted by a network of more than 2,000 educational and cultural sites

ELDERHOSTEL SCHOLARSHIPS

Elderhostel offers a limited number of full or partial scholarships, to be used only in the U.S., for people who find the tuition costs of the programs beyond their means. Funds to cover travel costs are not included and eligibility is determined upon completion of an application that includes a confidential questionnaire. Scholarship programs in Alaska and Hawaii are available only to residents of those states.

For information: Write to Elderhostel, 11 Avenue de Lafayette, Boston, MA 02111. Attention: Scholarships.

including colleges and universities, conference centers, state and national parks, museums, outdoor educational centers, and many others, in all 50 states and more than 100 countries.

The only requirement for participation is that you must be 55 or older. An accompanying spouse or adult companion may be younger. No previous educational background is required and there are no exams or grades and only occasional homework. The one- to four-week programs with classes on every conceivable topic are taught by the host institutions' faculty, staff, and local experts and include excursions and social activities.

Accommodations range from hotels or college dormitories to conference centers, cruise ships, barges, rustic cabins, and resorts. Meals are included. Most domestic programs last for five or six nights, while the overseas programs are planned for one to four weeks and include transportation. New this year: weekenders that run Thursday or Friday evening to Sunday or Monday noon and take place in major American cities.

The many course offerings are listed in voluminous seasonal catalogs. You may also view them 24 hours a day, 7 days a week, on the Web at www.elderhostel.org, where you may search by subject, date, or location.

Many of the programs include sports and other outdoor activities such as canoeing, skiing, biking, rafting, golfing, and walking (see Chapter 13). The service programs (see Chapter 18) connect you to a wide variety of volunteer organizations that provide significant services all over the world.

Elderhostel's Train Treks programs use trains as moving classrooms, combining rail travel with learning as you explore large expanses of territory, from Canada and the U.S. to China. The Adventures Afloat program uses ships as a way to visit and study remote places. And the new escorted Motor Coach programs give you an easy way to learn and explore by providing transportation from your own area—New York, San Francisco, Phoenix, Philadelphia, Boston, and other major cities—to destinations within a reasonable distance from home for courses and exploration.

Intergenerational programs for members and their children or grandchildren are another option, along with many others. For a more independent experience, the City Highlights programs in foreign countries allow you an opportunity to explore on your own after information sessions with the group.

Elderhostel's Exploring North America programs feature on-the-move itineraries from the mid-Atlantic and the South to the Pacific, listed by geographic region and theme. Themes currently include American heritage, American landscapes, cultural arts, food and wine, houses and gardens, national parks, and signature cities. On these trips, you usually move from place to place, spending time in two or three locations, studying and exploring as you go.

For information: Elderhostel, 11 Avenue de Lafayette, Boston, MA 02111; 877-426-8056 or 617-426-7788; www.elderhostel.org.

INTERHOSTEL

Interhostel was the first major provider of educational travel programs for adults 50+. Founded in 1982 by the University of New Hampshire, it offers all-inclusive, one-week travel programs in the U.S. and two-week adventures packed with activities everywhere from New Zealand, Germany, France, Canada, and Turkey to the Slovak Republic. New destinations are added every year. Each program is hosted by a university or educational institution in the region you're visiting, and their faculty and other experts lead the lectures and field trips.

On the overseas trips, you lodge in three- to four-star hotels, eat the local food, and get a first-hand look at the world, accompanied by a UNH faculty or staff member. The moderate cost covers airfare, accommodations, meals, tuition, ground transportation, and all of the activities from bus tours to boat trips and concerts. See Chapter 13 for Interhostel's walking tours abroad.

Recent programs in the U.S. have taken their 50-plus travelers (and spouses over 40) to the Southwest, New Orleans, Florida's sun coast, Arizona, Hawaii, Alaska, and more. They too are moderately priced and are all-inclusive.

The University of New Hampshire also offers Family-Hostel Learning vacations for grandparents and/or parents and school-age children. See Chapter 10.

For information: Interhostel, 6 Garrison Ave., Durham, NH 03824; 800-733-9753 or 603-862-1147; www.learn.unh .edu.

NATIONAL ACADEMY OF OLDER CANADIANS (NAOC)

Based in Vancouver, the NAOC's mission is to involve Canadians over the age of 45 in lifelong learning and to help them keep pace with modern technology. It offers computer classes with "senior-friendly" courses. The membership fee is $17 (Canadian) a year or $10 for six months.

For information: National Academy of Older Canadians, 411 Dunsmuir St., Vancouver, BC V6B 1X4; 604-681-3767; www.vcn.bc.ca/naoc.

OASIS

OASIS is a nonprofit organization sponsored by the May Department Stores Company in collaboration with local hospitals, medical centers, government agencies, and other participants through a network of centers in 25 cities across the nation. Its purpose is to enrich the lives of people over 55 by providing programs in the arts, humanities, wellness, and technology, and volunteer opportunities to its members. At its centers, OASIS offers classes ranging from French conversation and the visual arts to dance, bridge, creative writing, history, exercise, classical music, points of law, and prevention of osteoporosis. There are also special events such as concerts, plays, museum visits, lectures, and even trips and cruises. Membership is free.

For information: The OASIS Institute, 7710 Carondelet Ave., Ste. 125, St. Louis, MO 63105; 314-862-2933; www.oasisnet.org.

SEMESTER AT SEA

A 100-day educational voyage around the world, Semester at Sea, academically sponsored by the University of Pittsburgh and administered by the Institute for Shipboard Education, takes more than 600 college students and about 60 "senior scholars" on a unique learning experience that is designed to advance the exchange of understanding and knowledge among cultures. The *S.S. Universe Explorer*, a former passenger ship refitted as a floating campus, circumnavigates the earth twice a year, visiting countries that have included Japan, China, India, Malaysia, Kenya, Brazil, Venezuela, Egypt, Israel, South Africa, Greece, Turkey, Vietnam, and Morocco.

While the college students earn credit hours toward an undergraduate degree, the older participants may audit classes or enroll for full credit, choosing from among 60 courses taught by faculty from various universities. Onboard courses range from anthropology and biological sciences to economics, fine arts, philosophy, political science, and religion. Lengthy stays in each port of call give students a chance to experience the peoples and cultures firsthand.

Amenities include an adult coordinator; entertainment; buffet-style meals; lectures; discussion groups; and guest scholars with expertise in local cultures, films, art shows, sports, and more.

In addition to the long voyage scheduled during the spring and fall, a new, condensed 65-day summertime Semester at Sea combines a smaller number of college students and seniors. From Vancouver, B.C., to Sitka, Alaska, then to Vladavlostok, Pusan, Shanghai, Hanoi, Keelung, Osaka to Seattle, the group travels aboard the *MTS Explorer* learning all the way.

For information: Semester at Sea, 811 William Pitt Union, University of Pittsburgh, Pittsburgh, PA 15260; 800-854-0195 or 412-648-7490; www.semesteratsea.com.

SENIOR SUMMER SCHOOL

In this program, you can spend two to ten weeks in the summer taking classes at your choice of ten college campuses in vacation locations: San Diego State University; University of Wisconsin; University of California at Santa Barbara; University of California at La Jolla; West Virginia University at Morgantown; University of Judaism in Los Angeles; Marymount-Manhattan College in New York; Green Mountain College in Killington, Vermont; Appalachian State University in Boone, North Carolina; and Mount Allison University in New Brunswick, Canada.

The courses are college level but there are no grades, compulsory papers, or mandatory attendance. Accommodations and meals are in student residence halls. Sightseeing trips, excursions, classes, weekly housekeeping, and social activities are all part of the deal. While most students are in their mid-60s, people of any age are welcome to enroll. There are no previous educational requirements.
For information: Senior Summer School, PO Box 4424, Deerfield Beach, FL 33442; 800-847-2466; www.seniorsummerschool.com.

SENIOR VENTURES IN OREGON

Southern Oregon University in Ashland is where you can sign up for one- or two-week educational theater programs exclusively for people at least 50 years of age (and companions who may be younger). The summer programs coincide with Ashland's famous annual Oregon Shakespeare Festival and classes are taught by actors, backstage professionals, and Shakespearean scholars. You stay on campus and eat your meals there. Added bonus: theater tickets to current productions. A few travel adventures, such as a Canadian theater expedition, are also offered.

For information: Senior Ventures, Southern Oregon University, 1250 Siskiyu Blvd., Ashland, OR 97520; 800-257-0577 or 541-552-6285; www.sou.edu/seniorventures.htm.

TRAVELEARN

The upscale learning vacations by TraveLearn take small groups of adults all over the world, putting you up in first-class or deluxe accommodations and providing local lecturers and escorts who are experts in their fields and in-country guides from cooperating universities and colleges in each destination. You'll learn through on-site lectures, seminars, meals with local families, visits to homes and workplaces, and field trips. Destinations include Ireland, Egypt, Kenya, China, Morocco, Greece, Italy, Turkey, South Africa, Costa Rica, Peru, Belize, Australia, and Central Europe. If you are traveling alone and wish to share a room with another single traveler, you are guaranteed the double rate if you register 90 days in advance, even if a roommate is not found for you.

For information: TraveLearn, PO Box 315, Lakeville, PA 18438; 800-235-9114 or 570-226-9114; www.travelearn.com.

UNIVERSITY VACATIONS

Summer scholars may attend a range of six-day study programs, arranged by University Vacations, at prestigious institutions such as the Sorbonne in Paris, the University of Bologna in Italy, Trinity College in Dublin, and Cambridge and Oxford Universities in England. In-depth classroom lec-

LEARN COMPUTER TECHNOLOGY

SeniorNet is a national nonprofit organization dedicated to teaching older adults how to use computers and understand computer technologies. It sponsors more than 200 local SeniorNet Learning Centers all across the country, staffed by volunteers, where members may take classes and use the facilities. Independent members participate through the organization's electronic community, SeniorNet Online.

To take the classes at a learning center, you must join SeniorNet for $40 a year, which gives you other benefits as well: a quarterly newsletter; discounts on computer-related books, software, and hardware; and invitations to national conferences and regional meetings.

Without cost, you can access SeniorNet Online, where you may join any of about 600 discussion groups and share information and opinions about everything from computers to politics, finance, news, social concerns, the arts, leisure, and health.

For information: SeniorNet, 121 Second St., San Francisco, CA 94105; 800-747-6848 or 415-495-4990; www.seniornet.org.

tures by university faculty are augmented by field trips, walking tours, excursions, and notable meals. Students live on campus or in nearby hotels and eat in fine restaurants. The programs are open to all ages but are largely attended by older students.

For information: University Vacations, 3660 Bougainvillea Rd., Coconut Grove, FL 33133; 800-792-0100 or 305-567-2904; www.universityvacations.com.

UTAH STATE UNIVERSITY SUMMER CITIZENS

Spend three months—May to August—at Utah State University in Logan where about 1,000 seniors participate in the Summer Citizens Program and choose from a variety of courses taught by university professors and local experts, attend cultural events, live in student housing, participate in recreational activities, and enjoy the pleasant temperatures.

An ID card that costs $55 is your ticket to the program and gets you into all parts of the campus from theaters to libraries, computer labs, exercise rooms, tennis courts, parking lots, and the swimming pool. You get a one- to three-week course free with the card, then pay $30 to $60 for others. Your housing may be on campus or off, and free shuttles and buses take you everywhere you want to go at the university or in the city. Housing costs range from $1,000 to $2,000 for the three months, depending on the amenities.

Three-week packages are also available for those with less time to spend getting smart.

For information: Summer Citizens Program, Utah State University, 5005 Old Main Hill, Logan, UT 84322; 800-538-2663 or 435-797-7573; www.summercitizens.com.

WORLD OF KNOWLEDGE TOURS

This company's tours are exclusively for active people over the age of 50 who want to sail the earth's seas and oceans and learn at the same time. You'll travel with a small group of peers aboard a first-class cruise ship to such destinations as the Galapagos Islands, the Panama Canal, Alaska, the

Mediterranean, and Northern Europe and Russia. Your group dines together every evening and is accompanied by two guides who conduct shipboard seminars about the history, culture, art, geology, and wildlife of the area.

For information: World of Knowledge Tours, 107 222nd St. SW, Bothell, WA 98021; 800-453-9283; www.knowledge tours.com.

INSTITUTES FOR LEARNING IN RETIREMENT (ILR)

Another way to learn with a group of contemporaries is to join an ILR, a community-based organization of retirement-age learners for local people who commute to the program. Located in more than 220 communities across the U.S., most of these institutes are member-run under the auspices of a host college or university. Each is independent and unique, providing noncredit academic programs developed and often led by the members themselves. The institutes have an open membership for retirement-age students regardless of previous education and charge modest membership fees.

For a directory of ILRs, or information about starting a new program in your community, contact the Elderhostel Institute Network (EIN) which helps community groups set up their own learning programs.

For information: Elderhostel Institute Network, 11 Avenue de Lafayette, Boston, MA 02111; 617-422-0784; www.elder hostel.org.

13

Good Deals for Good Sports

Real sports never give up their sneakers. If you've been a physically active person all your life, you're certainly not going to become a couch potato now—especially since you've probably got more time, energy, and maybe funds than you ever had before to enjoy athletic activities. Besides, you can now take advantage of some interesting special privileges and adventures offered exclusively to people over the age of 49.

ELDERHOSTEL

Many Elderhostel programs (see Chapter 12) include a wide selection of outdoor and sports activities for beginners as well as experienced athletes. Among the choices are golf, birding, walking and trekking, tennis, hiking, biking, sea kayaking, sailing, whitewater rafting, wilderness canoeing, skiing, snowshoeing, and trail biking.

For information: Elderhostel, 11 Avenue de Lafayette, Boston, MA 02111; 877-426-8056 or 617-426-7788; www.elderhostel.org.

EXPLORATIONS IN TRAVEL

Specializing in outdoor and cultural vacations for women over 40, Explorations in Travel's action-filled itineraries are geared for women with energy who love the outdoors and like to travel with contemporaries, leaving the men at home. Typical trips include inn-to-inn hiking and rafting in New England, wildlife-watching in Ecuador, cycling in Ireland, spotting butterflies in Mexico, cruising the canals in England, and exploring Namibia or the Florida rivers.

Several multigenerational trips are planned every year for mothers and daughters, grandmothers and granddaughters, aunts, and other female friends and relatives. The rule is that one participant is over 40, the others 21 or over.

For information: Explorations in Travel, 2458 River Rd., Guilford, VT 05301; 802-257-0152; www.exploretravel.com.

THE OVER THE HILL GANG (OTHG)

This is a club that welcomes fun-loving, adventurous people from 50 to 90-plus (and younger spouses or companions) who are looking for action and contemporaries to pursue it with. No naps, no rockers, no sitting by the pool sipping planter's punch. OTHG started as a ski club many years ago (see Chapter 14) but its members can now be found participating in all kinds of activities when the ski season ends. Recent trips have included fully escorted trips to ski areas in the West, Europe, and South America. Other options include whitewater rafting in Idaho, biking in Nova Scotia, hiking in Italy, and golfing in Ireland.

The club currently has about 6,000 members in 50 states and 14 countries and 12 regional "gangs" (chapters). Each local gang decides on its own activities. If there's no chapter in your vicinity, you may become a member-at-large and participate in any of the happenings.

The annual membership fee ($50 single, $80 for a couple) brings you a quarterly magazine, discounts, information about national and chapter events, and a chance to join the fun. The local gangs charge small additional yearly dues.

For information: Over the Hill Gang International, 1820 W. Colorado Ave., Dept. G, Colorado Springs, CO 80904; 719-389-0022; www.othgi.com.

ADVENTURES FOR BIKERS

Biking has become one of America's most popular sports, and people who never dreamed they could go much farther than around the block are now pedaling up to 50 miles in a day. That includes over-the-hill bikers as well as youngsters of 16, 39, or 49. In fact, some tours and clubs are designated specifically for over-50s.

CAPE COD BICYCLE ADVENTURES

A few of this company's many bicycle tours on Cape Cod during the warm months are planned exclusively for 50-plus bikers, covering about 30 miles a day on leisurely pedals through the cape's towns and dunes. You bike in a group with a guide to three different elegant inns in your five-night tour. Included are your bicycle, four dinners, all breakfasts, a boat tour, and a few lunches, plus a support vehicle that carries your luggage and stands ready to give you a lift if you want one.

For information: Cape Cod Bicycle Adventures, 2533 State Hwy., Wellfleet, MA 02667; 888-644-4566 or 508-349-8005; www.capecodbybike.com.

COMPASS HOLIDAYS

For a "cycling break" in the heart of England—the Cotswolds, Bath and Wiltshire, Cornwall, The Severn Vail, and the Lake District—look into the guided or self-planned biking tours from Compass Holidays. With a guide you can ride for three days, for example, around Bourton-on-the-Water, or seven days in the Cotswolds, starting and ending in Cheltenham. You can also ride on your own with maps, planned accommodations, and luggage transfers, on circular routes along quiet country roads from village to village near Bath or Malmesbury. Your luggage is transported for you. For bikers over 50, this tour company—which also schedules walking tours—offers a 10 percent discount if you take a seven-night tour and 5 percent on tours of two nights or more—and a mention of this book. Take your own bike or rent one there.

For this company's walking excursions, see Walking Tours later in this chapter.

For information: Compass Holidays, Cheltenham Spa Railway Station, Queens Rd., Cheltenham, Glos GL51 8NP, UK; www.compass-holidays.com.

THE CROSS CANADA CYCLE TOUR SOCIETY

This is a bicycling club for retired people who love to jump on their bikes and take off across the countryside. Most of the club's members are over 60, with many in their 70s and 80s and only a few under 50. Says the society, "Our aim is to stay alive as long as possible." Now there's a worthwhile goal.

Based in Vancouver, B.C., with members—both men and women, skilled and novice—mostly in B.C., Ontario, and Alberta, but many in the U.S., it organizes many trips a year, all led by volunteer tour guides. Membership costs $25 single or $35 per couple per year and includes a monthly newsletter to keep you up to date on happenings. Several times a week, local members gather for day rides, and several times a year there are longer club trips to such far-ranging locations as South Africa, Germany, Switzerland, and U.S. national parks. Every few years a group of intrepid bikers pedals clear across Canada, an adventure that takes a few weeks to accomplish, with some members dropping in and out along the way. Many of the longer trips are tenting or camping tours, while others put you up in hostels, motels, or hotels.

For information: Cross Canada Cycle Tour Society, 6943 Antrim Ave., Burnaby, BC V5J 4M5; 604-433-7710; www.vcn.bc.ca/cccts.

ELDERHOSTEL BICYCLE TOURS

Elderhostel's famous educational travel programs include both domestic and foreign bicycle tours among its many offerings. These vary by the season and year and are all listed in the organization's frequent and voluminous catalogs. Recent programs in the U.S. have included six-day inn-to-inn pedals along the Erie Canal in New York, the northwest corner of Arizona, and the rolling hills of Texas. Lectures and sight-seeing excursions are included.

Bike tours in foreign lands are scheduled weekly from April through September in Canada, Denmark, England, Italy, Germany, Austria, France, and the Netherlands. Led by a guide and riding as a group, you cover 25 to 35 miles a day and learn about the culture and history from local educators and other specialists. Three-speed bikes are provided, as are breakfast, dinner, and accommodations in small hotels. The support van that travels with the group to carry the luggage and repair equipment will carry you as well if you decide that you can't possibly make it up another hill.

For information: Elderhostel, 11 Avenue de Lafayette, Boston, MA 02111; 877-426-8056 or 617-426-7788; www.elderhostel.org.

INTERNATIONAL BICYCLE TOURS (IBT)

The Fifty Plus Tour by IBT is planned for bikers over 50 who are not interested in pedaling up mountains but love to hit the road on two wheels. It takes you to Holland on leisurely eight-day rides along bicycle paths and quiet country roads on flat terrain through farmland, forests, islands, and small villages. You cover only about 30 miles a day, so there's plenty of time for sightseeing, snacking, shopping, and relaxing. You lodge in small hotels and dine on local specialties.

Although these are the only IBT tours specifically designated as 50-plus, most of its trips in Europe and the U.S. are geared to older riders.

For information: International Bicycle Tours, PO Box 754, Essex, CT 06426; 860-767-7005; www.internationalbicycletours.com.

LAID BACK TOURS

To see New Orleans and its environs, check into Laid Back Tours that send you out to see the world on your choice of bikes that include standard hybrids, mountain bikes, or two- or three-wheeled recumbent bikes and trikes that let you lean back in comfort while you pedal. Laid Back schedules several trips a year, anywhere from three hours to six days, just for people 50 and over. You'll pedal through the historic neighborhoods of New Orleans, along bayous and swamps, and the Mississippi River Levee Bike Path. Included in the tour is lodging, most of your meals, along with your bike.

For information: Laid Back Tours, 625 Hagan Ave., New Orleans, LA 70119; 800-786-1274 or 504-488-8991; www.laidbacktours.com.

OVER THE HILL GANG (OTHG)

This club, for energetic 50-plus adventurers whose main activity is skiing, schedules at least one group bike tour every year, usually in Europe along routes rated "easy" on gentle terrain. Bike during the day, sleep at small hotels along the way at night. See more information about the club and its activities earlier in this chapter.

For information: Over the Hill Gang International, 1820 W. Colorado Ave., Dept. G, Colorado Springs, CO 80904; 719-389-0022; www.othgi.com.

SIERRA CLUB OUTINGS

Every year, as part of this respected environmental organization affordable outings, a few backpacking treks through wilderness areas are targeted for experienced and fit backpackers age 50 or over. The one-week trips are led by volunteers and vary from year to year. Recent destinations have included national wilderness areas in Colorado and Wyoming.

Participants must be members of the club, and, if you consider yourself a "senior," your yearly membership costs you only $24, compared to $39 for other adults. Two seniors in the same household can join the Club for $32 a year, compared to $47.

For information: Sierra Club Outings, 85 Second St., San Francisco, CA 94105; 415-977-5522; www.outings.sierra club.org.

VBT BICYCLING VACATIONS

This venerable bike company, now an affiliate of Grand Circle Travel, an agency that specializes in travel for people over the age of 50, has tailored many of VBT's trips for the same fast-growing age group. Although challenging routes remain for those who want them, many of the itineraries in the U.S. and overseas are less demanding and their schedules more relaxed. VBT's biking vacations currently include a number of trips eminently suitable for older bikers who

SENIOR CYCLING

Exclusively for bikers over 50 who prefer to travel with congenial contemporaries, the bicycle adventures by Senior Cycling (a.k.a. Old Folks on Spokes) may do the job. You'll do the miles but at slower speeds than 20-somethings, taking time to enjoy the journey and make stops along the way. When overnights are required, you'll stay at local hotels or B&Bs and dine at local eateries. Trips range from local one- or two-day ventures out of the Washington, D.C., area to a seven-day spin along the Erie Canal from Buffalo to Albany in New York State. Other choices, two to six days, include the Florida Keys, the Katy Trail in Missouri, Pennsylvania's Amish country, and the towpaths of the C & O Canal in Maryland.

The trips are rated for difficulty, with several featuring flat easy terrain for rank beginners. Groups are small, from 6 to 12 participants, plus a guide and a support vehicle to carry luggage, lunch, and you, if necessary. Accommodations and most meals are included. Bring your own bike or rent one. ***For information:*** Senior Cycling, 37419 Branch River Rd., Loudon Heights, VA 20132; 540-668-6307; www.senior cycling.com.

seek adventure without all that much physical stress, such as the Salzburg Sojourn, which takes participants on flat bicycle paths and easy descents in the Austrian Alps. Or a tour of Tuscany traveling along the coast on less-traveled roads.

For information: VBT, 614 Monkton Rd., Bristol, VT 05443; 800-245-3868 or 802-453-4811; www.vbt.com.

WANDERING WHEELS

This program established in 1966 was created to work with local churches to provide long-distance bike tours for all ages and has since attracted people from all walks of life and with various beliefs. Its trips include a 2,600-mile coast-to-coast ride every spring geared specifically for people who are middle-aged or older.

For information: Wandering Wheels, PO Box 207, Upland, IN 46989; 765-998-7490; www.wanderwheels.com.

WOMANTOURS

Bicycle trips for women are the specialty of this group that schedules many trips suitable for older bikers with moderate terrain and easy mileage. Recent trips have gone to the Teton Mountains, the Canadian Rockies from Banff to Jasper, or the Vermont Champlain Valley. A van goes along with every group to carry the luggage and repair equipment and give weary riders a lift. Exclusively for women over 50 is a much more ambitious 83-day, 4,250-mile trip across the entire country, from San Diego, California, to St. Augustine, Florida. Mileage averages 65 miles a day, mostly on fairly flat terrain, with one rest day per week. For this trip you'd better be in good shape!

For information: WomanTours, PO Box 746, Driggs, ID 83422; 800-247-1444 or 208-354-2652; www.womantours.com.

TENNIS, ANYONE?

An estimated three million of the nation's tennis players are over 50, with the number increasing every year as more of us decide to forgo sitting by the pool for a few fast sets on the courts. You need only a court, a racquet, a can of balls, and an opponent to play tennis, but, if you'd like to be competitive or sociable, you may want to get into some senior tournaments.

UNITED STATES TENNIS ASSOCIATION (USTA)

The USTA offers a wide variety of tournaments for players over the advanced age of 35, at both local and national levels. To participate, you must be a member ($25 per year). When you join, you will become a member of a regional section, receive periodic schedules of USTA-sponsored tournaments and events in your area for which you can sign up, get a discount on tennis books and publications, and receive a monthly magazine and a free subscription to *Tennis* magazine.

In the schedule of tournaments, you'll find competitions listed for specific five-year age groups: for men from 35 to 90-plus and for women from 35 to 85-plus. In addition, self-rated tournaments match you up with people of all ages who play at your level. If you feel you're good enough to compete, send for an application and sign up. There is usually a modest fee.

For information: USTA, 70 W. Red Oak Ln., White Plains, NY 10604; 800-990-8782 or 914-696-7000; www.usta.com.

USA LEAGUE TENNIS, SENIOR DIVISION

If you want to compete with other 50-plus tennis players in local, area, and sectional competitions, culminating in a national championship, join the Senior Division of the USA

League Tennis program. Your level of play will be rated in a specific skill category ranging from beginner to advanced, and you'll compete only with people on your own ability level. You must join USTA ($25 a year) for the privilege and the details.

For information: USTA, 70 W. Red Oak Ln., White Plains, NY 10604; 800-990-8782 or 914-696-7000; www.usta.com.

VAN DER MEER TENNIS UNIVERSITY

Van der Meer Tennis University offers five-day Seniors Clinics from September to May every year at its Van der Meer Shipyard Tennis Resort on Hilton Head Island. Specifically for 50-plus players, beginning or experienced, the clinics provide more than 16 hours of instruction, including video analysis, tactics and strategies for singles and doubles, match play drills, plus round robins, social activities, and free court time. The goal is to improve your strokes and game strategy so you'll get more enjoyment out of your game. Discounted accommodations are available for participants, making a week's package quite inexpensive.

For information: Van der Meer Tennis University, PO Box 5902, Hilton Head Island, SC 29938; 800-845-6138 or 843-785-8388; www.vdmtennis.com.

WALKING TOURS

Walking tours have become remarkably popular among people of all ages but especially ours—those of us who are old enough to appreciate the close encounters with the world and its wonders that moving along at a leisurely pace on our own two feet allows. Among the many tour companies that plan walking tours are some that specialize in travel on foot for mature participants.

APPALACHIAN MOUNTAIN CLUB (AMC)

Every year this famous hiking club, the oldest conservation and recreation organization in the U.S., schedules a few inexpensive two- to five-day treks for people over the age of 50. You'll hike two to eight miles a day at an easy pace in New Hampshire's White Mountains or the Catskills in New York and sleep in a comfortable lodge at night, with plenty of time to savor the scenery and glimpse the wildlife. Routes vary from year to year. Yearly membership fee in AMC for adults is $40 ($65 per family) but if you are 69 or more, you pay only $25.

For information: Appalachian Mountain Club, 5 Joy St., Boston, MA 02108; or 617-523-0636; www.outdoors.org.

COMPASS HOLIDAYS

This company specializes in walking holidays in the English countryside, with or without a guide. You'll enjoy walks through quiet villages, bustling towns, and pastoral countrysides for three to eight days, covering only a few or many miles, stopping each evening at a small family hotel for local food and a comfortable night's sleep. If you are over the age of 50 and you sign up for seven-night break, you'll get a 10 percent discount if you remember to mention this book. Compass also offers many bike tours in England.

For information: Compass Holidays, Cheltenham Spa Railway Station, Queens Rd., Cheltenham, Gloucestershire GL51 8NP, UK; www.compass-holidays.com.

ELDERHOSTEL WALKING & HIKING PROGRAMS

Both Elderhostel's domestic and international programs include walking and hiking tours for which you should be practiced walkers with energy and good health. Accompanied by guides, lecturers, and local specialists, the overseas walkers, carrying small day packs, cover 4 to 12 miles a day, rain or shine. You'll stay and dine mostly in small hotels, while lunch is taken en route. Educational programs are part of the package. Trekking trips are also on Elderhostel's menu, taking you up to eight miles a day on footpaths in Nepal or Switzerland. For these you must be in even better physical shape and accustomed to vigorous exercise.

For information: Elderhostel, 11 Avenue de Lafayette, Boston, MA 02111; 877-426-8056 or 617-426-7788; www.elderhostel.org.

ELDERTREKS

On these trekking trips in exotic lands, most of them in the Far East, you will hike overland on foot and, in many cases, sleep on an air mattress in a village house or a tent. The trips are rated for difficulty so you may choose one that matches your abilities. For more, see Chapter 9.

For information: ElderTreks, 597 Markham St., Toronto, ON M6G 2L7; 800-741-7956 or 416-588-5000; www.eldertreks.com.

EXPLORE HOLIDAYS

A specialty of this Canadian company is its 50-plus Mountain Tours, fully catered and guided camping and hiking tours of the Canadian Rocky Mountains for adventurers over 50. Starting and ending in Calgary, the 10-day tours are scheduled in the summer months and take groups of no more than 10 participants accompanied by 2 staff members to campsites in Kananaskis country and Lake Louise, where they settle down in large stand-up tents furnished with comfortable cots. Meals, served up by the cook, are eaten in a dining tent. Each day, there's a three- to five-mile hike deep into mountain passes and glacier-filled valleys.

For information: Explore Holidays, PO Box 607, 743 Railway Ave., Canmore, AB T1W 1P2; 403-609-4101; www.exploreholidays.com.

INTERHOSTEL

If you love to amble along, taking a good look at the world, sign on for one of Interhostel's educational walking tours for people over 50. Foreign itineraries currently include vacations around Galway and Killarney in Ireland and Stirling and Edinburgh in Scotland. Itineraries in the U.S. include California, Colorado, Alaska, and more. Traveling from place to place by van, you explore on foot and cover perhaps three to five miles a day on gentle terrain that includes some hills and lodging in small hotels or student residences. See Chapter 12 for more about Interhostel's programs.

For information: Interhostel, 6 Garrison Ave., Durham, NH 03824; 800-733-9753 or 603-862-1147; www.learn.unh.edu.

NIFTY OVER FIFTY TOURS

From Pacific Pathways, these wildlife, horticultural, and botanical tours, specifically for energetic people over 50, take small groups—or just two of you—to less-traveled scenic and perhaps remote areas of New Zealand. On your daily relaxed walks in a variety of terrains, you'll observe the native forest and its bird life; view the animals; study the plants; learn about local culture and customs; and meet the people through farmstays, home visits, shared meals, private garden tours, birding trips, and hikes in a variety of forest, alpine, bush, and coastal locations. There's time too to explore the cities of Auckland and Christchurch.

For information: Nifty Over Fifty Tours, Pacific Pathways, 1919 Chula Vista Dr., Belmont, CA 94002; 650-595-2090; www.pacificpathways.com.

RIVER ODYSSEYS WEST (ROW)

If you love wilderness rivers but aren't into whitewater rafting (see Chapter 9), consider ROW's raft-supported walking tours along trails that follow the course of the Middle Fork of the Salmon River in Idaho or the Snake River in Hells Canyon on the Oregon border. Carrying only a day pack and led by a guide, you hike six or eight miles a day with plenty of time to smell the flowers and spot the wildlife. A cargo raft carries all the camping gear and your luggage as well as the food and other supplies, and a smaller support raft floats along at the group's pace to act as a sag wagon for tired walkers. When you arrive at camp each afternoon, the staff has already set up the roomy tents and the kitchen and has started cooking dinner, giving you time to relax, fish, or explore.

For information: River Odysseys West, PO Box 579-UD, Coeur d'Alene, ID 83816; 800-451-6034 or 208-765-0841; www.rowinc.com.

SILVER SNEAKER EXCURSIONS

Silver Sneaker walking tours, many of them exclusively for people over 50, are led by a couple of experienced outdoor adventure guides. In the U.S., their trips vary from weekends to 18-day adventures, including hikes from inn to inn in Vermont as well as walks on Rhode Island's beaches; in Sedona and the Grand Canyon in Arizona; on the coast of Maine; and around the famous resort city of Newport, Rhode Island. Abroad, they offer longer hiking trips in Wales or England's Cornwall as well as the Copper Canyon in Mexico, Bolivia and Peru, Ecuador and the Galapagos Islands, and Costa Rica.

For information: Silver Sneaker Excursions, 100 Worsley Ave., N. Kingstown, RI 02852; 401-295-0367; www.silversneakerexcursions.com.

WALK YOUR WAY

Walk Your Way Into the Heart of England tours always include a few trips per year just for older walkers. These are 12- to 15-day tours off the beaten path in quaint and picturesque areas of Deven and Dorset, the Lake District, the Dales of Yorkshire, or the Cotswolds in England as well as the Highlands of Scotland and the Republic of Ireland. Some walks are circular, beginning and ending in the same village, averaging five miles a day. Others are linear, covering eight to ten miles a day. The group is never larger than ten, lodging is in family guest houses or bed-and-breakfasts, and evening meals are eaten in local pubs.

For information: Walk Your Way, PO Box 231, Red Feather Lakes, CO 80545; 970-881-2709; www.acqr43.ukgateway.net

WALKING THE WORLD

Anyone over 50 who loves adventure and is in good physical shape is invited to participate in Walking the World's explorations. These are 8- to 19-day backcountry treks, covering six to ten miles a day, that focus on natural and cultural history. On some trips, you'll camp out and, carrying only a day pack, hike to each new destination. On others, you will lodge in small country inns, hotels, or bed-and-breakfasts, setting forth on daily walks into the countryside. Groups are small, from 12 to 18 participants plus two local guides, and there's no upper age limit. No previous hiking experience is necessary.

Destinations include Arches and Canyonlands National Parks in Utah; Banff and Jasper National Parks in the Canadian Rockies; plus trips in Maine, Arizona, Scotland, England, Norway, Wales, Switzerland, Ireland, Portugal, New Zealand, Hawaii, Tahiti, Peru, Ecuador, Costa Rica, and Italy. ***For information:*** Walking the World, PO Box 1186, Fort Collins, CO 80522; 800-340-9255 or 970-498-0500; www.walkingtheworld.com.

NATURAL HISTORY TOURS

ELDERHOSTEL BIRDING PROGRAMS

Among Elderhostel's many outdoor programs are trips specifically designed for bird-watching in the field in Australia, Costa Rica, Ecuador, Iceland, Kenya, Mexico, Peru, and Norway. Here in the U.S. there are many Elderhostel programs that include this popular activity among their courses.

For information: Elderhostel, 11 Avenue de Lafayette, Boston, MA 02111; 877-426-8056 or 617-426-7788; www.elderhostel.org.

SNOWMOBILE TOURS

SENIOR WORLD TOURS

Explore the winter wonders of Yellowstone National Park or the Black Hills of South Dakota aboard your own snowmobile on a seniors-only six- or seven-day adventure trip planned by Senior World Tours. All tours travel on roadways already groomed for the use of park personnel—and never off-road, where snowmobiles can damage the environment. Included in the package are driving lessons, snowmobiles, fuel, boots, gloves, helmets, cross-country skis, meals, and trusty guides. No experience is necessary, but don't even think of going unless you enjoy the snow and are in good physical condition.

By the way, if you go with a companion who does not care to ride alone, you may choose a two-up machine that allows the two of you to travel tandem.

On the Yellowstone National Park trip, you'll begin your adventure at Togwotee, near Jackson, Wyoming, riding your snowmobile through the park to view the wildlife, geysers, hot springs, mountain passes, awesome views, and splendid scenery. You'll make many stops along the way to see the sights and overnight in wilderness lodges and resorts. If you choose to ride in the Black Hills of South Dakota, your tour begins at Rapid City, then takes you to Mt. Rushmore, Crazy Horse Memorial, and on to Spearfish Canyon, and through

the Hills to an overnight in Lead and a stop at the gambling casinos in the historic town of Deadwood.
For information: Senior World Tours, 2205 N. River Rd., Fremont, OH 43420; 888-355-1686; www.seniorworld tours.com.

SNOWSHOEING/CROSS-COUNTRY SKIING

APPALACHIAN MOUNTAIN CLUB (AMC)

Famous for its hiking programs in New England (see page 213), AMC also schedules several affordable cross-country skiing and snowshoeing courses for grownups every winter. The 50+ Cross Country Skiing for Beginners gives you a chance to join a small group of peers for two nights at an inn in the Catskills or the White Mountains where you'll get accommodations, meals, and lessons on groomed trails. The 50+ Snowshoe Adventure is a similar program for beginners who want to learn the basics about navigating on top of the snow. To participate, you need to be in good physical condition and able to carry a full day pack. Members of the club are entitled to a 10 percent discount on the cost of these adventures. The annual adult membership fee for AMC is $40 ($65 for family) but only $25 for those 69 or over.
For information: Appalachian Mountain Club, 5 Joy St., Boston, MA 02108; 617-523-0636; www.outdoors.org.

SILVER SNEAKER EXCURSIONS

Every winter, Silver Sneaker Excursions adds a couple of cross-country skiing and snowshoe packages in Vermont to its list of adventures specifically for people over 50. For both beginners and intermediates, the packages include five nights, meals, and aprés ski parties. All are led by experienced outdoor adventure guides.

For information: Silver Sneaker Excursions, 100 Worsley Ave., N. Kingstown, RI 02852; 401-295-0367; www.silversneakerexcursions.com.

MOTORCYCLE HEAVEN

BEACH'S MOTORCYCLE ADVENTURES

If motorcycling is your passion and adventure is in your blood, look into the motorcycle tours offered by the Beach family who has been conducting cycling tours since 1972. All ages, including yours, may choose trips in "the world's best motorcycling areas" in the Alps, Norway, and New Zealand. You must, of course, have a valid motorcycle license. Motorcycles are provided in your choice of available models and there is no mileage charge. A guide goes along with you, and your luggage is carried by a van. By the way, both bikes and automobiles are welcome on these tours, so if friends or family want to join you they may go along in a car.

You're on your own during the day, following a tour book that gives daily itineraries, road maps, distances, estimated en route times, business hours, sight-seeing ideas, good (and bad) roads, suggestions for activities, driving tips, and directions to the hotel of the night. The daily routing, pace, and stops are up to you. There are several riding options each day, so you may decide to cruise along or ride

long and hard. Every evening, you'll meet the group and your guide at a hotel or family farm where you'll eat dinner that night and have breakfast the next morning.
For information: Beach's Motorcycle Adventures, 2763 W. River Pkwy., Grand Island, NY 14072; 716-773-4960; www.beachs-mca.com.

RETREADS MOTORCYCLE CLUB

Retreads, an association of motorcycle enthusiasts with an average age of 60 and a few members in their 80s, get together for state, regional, and international rallies to talk cycling and ride together. Each state association and local chapter (there are more than 40 in Florida) also has regular get-togethers for short jaunts and socializing. Started as a correspondence club in 1969, Retreads has grown to more than 15,000 members—men and women—in the U.S., Canada, and several other countries including Japan, England, New Zealand, and Australia. Annual contribution is $15 a year per person or $20 per couple. A club newsletter keeps members informed of the activities.
For information: Retreads Motorcycle Club International, 528 North Main St., Albany, IN 47320; 765-789-4070. From November 1 to May 31: 4504 Pittenger Dr., Sarasota, FL 34234; 941-351-7199; www.retreads.org.

GOLF VACATIONS

GREENS FEES

Most municipal and many private golf courses offer senior golfers (usually those over 65) a discount off the regular greens fees, at least on certain days of the week. Take along identification and always make inquiries before you play.

AMERICAN SENIOR GOLF SOCIETY (ASGS)

More than 1,500 golfers over 50—average age 63—belong to ASGS, which sponsors recreational and competitive four-day, midweek golf holidays once or twice a month at highly rated courses all over the country. The holidays include accommodations, golf (including a 54-hole medal-play tournament), breakfasts, at least two dinners, and activities for nonplaying companions. Recent locations have included Pebble Beach Resorts in California; Kiawah Island, South Carolina; Banff Springs in Canada; and The Equinox in Vermont. Longer golf holidays are scheduled once a year to more far-flung locations such as Scotland and Portugal.

Membership in ASGS costs $35 a year or $75 for three years, includes your spouse, entitles you to participate in the trips, and gets you a voluminous monthly newsletter. The three-year membership includes discounts at selected golf courses around the country.

For information: ASGS, 1 Airport Rd., Princeton, NJ 08540; 800-282-6772 or 609-279-0024; www.asgs.net.

GOLF ACADEMY OF HILTON HEAD ISLAND

Golfers over 50 will get a 15 percent discount on the three-day golf schools at the Golf Academy of Hilton Island at Sea Pines if they mention this book when they make their reservations. The school includes five hours of daily instruction

from Class A PGA professionals each morning, followed by 18 holes of golf in the afternoon. Also included are on-course instruction, video analysis with a take-home tape, a personalized improvement manual, plus breakfast and lunch all three days.
For information: Golf Academy of Hilton Head Island, PO Box 5580, Hilton Head Island, SC 29938; 800-925-0467 or 843-785-4540; www.golfacademy.net.

THE GOLF CARD

Designed especially for senior golfers, the Golf Card entitles members to two complimentary rounds of golf per year per course at more than 1,400 courses in the country; up to half off the player's fees at 1,900 additional courses; and savings at 250 stay-and-play packages at more than 250 golf resorts in the U.S., Canada, the Bahamas, Jamaica, and the Dominican Republic. Current membership fees are $75 the first year for a single or $120 for a couple, thereafter $70 a year for solo players and $99 for a couple. A subscription to *Golf Traveler*, a magazine that serves as a guide to the participating courses and resorts, is part of the package.
For information: The Golf Card, PO Box 7021, Englewood, CO 80155; 800-321-8269 or 303-790-2267; www.golfcard.com.

JOHN JACOBS GOLF SCHOOLS

Golfers over the age of 62 get a discount of 10 percent on the cost of golf vacations offered July through December at any John Jacobs Golf School. You'll learn how to improve your game while you play at some of the finest courses in the country. Most packages include lodging, breakfast and din-

ner, instruction, course time, greens fees, and cart. Commuter packages are available, too, at all 45 schools.
For information: John Jacobs Golf Schools, 7825 E. Redfield Rd., Scottsdale, AZ 85260; 800-472-5007; www.jacobsgolf.com.

OVER THE HILL GANG (OTHG)

In the off-season when there's little or no snow for its members to ski upon, this club for peppy people over the age of 50 always plans at least one group golf vacation every year at a well-known golf resort. See more information about the club and its activities earlier in this chapter.
For information: Over the Hill Gang International, 1820 W. Colorado Ave., Dept. G, Colorado Springs, CO 80904; 719-389-0022; www.othgi.com.

SENIOR GOLF ASSOCIATION OF AMERICA (SGA)

An association of amateur senior and super-senior golfers, SGA invites its members, all of them 50 or older, to travel to some of the best golf resorts in the country, stay in deluxe accommodations, and compete in friendly tournaments. Vacations include four nights lodging and dinner reservations, three or four days of golf, plus banquets, award ceremonies, dances, cocktail parties, tours, shopping sprees, special events for non-golfing spouses, you name it. SGA handles all the details but you must provide your own transportation to the resort.

Tournaments at the resorts are based on your handicap and your age, with Senior (50+), Grand Senior (70+), and Legendary Senior (80+) championships and prizes. Annual

membership costs $60 for an individual and $100 for a couple (one of you must be at least 50). Members must agree to abide by the "slow play" rules.
For information: Senior Golfers Association of America, 3013 Church St., Myrtle Beach, SC 29577; 800-337-0047 or 843-626-8100; www.seniorgolfersamerica.com.

SENIORS GOLF TOURNAMENT

Golfers over the age of 50, with a maximum handicap of 24 for men and 36 for women, can sign up for the Annual Seniors Golf Tournament held every winter at the Port Royal Golf Course on Bermuda's southwest coast. A special package includes five nights at the Pompano Beach Club, breakfasts and dinners, three rounds of golf, parties, and more.
For information: Pompano Beach Club, Bermuda Hotels, PO Box 78, Wayland, MA 01778; 800-343-4155; www.pompanobeachclub.com.

EVENTS FOR RAPID RUNNERS

FIFTY-PLUS FITNESS ASSOCIATION

This is not a club, although it occasionally sponsors athletic events for its over-50 members. It is an organization formed by exercise researchers at Stanford University as an exchange of information about fitness and its benefits for those who are 50 or more. Its members, from almost every state and several foreign countries, also serve as volunteers for ongoing studies of activities such as running, swimming, biking, and racewalking. Each is asked to contribute $50 a year, tax-deductible, to defray costs and receives a newsletter. The association sponsors many events throughout the U.S. but mostly in northern California. These include walks, runs, swims, bike rides, and seminars and conferences on aging.

For information: Fifty-Plus Fitness Association, PO Box 20230, Stanford, CA 94309; 650-323-6160; www.50plus.org.

OVER-50 SOFTBALL

INTERNATIONAL SENIOR SOFTBALL ASSOCIATION (ISSA)

ISSA, an association that was founded to promote softball for men and women over the age of 50, conducts the World Championship Tournaments every year in Virginia for more than 300 senior teams. Players who are members of senior leagues and local softball associations all over the U.S. may join and so may individuals without affiliation. Members receive a master nationwide tournament schedule, the results of all national tournaments, and the rankings of all senior softball teams.

For information: ISSA, 9401 East St., Manassas, VA 20110; 703-368-1188; www.seniorsoftball.org.

NATIONAL ASSOCIATION OF SENIOR CITIZEN SOFTBALL (NASCS)

The NASCS is an organization composed of several thousand softball players and hundreds of teams in the U.S. and Canada, with a goal of promoting a worldwide interest in senior softball. To play ball on one of its teams, you must be at least 50 years old. There's no upper age limit, and both men and women are welcomed. NASCS runs qualifying tournaments for the annual Senior Softball World Series, when more than 125 teams from the U.S. and Canada compete in a major ballpark. A semiannual magazine, *Line Drive*, keeps members up to date on happenings here and abroad. ***For information:*** NASCS, PO Box 1085, Mt. Clemens, MI 48046; 586-792-2110.

SENIOR SOFTBALL-USA

This organization, the largest senior softball group in the world, conducts softball tournaments all over the country and organizes international tournaments as well, including the Senior Softball World Championship Games held in September. Anyone over 50, man or woman, in the U.S. and Canada may join for a $25 registration fee, and many thousands have. Members get assistance finding teams in their areas and may subscribe to the *Senior Softball News*, which keeps them up to date on tournaments and other news. They are eligible to take part in an annual international tour that takes teams to play ball in foreign lands. ***For information:*** Senior Softball-USA, 2701 K St., Ste. 101A, Sacramento, CA 95816; 916-326-5303; www.seniorsoftball.com.

SOFTBALL WINTER CAMP

Softball Winter Camp is an annual event held every winter in Altamonte Springs, Florida, (10 miles from Orlando). Older amateur players gather for five days to train, get batting and fielding practice, play eight umpired games, compete in a mini-tournament, join an exercise program, and socialize. Men of all ages and abilities participate, with wives invited to come along to enjoy the fun. Lunch every day, a couple of breakfasts, an awards banquet, an equipment bag, a team shirt, and a cap are included in the fee as are special hotel rates.

For information: Softball Winter Camp, Active Life Styles, 11465 Kanapali Lane, Boynton Beach, FL 33437; 888-335-3828; www.softballcamp.com.

SENIOR GAMES

HUNTSMAN WORLD SENIOR GAMES

Every October, about 6,000 athletes—men and women, 50 and over, from the U.S. and many other countries—gather in St. George, Utah, for two weeks of competition in up to 20 events from basketball, mountain biking, golf, swimming, and tennis to track and field and triathlon. The registration fee (currently $79) includes participation in any of the athletic events and additional perks such as free health screenings, seminars on healthy living, receptions, band concerts, and ceremonial dinners.

For information: Huntsman World Senior Games, 82 W. 700 South, St. George, UT 84770; 800-562-1268 or 435-674-0550; www.seniorgames.net.

NATIONAL SENIOR GAMES ASSOCIATION (NSGA)

The NSGA is the organization that sanctions and coordinates the official senior games across the country. It sponsors the Summer National Senior Games/The Senior Olympics in odd-number years, attracting about 12,000 athletes over the age of 50 who compete in 18 sports. The Winter National Senior Games/The Senior Olympics, also held every other year, in even-number years, features competitions in alpine and cross-country skiing, curling, figure skating, ice hockey, and snowshoeing.

To compete in the national games, you must first qualify in authorized state competitions, which means you must be a medal winner in your age group or meet minimum performance standards in time and distance events.

For a free Qualifying State Games Directory, write to NSGA at the address below or download it from its website. You'll find a representative sample of the games in the following pages.

For information: National Senior Games Association, PO Box 82059, Baton Rouge, LA 70884; 225-766-6800; www.nationalseniorgames.org.

STATE AND LOCAL SENIOR GAMES

Most states hold their own senior games once or twice a year and send their best competitors to national events. If you don't find your state among those listed here, that doesn't mean there's no program in your area—many are sponsored by counties, cities, even local agencies and colleges. Check with your local city, county, or state recreation departments to see what's going on near you or contact the NSGA for a free list. You can find it too on NSGA's website. You don't have to be a serious competitor to enter these games but merely prepared to enjoy yourself. So what if you don't go home with a medal? At the very least, you'll meet other energetic people and have a lot of laughs.

ARIZONA

If you are 50 or more, resident of the state or a visitor, man or woman, a beginner or advanced athlete, you are invited to participate in the Arizona Senior Olympics held every year over about two weeks in February. Events include 29 sports from track to golf, biking, and swimming and are held in several venues in the Phoenix metropolitan area. Every two years you may compete in qualifying games for the national Senior Olympics. Festivities and medals are included.

Local senior games are also scheduled throughout the year in many Arizona cities, including Sierra Vista, Flagstaff, Prescott, and Tucson.

For information: Arizona Senior Olympics, PO Box 60425, Phoenix, AZ 85082; 602-261-8765.

COLORADO

The Senior Winter Games at the Summit take place each year during three days in the second week of February in Summit County. Anyone from anywhere who's over 50 and wants to compete against peers is welcome. Events include cross-country skiing, downhill slalom, speed skating, snowshoe races, biathlon, figure skating, and more, plus social activities. Age categories for the competitions begin at 50 to 54 and increase in five-year increments to 90-plus. A registration fee of $25 for state residents, $30 for others, allows you to participate in one event plus $5 for each added event.

The summer Rocky Mountain Senior Games are held in Greeley the first week in August and include more than 20 competitions in sports ranging from basketball and rac-

quetball to golf, softball, bowling, cycling, and tennis. A registration fee of $35 for state residents, $40 for others, includes admission to eight different events, continental breakfast, and snacks. To participate, you must be at least 50 and you can compete no matter where you're from.
For information: Senior Winter Games at the Summit, PO Box 1845, Frisco, CO 80443; 970-453-2461; or Rocky Mountain Senior Games, 1010 6th St., Greeley, CO 80631; 970-350-9433; www.rmseniorgames.com.

CONNECTICUT

The Connecticut Senior Summer Olympics include not only competitive sport events but also a mini health fair and many physical fitness activities. Residents of Connecticut and neighboring states who are 50-plus converge on the town of Southington on the first weekend in June for three days of events such as the 5,000-meter run, the 100-yard dash, the mile run, the long jump, swimming, bocci, and tennis. These summer games require a small entrance fee.

The one-day Connecticut Senior Winter Olympics, held in February, are open to anyone from anywhere who's at least 50 and an amateur. The games feature downhill, giant slalom, and cross-country skiing, as well as snowshoe races, and take place at Ski Sundown.
For information: Connecticut Senior Olympics, Nutmeg Senior Games, 290 Roberts St., E. Hartford, CT 06106; 800-528-4588.

FLORIDA

Since 1974, the Golden Age Games have taken place in Sanford every November. Today, they host more than 1,500 athletes for a week of 40 different competitions, plus ceremonies, social events, and entertainment. If you are over 50, you are eligible to participate regardless of residency. In other words, you needn't be a Floridian to compete for the gold, silver, and bronze medals in sports such as basketball, biking, bowling, canoeing, checkers, dance, swimming, tennis, triathlon, track and field, canasta, and croquet. There is an entry fee of $6 for the first event and $2 for each additional event.

For information: Golden Age Games, PO Box 1298, Sanford, FL 32772; 407-302-1010; www.ci.sanford.fl.us.

MISSOURI

The St. Louis Senior Olympics have become an institution in Missouri by now. A five-day event in May that is open to anyone who lives anywhere and is at least 50 years old, it costs a nominal amount and is action-oriented. No knitting contests here—only more than 70 energetic events such as bicycle races, 200-meter races, standing long jumps, golf, basketball, free throw, sprints, tennis (singles and doubles), and swimming.

For information: St. Louis Senior Olympics, JCC, 2 Millstone Campus Dr., St. Louis, MO 63146; 314-432-5700, ext. 3217; www.stlouisseniorolympics.org.

MONTANA

Men and women over the age of 50, from Montana or otherwise, are invited to participate in the Montana Senior Olympics, held every year in June. Events range from archery, bowling, and basketball to swimming, tennis, cycling, and track.

For information: Montana Senior Olympics, 2200 Bridger Dr., Bozeman, MT 59715; 406-586-5543.

NEW HAMPSHIRE

For a week in August, you can compete with your peers in the Granite State Senior Summer Games in Manchester, where you can choose from 15 sporting events ranging from swimming to tennis, track and field, shuffleboard, and table tennis. In alternate odd-number years, these are qualifying games for the National Senior Games. Sign up if you are a man or a woman who is at least 50 and in good operating condition. The cost is minimal.
For information: Granite State Senior Games, 610 Front St., Ste. B, Manchester, NH 03102; 603-622-9041.

NEW JERSEY

Held once a year, the New Jersey Senior Sports Classic games feature more than 1,000 seniors competing in 21 competitive sports such as archery, golf, tennis, and track and field.
For information: Senior Citizens Activities Network, Monmouth Mall, Eatontown, NJ 07724; 732-542-1326; www.scannj.com.

NEW YORK

The Empire State Senior Games, open to all New York residents who are 50 or over, are held in Cortlandt over four days in June. Winners may qualify for the National Senior Olympics. For a small registration fee, amateur athletes may compete in many events—swimming, bridge, basketball, softball, croquet, track and field, tennis, racewalking, cycling, and more. There are additional fees for golf and bowling. Participants are invited to social events each of the three nights.

For information: Empire State Senior Games, NYS Parks, 6105 E. Seneca Turnpike, Jamesville, NY 13078; 315-492-9654; www.empirestategames.org.

NORTH CAROLINA

After local games are held statewide, the winners travel to Raleigh for the North Carolina Senior Games State Finals and, perhaps, on to the national games. Most sports are on the agenda, plus an arts competition that celebrates artists in heritage, literary, performing, and visual arts. The state also sponsors the SilverStriders, a walking club for those 50 or better that gives its members logbooks for tracking progress, gifts and awards, and an annual report of their accomplishments.

For information: North Carolina Senior Games, PO Box 33590, Raleigh, NC 27636; 919-851-5456; www.ncsenior games.org.

PENNSYLVANIA

The Pennsylvania Senior Games "combine sports, recreation, and entertainment with fellowship." You can get some of each if you are a Pennsylvania resident who is 50 or older. The games are held over five days in July at Shippensburg University where you can get lodging and three meals a day at low cost. If you prefer to stay in a motel, you'll get a senior discount.

For information: Pennsylvania Senior Games, PO Box 3131, Wilkes-Barre, PA 18773; 570-823-3164, ext. 7; www.keystonegames.com.

UTAH

The Utah Winter Games, open to everyone whatever age, abilities, or home address, schedules more than 100 free clinics and events all over the state from November to January in a variety of winter sports. It includes a free Senior Ski clinic at Brighton Ski Resort in late November, where skiers over 50 are invited for a day of instruction and fun.

The Utah Summer Games Foundation holds annual Olympic-style competitions every June in 41 events from archery to track and field, all of them open to amateur athletes of all ages and skill levels.

For information: Utah Winter Games, 2175 W. 1700 S., Salt Lake City, UT 84104; 801-975-4515; www.utahwintergames.org. Utah Summer Games, 351 W. Center St., Cedar City, UT 84720; 435-865-8421; www.utahsummergames.org.

VERMONT

If you are over 50 years old and an amateur in your sport, you are invited to become a member of the Green Mountain Senior Games (GMSG) for $10 a year per person or $15 per couple. At the summer games, held throughout the summer months at several locations and at the three-day games at Green Mountain College in Poultney every fall, you may compete in sports ranging from golf and tennis to swimming, walking, softball, biking, basketball, and table tennis. The winter games are usually held in January at two sites—

cross-country and snowshoeing events take place at Blueberry Hill, and the downhill skiing events are held at Stratton Mountain.

For information: Green Mountain Senior Games, 131 Holden Hall, Weston, VT 05161; 802-824-6521.

VIRGINIA

The Virginia Senior Games are an annual four-day event held each spring on a college campus, where older athletes compete to qualify for the U.S. National Senior Olympics—or just for the fun of it. It is a combination of social events and entertainment with sports competitions, open to anybody over the age of 50. Spouses are invited to come along and enjoy the hospitality, which includes parties, dances, tours of local sites, and other festivities. The fees are low, lodging and meals are cheap, and the sporting events are many, ranging from rope jumping, miniature golf, and riflery to swimming, running, and tennis for age groups from 55 upwards.

For information: Virginia Senior Games, Virginia Recreation and Park Society, 6038 Cold Harbor Rd., Mechanicsville, VA 23111; 804-730-9447; www.vrps.com.

14

Adventures on Skis

Downhill skiing is one sport you'd think would appeal only to less mature, less wise, or less breakable people. On the contrary, an astounding number of ardent over-50 skiers would much rather glide down mountains than sit around waiting for springtime. In fact, many of us ski more than ever now that we're older because we can go midweek when the crowds are thinner and get impressive discounts on lift tickets, especially after the age of 65. A lot of us, too, are taking up the sport for the first time. Ski schools all over the U.S. and Canada are reporting an increase of older students in beginner classes.

The truth is, you're never too old to learn how to ski or to improve your technique. Once you get the hang of it, you can ski at your own speed, choosing the terrain, the difficulty level, and the challenge. You can slide down cliffs through narrow icy passes or wend your way on gentle slopes in a more leisurely fashion, aided by the new improved skis and boots. You'll find clearly marked and carefully groomed trails and sophisticated lifts that take all the work out of getting up the mountain.

Besides, ski resorts are falling all over themselves catering to older skiers, offering discounts on lift tickets, cheaper season passes, and other engaging incentives. In fact, it is a rare ski area that does not give a substantial break to skiers over a certain age.

CLUBS FOR MATURE SKIERS

THE OVER THE HILL GANG (OTHG)

OTHG is a club for energetic men, women, singles, and couples over 50 (the average age of members is 63) that schedules a wide assortment of guided ski trips every year in this country and abroad. Members—about 6,000, with 97 percent of them active skiers to date—are entitled to reduced rates for lift tickets, lessons, rentals, services, equipment, lodging, car rentals, dining, and transportation at nearly 100 of the top ski area, in most cases, whether or not they are skiing with the club on their own.

The club's 12 regional "gangs," or chapters, in the U.S. run their own ski trips as well, and all members everywhere are invited to go along. At some ski areas, local and visiting members meet regularly to ski in small groups with similar ability, each group led by its own guide. At Steamboat, for example, they gather four days a week during the season. At Vail, they ski together on Mondays; at Breckenridge on Tuesdays; at Winter Park on Wednesdays; and at Keystone on Thursday mornings. Out-of-town members and anyone else over 50 are invited to come along.

Members who reach their 70th birthday (and are willing to admit it) are part of the "Over 70 Gang," and members who have turned 80 are included in the "Over 80 Gang." They receive special shoulder patches and a discount on their next membership renewal or their next trip with the club.

When ski season ends, you may join OTHG for other activities including biking, rafting, hiking, and golfing (see Chapter 13).

Annual membership fee: $50 single, $80 per couple, plus chapter dues if you join a local gang.

For information: Over the Hill Gang International, 1820 W. Colorado Ave., Dept. G., Colorado Springs, CO 80904; 719-389-0022; www.othgi.com.

70+ SKI CLUB

Once you hit 70, you're eligible to join the 70+ Ski Club for an annual fee of $10 ($15 for couples)—until you're 90, when you pay only a one-time $10 fee. Don't laugh. Among the approximately 16,000 registered members worldwide, 174 are over the age of 90 and almost 4,000 are between 80 and 90. Members get a selection of ski trips and special events every year at ski resorts in the Northeast and the West; at least one in Europe; and the others in New Zealand, Chile, or Argentina. Hunter Mountain in New York hosts the club's annual meeting each March. Here the 70+ Ski Races have become such a popular event that contestants are divided into three age groups: men 70 to 80, women 70 to 80, and anyone over 80. Awards are presented at a gala party at the lodge.

Founded in 1977, the club has always promoted the interests of senior skiers, especially those on limited incomes. Today, largely as a result of its efforts, most ski areas give seniors free or half-price lift tickets.

Proof of age is required with your application to join the club, and you may not apply earlier than two weeks before your 70th birthday. Members receive a patch, a membership card, a periodic newsletter, and a directory of areas around the country that offer discounts or free skiing.

For information: 70+ Ski Club, 1633 Albany St., Schenectady, NY 12304; 518-346-5505; E-mail: rtl70plus@aol.com.

COPPER MOUNTAIN OHG

At Copper Mountain, members of the OHG, an independent snow-sports adventure club, skis in guided groups on Tuesdays, Wednesdays, Saturdays, and Sundays from mid-November to mid-April except for breaks during the major holidays. They gather for lunch and ski again in the afternoon, ending with an après ski social for members and guests. Throughout the year, members organize potluck dinners, banquets, hikes, bike rides, golf outings, tennis tournaments, and other activities, and a monthly newsletter keeps members up to date on coming activities. Anybody may join or participate as a guest.

Membership dues are $175 for a single, $330 for a couple. A four-day ski membership is $50 per person. For those who don't ski, a summer/social membership is offered for

$50 a year. It includes the newsletter and all summer and social activities but does not include skiing with the gang.
For information: OHG, PO Box 3488, Copper Mountain, CO 89443; 970-968-2318, ext. 38886; www.coppercolorado.com.

SKIMEISTERS

A group of 55-plus skiers based in Denver, the SkiMeisters ski together at Colorado's Winter Park in small groups led by volunteer guides. They ski every Wednesday, Thursday, and Sunday from November to April. Guided cross-country ski days are included as well as group trips to other resorts. With 400 members and a waiting list, the club charges a one-time fee of $100, then $50 a year. Guests are permitted but they may ski with the club only twice during the season. To keep themselves busy when the ski season is over, members get together for biking, hiking, rafting, tennis, and golf.
For information: SkiMeisters, PO Box 620625, Littleton, CO 80162.

THE WILD OLD BUNCH

Skiers who frequent Alta in Utah are advised to search out members of the Wild Old Bunch, an informal group of longtime skiers who hang out together on the mountain and welcome anyone who wants to join them. There are no rules, no regulations, no meetings. The only requirement is that you must be over 55. The group grows haphazardly as members pick up stray mature skiers on the slopes. Lunch is usually at 11 A.M. on the deck of the mid-mountain Alps Inn.

For information: Look for the Wild Old Bunch on the slopes.

GOOD DEALS EVERYWHERE FOR SKIERS

The older you are, the less it costs to ski. There's hardly a ski area in North America today that doesn't give mature skiers a break. Many cut the price of lift tickets in half for skiers at age 60 or 65, and most stop charging altogether at 70, although a few—Alta in Utah, Mt. Tom in Massachusetts, and Diamond Peak in Nevada, for example—make you wait until you're 80 to ski free. A few areas charge anybody over the age of 65 only $5 a day for lift tickets, and most make offers on season passes that are hard to refuse. Others plan special senior programs specifically for mature skiers.

To give you an idea of what's out there, here is a sampling of the special senior programs, workshops, and clubs in the states where skiing is big business. This list does not include all areas, of course, so be sure to check out others in locations that interest you. Remember to carry proof of age with you at all times. The ski areas change their programs frequently, so while you can use the following information as a guide, you must do your own research, too.

CALIFORNIA

Ski in California and you'll get good deals on lift tickets and season passes almost everywhere. Plus, there are some special programs designed especially for mature skiers, such as the following.

Every Thursday, Tahoe Donner offers skiers age 55 and over morning and/or afternoon clinics, lift ticket, and lunch with top senior instructors. The cost at this writing is $25.

Donner Ski Ranch's deal for skiers 65 through 69 is a daily lift ticket for $5. Skiers 70 or older ski free.

At Northstar-at-Tahoe, the Golden Stars Workshop offers three days of instruction and camaraderie to skiers 65-plus. The program is for intermediate or advanced level skiers and includes a lunch, an après ski party, a three-day lift ticket, and three hours of instruction daily. Current cost is $189 for seniors ages 65 to 69, and $135 for those 70 or more.

Royal Gorge Cross Country Ski Resort on Donner Summit schedules its Silver Streak Week every year, a week of specials for skiers 50 and older that offers reduced fees for trail passes and group lessons. You get a free trail pass for the entire season if you're 75.

Southern California's Mountain High has its Senior Days for 60-plus skiers on Wednesdays from 8 A.M. to 2 P.M. They include a lift ticket and two two-hour lessons. Up to age 69, the cost at this writing is $39 a day; at 70, it's only $25.

Adults, intermediate through expert, can take advantage of the Vertical Improvement Clinic, free with the purchase of a lift ticket morning and afternoon, any day they choose at Sierra-at-Tahoe. Although the clinic is not strictly for over-50 skiers, it attracts plenty of them.

At Heavenly Ski Resort, there are free four-hour workshops for skiers over 55. Mammoth Mountain offers three-day senior ski clinics.

Squaw Valley USA is offering a Just for Women Ski Clinic designed for women over the age of 50. The three-day clinic in January that provides older women the chance to learn new technology, skills, and techniques, features women-specific coaching, stretching techniques, video feedback, workshops, and evening socials. Cost, currently $545, includes all activities, lunch, and lift tickets.

By the way, Squaw Valley, which reduces lift tickets for skiers over 65 and gives free rides to those over 75, offers $5 in Squaw Bucks valid all over the mountain to anybody hitting the slopes over the age of 85.

COLORADO

Every ski area in Colorado offers discounted lift tickets to seniors, some starting at 60, others at 65, and almost every ski area charges nothing at all to ski after you reach age 70. And many special programs, lessons, and clubs are especially designed for mature skiers.

Aspen Mountain offers skiers over 70 a Silver Pass for $149. It allows unlimited skiing there and also at Snowmass, Ajax, Buttermilk, and Aspen Highlands.

For $99, Vail Resorts sells a 70-plus pass for unlimited skiing all winter at Vail, Beaver Creek, Breckenridge, Keystone, and Arapahoe Basin.

At Breckenridge, two-day Silver Skiing Seminars in January and February for skiers over 50 of all abilities, taught by seniors, include lift tickets, lessons, video analysis, and a group dinner.

Breckenridge is the place where members of the local Over the Hill Gang, plus any other visitors 50 and over, get together on Tuesdays for a day on the slopes with their own guide.

It's Thursday mornings at Keystone for Gang members and visitors to ski with volunteer guides.

Also at Keystone, Senior Winter Games are organized by local skiers and held in February every year. Downhill skiing and skating events are held at K Resort.

At Vail, any skier over 50 is welcome to meet on Mondays and ski with OTHG members.

At Steamboat, led by local guides, they gang up on the slopes every day from Sunday through Friday during the season. Steamboat also gives skiers 65+ a 20 percent discount on most ski programs.

Ski at Arapahoe Basin at 70-plus and you get a season pass for $30.

Join the Over the Hill Gang (OHG) at Copper Mountain and you can ski with volunteer guides on Tuesdays, Wednesdays, Saturdays, and Sundays; party with the members; and participate in other activities such as golf outings, bike rides, tennis tournaments, and social events. (See more about the club earlier in this chapter.)

The good news at Crested Butte Mountain Resort is that anybody 70 and over skis and snowboards free while those ages 65 to 69 pay only half-price for lift tickets. All 65+ skiers also get 50 percent off group lessons and 25 percent off private lessons.

Sunlight Mountain Resort in Glenwood Springs has its 100 Club, open to couples whose combined ages total 100 years or more, and singles who are 50 or older. Club members, beginners to experts, meet here each Wednesday and sometimes at other areas on weekends during the season to ski in the morning and stay for lunch. They often plan trips to other area resorts as well and after the ski season get together for tennis, golf, hiking, and mountain biking. Cost for membership is currently $8 a year and includes a monthly newsletter.

At Powderhorn Resort, just show up any Tuesday morning during the season and join the Seniors Clinic, an informal group of mature skiers who ski together and work to improve their skills. Cost right now is $20 per lesson.

At Eldora, skiers and snowboarders 65 and older can participate in Senior Ski every Tuesday. Senior Days at Ski Cooper gives you a day lift ticket, free racing, and an après-ski party.

Every winter, Purgatory Resort in Durango schedules two one-week skiing and social events for skiers over 50. Called the Snowmasters Classic, each session, which currently costs $75, includes daily continental breakfast, two wine and cheese parties, and three half-day clinics. The clinics are chosen from the following subjects: shaped skis, powder skiing, racing, mogul skiing, and ski improvement. Participants get discounts on lift tickets, rentals, accommodations, food, and more.

The SkiMeisters (see details earlier in this chapter) ski together at Winter Park every Wednesday, Thursday, and Sunday from November to April. A membership club with a one-time fee of $100 and then an annual fee of $50, it has about 400 members and a waiting list.

The two Ski Forever Weeks held at Telluride each winter cater to mature skiers, intermediate to expert. The five-day session, which currently costs $575, includes five hours a day of on-snow instruction, an alignment session, professional speakers, video analysis, races, and a farewell dinner.

IDAHO

Sun Valley's Prime Time, a week reserved for older skiers, is scheduled twice each winter. It includes seven nights' lodging, five days of lift tickets or a Nordic trail package, discount coupons, races, parties, special events, and a Big Band Buffet Dinner Dance. Skiers over 60 pay less for the package than those under 60.

Schweitzer Mountain's Prime Timers Club for skiers 55 and over is an informal club whose members ski together almost every day and get together for social gatherings on Thursday afternoons. In addition, there's a bargain senior ski week in March, the Snowmaster's Classic, a week of workshops, clinics, social activities, and race training for older skiers who are seeking to improve their technical abilities.

MAINE

At Sunday River, those who purchase the Perfect Turn Gold or Platinum Card and are over 50 may become members of the Prime Time Club. Members ski together every weekday at 10 A.M. and participate in many off-mountain field trips and parties too.

Shawnee Peak starts cutting costs for season passes at age 65, reduces them drastically at 70-plus, and charges skiers 80 and over $50.

MASSACHUSETTS

Ski every day all winter at Ski Butternut for only $99 if you've passed your 70th birthday, or pay $10 for a day ticket. At ages 50 to 69, you can buy a full-day lift ticket on any non-holiday Monday or Tuesday for $15.

At Jiminy Peak in Hancock, you may join the Silver Sliders every Thursday morning for coffee and a two-hour lesson. The six-week program is designed exclusively for people over 50, expert or novice, who want to perfect their technique of skiing or snowboarding.

MICHIGAN

The Silver Streak program at Crystal Mountain for skiers 60 or older offers free skiing when you book midweek lodging, excluding holidays. Other privileges for mature skiers include half price on lift tickets, cross-country trail passes, rental equipment, and group lessons, again excluding holidays.

At Caberfae Peaks Ski Resort in Cadillac, every Tuesday, Wednesday, and Thursday (except during the major holiday weeks) are Silver Streak Days, when anybody over the age of 50 is allowed to ski all day for only $15. In addition to the lift ticket, you will receive free rental skis and a one-hour lesson.

NEW HAMPSHIRE

It's a rare ski area in this state that does not offer older skiers an impressive break on lift tickets. Many also have special programs for senior skiers.

If you're 55 or more, you can join the Silver Streaks, a program for alpine skiers, cross-country skiers, and snowboarders, at Waterville Valley, paying an annual membership fee of $65. You'll get to ski or board the slopes with a guide four mornings a week and participate in races, clinics, and parties. Silver Streaks for cross-country skiers meets at the Nordic Center on Wednesdays to explore the White Mountain National Forest led by retirees from the U.S. Forest Service.

Loon Mountain's Flying 50s Plus meets every Thursday and Friday morning except on holidays for two-hour group skiing with friends and an instructor. Members pay $109 for the season.

At Cannon Mountain, the Cannon Cruisers for skiers over 50 meet Monday mornings to ski for two hours with instructors at $10 per session or $79 for 10 sessions.

Skiers 50-plus get a lift ticket and lesson at Wildcat for $35 on nonholiday Tuesday mornings.

And at Mount Sunapee, Senior Cruisers for skiers and boarders age 50 and over meet on nonholiday Wednesday mornings throughout the season for skiing and a little socializing.

NEW MEXICO

Sign up for a Masters Ski Week at Taos Ski Valley if you are 50-plus and you get six consecutive mornings of instruction, all-day lift tickets for the week, and après-ski seminars.

NEW YORK

Skiers over 50 are invited to join the Senior Skier Program at Ski Windham for eight weeks of Tuesdays in January and February. The purpose is to strengthen skiing skills, socialize, and meet new people. Join for all eight weeks or by the day, if you prefer. What you get is morning coffee, guest speakers, two-hour morning and afternoon on-snow lessons, and a midweek nonholiday season pass to Ski Windham. For information, call 518-734-5070.

UTAH

Virtually all of Utah's ski areas give senior skiers reduced rates on lift tickets at 55, 60, or 65, with Sundance and Elk Meadows offering free rides to those over 65. Most others stop charging at 70—except Alta, where you must wait until you are 80!

By the way, don't forget to check out Alta's Wild Old Bunch that gets together informally to ski almost every morning. Anybody 55 or over is welcome to join the group on the slopes and then eat an early lunch at the mid-mountain Alps Inn.

At Snowbird, any intermediate or expert skier 62 or more may join the famous instructor Junior Bounous for a complimentary ski outing for a couple of hours on Tuesday mornings. If you like, you can continue to ski with him in the afternoon for more ski tips and instruction.

Sundance sells an all-day pass to seniors 65 or older for $10 and a season pass for $150.

As for Brighton Ski Resort, the Senior Workshop, a three-day program for "seasoned skiers" over 50, focuses on terrain, snow conditions, weather, conditioning, and motivation. It includes lessons and a lift ticket.

VERMONT

Vermont's ski areas were the first to cater to older skiers. It is highly unlikely that there are any resorts there that don't give seniors a decent break on lift tickets and season passes. Along with special rates, several areas offer special senior programs as well. Here's a sample.

Stratton Mountain's Trailblazers, open to skiers or snowboarders over 50 (and their partners), schedules activities for its hundreds of members almost every day of the week, starting with bridge or canasta on Mondays, snowshoe and cross-country activities on Wednesdays, recreational racing on Fridays, and après-ski parties whenever. Members may also participate in a special 50-plus ski clinic program that comes in two versions. The first, for full-time residents of the area, meets Monday, Wednesday, and Friday mornings (except on holidays) to ski in small groups with an instructor; the second is a weekend program that meets on Saturday mornings for 14 weeks. Basic membership fee is $25 a year per person, with an extra charge for participation in the ski clinics.

At Jay Peak any skier over the age of 55 is invited to join Silver Peaks, a group that skis together every Tuesday. For a nominal fee, you are entitled to a day that includes your lift ticket, guide, coffee and doughnuts, and après-ski activities. By the way, if you're over 65, you may ski here any time for $12 a day.

The Prime Time Club at Sugarbush offers skiers age 50 years and up, levels five to eight, a chance to meet, ski, and learn with a group of their peers. The club meets Tuesday and Thursday mornings for skiing on a variety of terrains.

Mount Snow's Prime-Time Seniors program, also for skiers and snowboarders 50 and over, meets once a week in February and March and offers clinics and a specialized video as well as resort savings.

The Silver Griffins at Bromley Mountain meet every nonholiday Monday through Friday for group skiing, clinics, fun races, picnics, and parties. Members of the group get preferred parking midweek and discounts on food, equipment, and lessons. Annual fee is $15.

Okemo's Trailblazers Program for intermediate and advanced adult skiers runs for a six-week series on Sunday mornings. Come as a single or put your own group of peers together. You'll meet in the morning for coffee and then ski with others of similar ability and pace with the guidance of a teaching professional. Skiers 65-plus get a half-price discount on group ski and snowboard lessons and a good break on lift tickets.

Members of Smuggler's Notch 55-Plus Club meet every Wednesday morning for coffee and bagels, then head to the slopes, finishing the day with a presentation from a guest speaker. The club also organizes summer activities and a trip to another ski resort in New England or Canada during the winter. Those who are 55 to 69 can ski on Wednesdays at 50 percent off the regular lift prices, while skiers over 70 ski free any time they wish. All members also get half price on rentals, group lessons, and cross-country trail fees on Wednesdays, as well as 20 percent on merchandise in the ski shop. If you want to join the Club, the cost is $25 for the season.

WISCONSIN

Skiers over 55 get a lift ticket, day or night, Monday through Friday, for $10 at Cascade Mountain Ski Area in Portage.

15

Perks in Parks and Other Good News

All over the U.S. and Canada, enterprising officials in states, provinces, and cities have initiated some enticing programs designed to capture the imagination of the mature population. Often they are expressing their appreciation of our many contributions to society and simply want to do something nice for us. And sometimes they are trying to attract us and our vacation dollars to their neighborhoods, having discovered that we're always ready to enjoy ourselves and know a good deal when we see one.

But, first, keep in mind:

- Before you set off for a new place, send ahead for free maps, calendars of events, booklets describing sites and scenes of interest, accommodation guides, and perhaps even a list of special discounts or other good things that are available to you as a person over 50. For state-by-state tourism information online, go to the website operated by the Travel Industry of America, www.seeamerica.org and click on "Tour America Map."

- Many states offer passes for admission to their state parks and recreation facilities for free or at reduced prices to people who are old enough to have learned how to treat those areas respectfully.
- Following the section on national parks, you'll find information about state park passes and special events in many states. There may be other good deals that have escaped our attention, but those in this chapter are probably the cream of the crop.

NATIONAL PARKS

CANADIAN NATIONAL PARKS

The national parks and national historic sites throughout Canada charge modest entry fees for adults and take about 20 percent off those for visitors over 65. The same is generally true for provincial parks.

GOLDEN AGE PASSPORT

Available for $10 to U.S. citizens or permanent residents who are at least 62, the Golden Age Passport is one of the best senior travel bargains around. Good for a lifetime, it admits you free of charge to most national parks, forests, refuges, monuments, and recreation areas. A whole carload of family and friends, whatever their ages, also get free admission when you enter in a private car, so one pass is enough if you are a couple or a group traveling together.

Turn up at the gate in a commercial vehicle such as a bus, and the passport admits you, your spouse, and your children without cost.

It also gives you a 50 percent discount on fees charged for facilities and services such as camping, swimming, boat launching, parking, and cave tours. It does not, however,

ESCAPEES CLUB

Escapees is a club dedicated to providing a support network for RVers, full-time or part-time, many of whom are on the far side of 50. It publishes a bulky bimonthly magazine filled with useful information for travelers who carry their homes with them; organizes rallies in the U.S., Canada, and Mexico; and hosts five-day seminars on RV living. Its almost 50 regional chapters also coordinate rallies and host get-togethers, and its Birds of a Feather (BOF) groups connect members who have common interests.

Benefits include discount RV parks and campgrounds, emergency road service, mail service, calling card service, vehicle insurance, and voice message service. After a $10 enrollment fee, the annual membership fee is $60 a year per family with a U.S. address.

The club has established its own CARE Center (Continuing Assistance for Retired Escapees), a separate RV campground where retired members can live independently in their own RVs while receiving medical and living assistance, housekeeping, and transportation services as needed.

For information: Escapees, Inc., 100 Rainbow Dr., Livingston, TX 77351; 888-757-2582 or 936-327-8873; www.escapees.com.

cover or reduce special recreation permit fees charged by concessioners.

The passport is not available by mail but must be purchased in person at any federal area where entrance fees are charged or at regional offices of the National Park Service, the U.S. Forest Service, or the Fish and Wildlife Service. You must provide proof of age. Your driver's license will do just fine.

The free Golden Access Passport provides the same benefits for the disabled of any age.

If you're under 62, you can buy a National Parks Pass that costs $50 and is good for a year. When a per-vehicle fee is charged at a national park, the pass admits you and your passengers in a private vehicle; when a per-person fee is charged, it admits you, your spouse, your children, and even your parents. It may be purchased online or by telephone. If you are a member and order it on AARP's website, it will cost you only $45.

For information: National Park Service, Office of Public Inquiries, U.S. Dept. of Interior, 1849 C St. NW, Washington, DC 20013. For National Parks Pass only: 888-GO-PARKS (888-467-2757); www.nationalparks.org.

OFFERINGS FROM THE STATES

Virtually every state has a special senior rate for hunting and fishing licenses for people over a certain age (usually 65). Some states require no license at all for seniors, while others give you a reduced fee (usually half). Most require that you are a resident of the state in order to get these privileges.

Most states also offer state park discounts to seniors, usually only residents, reducing or eliminating entrance fees and marking down camping rates. A few have other privileges to offer, such as shopping discounts. To check out the regulations and offers in your state or a state you are visiting, contact the state or local parks department or the state tourism office.

CALIFORNIA

At California State Parks, anybody 62 and over saves $2 on overnight camping fees and $1 on parking. Just show proof of age at the gate. And, for $10, seniors may buy a Limited Use Golden Bear Pass that gives them free parking between Labor Day and Memorial Day.

For information: California Parks and Recreation, 800-444-7275; www.parks.ca.gov.

COLORADO

The Aspen Leaf Annual Pass entitles Colorado residents 62 and over to free year-round entrance to state parks any day and reduced fees for camping Sundays through Thursdays except on holidays. The pass costs $10 per year.

For information: Colorado Division of State Parks, 1313 Sherman St., Room 618, Denver, CO 80203; 303-866-3437; www.parks.state.co.us.

CONNECTICUT

Residents of Connecticut who are over 65 get a free lifetime Charter Oak Pass that gets them into all state parks and forests plus Gillette Castle, Dinosaur Park, and Quinebaug

Valley Hatchery for free. To get your pass, write to the address below and send along a copy of your current Connecticut driver's license.

For information: DEP, Charter Oak Pass, State Parks Division, 79 Elm St., Hartford, CT 06106; 860-424-3200; www.dep.state.ct.us.

FLORIDA

Orlando, one of the most popular destinations in the U.S. today, is visited by more than seven million mature travelers a year. To accommodate them, the Orlando/Orange County Convention and Visitors Bureau offers a free vacation planning kit that includes the *Mature Travelers Guide*. It features discounts for visitors age 55 or older at about 50 establishments in the area, including restaurants, attractions, and accommodations. Whatever your age, ask for the free Orlando Magicard too. It's valid for up to six people, any age, and provides even more discounts.

For information: For the *Mature Travelers Guide*, call 800-551-0181, or order online at www.orlandoinfo.com. Or request both the guide and the Magicard at the Official Visitor Center at 8723 International Drive in the Gala Center; 800-643-9492 or 407-363-5872.

Visit or take up residence in Panama City Beach in the winter and you can enjoy the programs and discounts offered by the free Winter Resident SunCard. Get one by stopping into the Visitors Information Center, or call the number below.

For information: Panama City Beach Convention & Visitors Bureau, 800-PCBEACH (722-3224) or 850-233-5070; www.pcbeach.com.

The thick little coupon booklet, *$1,000 Worth of the Palm Beaches Free*, is not exclusively for visitors over 50 but it is included here because it offers many ways to save money in the off-season, April to mid-December, such as discounts, two-for-one deals, and complimentary offers on shopping, dining, sporting activities, and attractions. To order, call the toll-free number.

For information: Palm Beach County Convention and Visitors Bureau, 1555 Palm Beach Lakes Blvd., West Palm Beach, FL 33401; 800-554-PALM; www.palmbeachfl.com.

HAWAII

Hawaii caters to the over-50 crowd, and there are discounts for almost everything, including hotels, golf courses, rental cars, and movies. If you live in Oahu and are 65-plus, take advantage of an offer from TheBus, the municipal bus system. This is a pass good for two years of unlimited travel on the island for only $25. Or simply pay half fare (75 cents) after presenting your Medicare card to the driver when you board the bus. Yet another choice is the Visitor Pass, which is available for all ages and costs $15 for four days of unlimited travel.

For information: TheBus Customer Service, 811 Middle St., Honolulu, HI 96819; 808-848-5555; www.thebus.org.

INDIANA

The Golden Hoosier Passport admits Indiana residents over the age of 60 and fellow passengers in a private vehicle to all state parks and natural resources without charge. An application for the passport, which costs $11 a year, is available at all state parks.

For information: Indiana State Parks Dept., 402 W. Washington St., Indianapolis, IN 46204; 800-622-4931 or 317-232-4124; www.dnr.state.in.us.

KANSAS

If you're over 65 and a Kansas resident, show proof of age at the gate and you'll pay only half of the usual adult entry fee at all state parks. In addition, at the same age residents of the state no longer require a hunting and fishing license, although they must pay for special permits to hunt certain game.

For information: Kansas Department of Wildlife and Parks, 900 SW Jackson, Topeka, KS 66612; 785-296-2281; www.kdwp.state.ks.us.

MAINE

Pick up your Senior Citizen Pass at age 65 and you will get free admission to all state parks and historic sites. The pass is available at no cost at any state park or by writing to the Bureau of Parks and Lands. Be sure to include proof of your age.

For information: Maine Bureau of Parks and Lands, State House Station 22, Augusta, ME 04333; 207-287-3821; www.state.me.us/doc.

MICHIGAN

You can get some good deals in Michigan if you are a resident who's reached the age of 65. These include a motor-vehicle permit for $5 a year that gets you into all state parks and a fishing or hunting license for $5.60 a year.

For information: Call the Department of Natural Resources at 517-373-9900; www.michigan.gov/dnr.

MISSOURI

Missouri residents over the age of 60 are entitled to a free Silver Citizen Discount Card that gives discounts at restaurants, stores, pharmacies, and other businesses throughout the state. To get a card, call the toll-free number below.

For information: Missouri Dept. of Health and Senior Services, PO Box 570, Jefferson City, MO 65102; 800-235-5503.

MONTANA

Montana residents need pay only half the usual camping fee in Montana's state parks if they are over the age of 62.

For information: Montana Fish, Wildlife, and Parks Dept., 1420 E. 6th Ave., Helena, MT 59620; 406-444-3750; www.fwp.state.mt.us.

NEVADA

In Carson City, you will strike silver without doing any digging—if you are over 50 and join the free Seniors Strike Silver Club. You'll get a list of discounts in town, plus a membership card to present as identification to participating lodgings.

For information: Carson City Convention & Visitors Bureau, 1900 S. Carson St., Carson City, NV 89701; 800-NEVADA-1 (800-638-2321) or 775-687-7410; www.visitcarsoncity.com.

NEW YORK

Simply by presenting your current valid New York driver's license or a New York nondriver's identification card, you will be entitled to all of the privileges of the Golden Park Program for residents over the age of 62. The program offers, any weekday except holidays, free vehicle access to state parks and arboretums; free entrance to state historic sites; and reduced fees for state-operated swimming, golf, tennis, and boat rentals. Just show your driver's license or ID card at the entrance of the facility.

For information: State Parks, Albany, NY 12238; 518-474-0456.

At age 65, you can ride the commuter railroads and most bus lines in New York State by simply showing proof of age. You can also buy a reduced-fare MetroCard that entitles you to half fare on New York City's local buses and trains 24 hours a day, and on express buses a fare of $1.50 between the hours of 10 A.M. and 3 P.M. Call the number below for an application and instructions. By the way, a Fun Pass, good for a day of unlimited travel in New York City, may be purchased by anyone of any age for $4. Buy it in any subway station.

For information: New York City Transit Reduced-Fare Line, 718-243-4999; www.mta.nyc.ny.us.

OHIO

You are in luck if you live in Ohio because the minute you turn 60, you may sign up for a free Golden Buckeye Card that gives you discounts on meals, prescription drugs, enter-

GOOD SAM CLUB

The **Good Sam Club** is an international organization of people who travel in recreational vehicles, mentioned here because the vast majority of those in rolling homes are over 50. Its goal is to make RVing safer, more enjoyable, and less expensive. Among the benefits are 10 percent discounts on nightly fees at more than 2,000 RV parks and campgrounds, plus more discounts on propane, parts, and accessories at hundreds of service centers.

The club offers a toll-free hotline, a lost key service, lost pet service, trip routing, mail forwarding, telephone message service, insurance, a magazine, and campground directories. Most important, it provides low-cost emergency road service anywhere in the U.S. and Canada, including Alaska. Social activities include Good Sam rallies and travel tours and cruises all over the world. And about 2,100 local chapters in the U.S. and Canada hold campouts and meetings and participate in local volunteer projects. Membership is $12 a year per family, $23 for two years, $30 for three.
For information: The Good Sam Club, PO Box 6885, Englewood, CO 80155; 800-234-3450; www.goodsamclub.com.

tainment, merchandise, and services at thousands of businesses all over the state. Some merchants offer daily discounts, some on certain days of the week, some during certain seasons of the year. For the location of a sign-up site near you, call the toll-free number below.
For information: and the sign-up site nearest your home: Golden Buckeye Card Program, Ohio Dept. of Aging, 50 W. Broad St., 9th floor, Columbus, OH 43215; 800-422-1976 (in Ohio) or 614-466-5500; www.goldenbuckeye.com.

PENNSYLVANIA

In Pennsylvania, the Lottery Fund pays for many good things for seniors. Among them is free statewide transportation. Anyone 65 or older, resident of the state or not, can acquire a special identification card that gets him or her aboard scheduled buses, trolleys, and subways without paying a cent. They must, however, travel off-peak: before 7 A.M., between 8 A.M. and 4:30 P.M., or after 5:30 P.M. on weekdays, and all day on weekends and some holidays.

On the Southeastern Pennsylvania Transportation Authority (SEPTA) regional rail lines in the Philadelphia area, those traveling within Pennsylvania with a valid ID pay only $1 to ride the trains during the same non-peak weekday hours as above and on all weekends and holidays.

Another perk is the Shared Ride Program, also funded by the state lottery, which provides door-to-door transportation, usually by van, at a discount of up to 85 percent to anybody over 65 who requests it and makes an advance reservation.

For information: Call your local transit agency or the Bureau of Public Transportation, Pennsylvania Department of Transportation, PO Box 3151, Harrisburg, PA 17105; 717-783-8025. SEPTA: 215-580-7478.

SOUTH CAROLINA

Residents of South Carolina who are 65 or older must merely show their driver's licenses to get free admission at all state parks, plus half off on both the camping fees at all parks and the greens fees at Hickory Knob and Cheraw State Parks.

For information: South Carolina Department of Parks, Recreation, and Tourism, 1205 Pendleton St., Columbia, SC 29201; 803-734-0166; www.discoversouthcarolina.com.

TENNESSEE

Anyone over the age of 62, state resident or not, gets a 10 percent discount on food at park restaurants, cabins, and rooms at the Resort Park Inns. Tennessee residents over 62 pay no greens fees at state golf courses on Mondays. Besides, they are charged only 50 percent of the regular camping fees, while out-of-state campers are entitled to a 10 percent reduction. Admission to all state parks is free, regardless of your age.
For information: Tennessee Parks and Wildlife, 401 Church St., LC Tower, Nashville, TN 37243; 800-421-6683; www.tnstatepark.com.

TEXAS

The Parkland Pass is free to all comers, residents of Texas or not, who are over the age of 65. If you turned 65 on or before August 31, 1995, the pass gives you free admission to state parks. If your 65th birthday was after that date, it admits you to the parks at half price. Pick up the pass at any park.
For information: Texas Parks and Wildlife, 4200 Smith School Rd., Austin, TX 78744; 800-792-1112; www.tpwd.state.tx.us.

If you are a winter snowbird in Galveston, be sure to stop at the Galveston Island Visitor Information Center and sign up for a free Special Winter Texan ID card. It gives you discounts or specials at more than 100 businesses on the island, including accommodations, attractions, auto services, banking services, retail stores, restaurants, medical services, fishing charters, and golf courses.

For information: Galveston Island Visitor Information Center, 2428 Seawall Blvd., Galveston, TX 77550; 888-425-4753 or 409-763-4311; www.galvestoncvb.com.

UTAH

The Silver Card issued by Park City, an old mining town known for its great ski mountains, is a summer (June through September) program of discounts that gives you 10 percent or more off on merchandise, tickets, and meals. Pick up your free ID card and an information packet for seniors at a participating hotel or the Park City Visitors Bureau.

For information: Park City Convention and Visitors Bureau, 1910 Prospector Ave., Park City, UT 84060; 800-453-1360 or 435-649-6100; www.parkcityinfo.com.

VERMONT

Vermont residents age 62 or over can purchase a Green Mountain Passport for $2 from their own town clerk. It is good for a lifetime and entitles them to free admission to all state parks and their state-sponsored events. Many local businesses offer discounts on merchandise and services to passport holders. In addition, residents 65-plus can get a lifetime hunting and fishing permit for $14.

For information: Vermont Dept. of Aging, 103 S. Main St., Waterbury, VT 05676; 802-241-2400; www.dad.state.vt.us. For hunting and fishing: Dept. of Fish and Wildlife, 802-241-3700.

VIRGINIA

Virginia offers many park passes just for those 62 and older. They include the Senior Lifetime Naturally Yours Passport Plus, good for parking and admission to state parks, and discounts on facilities and equipment, that costs $100 but lasts for life; the Senior Parking Passport, $20, good for a year of parking and admission for your park of choice; and the Senior Park/Launch Passport that comes in various versions.

In this state that abounds with historic sites, you will find senior discounts almost everywhere you go. You will get them, for example, at Colonial Williamsburg, Bush Gardens, Mount Vernon, the Edgar Allen Poe Museum, and the Virginia Air and Space Center.

For information: Virginia State Parks, PO Box 1895, Richmond, VA 23218; 800-933-PARK (in Richmond, 225-3867); www.dcr.state.va.us. For historic sites: Virginia Division of Tourism, 800-932-5827; www.virginia.org.

WASHINGTON

For $30, those 62-plus may buy an Off-Season Senior Citizen Pass that gives them free nightly camping or moorage from October 1 through March 31 and Sunday through Thursday in April.

For information: Washington State Parks, 800-902-8500; www.parks.wa.gov.

WASHINGTON, D.C.

If you're 65, it costs you only 50 cents to ride the buses (that's less than half the regular fare) in the nation's capital. Upon request by the driver you must show photo identification with your date of birth. An alternative is a Metrobus Weekly Senior Pass that costs $5 and allows unlimited travel. To get your special reduced fare on Metrorail trains, you must first acquire a Metro Senior ID Card, then a specially encoded reduced fare card that's available online or at a Metro sales office.

For information: Washington Metropolitan Transit Authority, 202-637-7000; www.wmata.com.

WEST VIRGINIA

Everybody who turns 60 in West Virginia gets a Golden Mountaineer Discount Card, which entitles the bearer to 10 percent discounts from more than 3,500 participating merchants and professionals in the state and a few outside of it. If you don't receive a card in the mail from the state soon after your 60th birthday, you may apply for one at your local senior center or by calling the number below. Flash it wherever you go and save a few dollars.

West Virginia's state parks are free to everyone, no matter what age.

For information: West Virginia Department of Parks, 1900 Kanawha Blvd., Charleston, WV 25305; 304-558-2764. Tourism hotline: 800-CALL-WVA; www.callwva.com.

WISCONSIN

This state's residents who are over the age of 65 pay only half the annual fee for fishing and small-game hunting licenses, and for the annual admission sticker that gets them into state parks. On a daily park pass, they save a dollar. Buy the stickers at the entrance to parking areas.

For information: For hunting and fishing licenses: Wisconsin Department of Natural Resources, PO Box 7924, Madison, WI 53707; 877-945-4236; www.dnr.state.wi.us. For state parks admission stickers: DNR Parks & Recreation, PO Box 7921, Madison, WI 53707; 608-266-2181.

16

Back to Summer Camp

Maybe you thought camp was just for kids, but if you are a grown-up person who likes the outdoors, swimming, boating, birds, and arts and crafts; and if you appreciate fields and forests and star-filled skies, you too can pack your bags and go off on a sleepaway. Throughout the country, many camps set aside weeks for adult sessions, while others offer adult programs all season long. More and more adults are getting hooked on summer camp, and many wouldn't miss a year.

ASSOCIATION OF JEWISH SPONSORED CAMPS

You can renew your spirits by spending a week or two during the summer with other 55- or 60-plus Jewish men and women at one of the five adult camping centers operated by this association. All are inexpensive, all but one serve kosher meals, put you up in lodges, and are located within a few hours of New York City. You'll be kept busy morning 'til night with activities and entertainment.

For information: Association of Jewish Sponsored Camps, 130 E. 59th St., New York, NY 10022; 212-751-0477; www.jewishcamps.org.

CHURCH-SPONSORED CAMPS

There are many adult camps and summer workshops sponsored by religious organizations—too many and too diverse to list here. One source of information is Christian Camping International that publishes a directory of about 1,000 camps and conferences in the U.S.

For information: Christian Camping International/USA, PO Box 62189, Colorado Springs, CO 80962; 719-260-9400; www.cciusa.org.

ELDERHOSTEL

Many of Elderhostel's programs are a combination of camp and college. In this wildly successful low-cost educational program (see Chapter 12 for details), you can spend a week or two camping in remote scenic areas, enjoying all the activities from horseback riding to crafts, boating, campfires, and sleeping in a cabin or under the stars.

For information: Elderhostel, 11 Avenue de Lafayette, Boston, MA 02111; 877-426-8056 or 617-426-7788; www.elderhostel.org.

RV ELDERHOSTEL PROGRAMS

On these programs, you take along your own housing—a recreational vehicle, travel trailer, or tent—and stay on the host campus or at nearby campgrounds. Classes, usually held on the campus, are included, as are meals and excursions. On most RV tours you join the group for classes, meals, and excursions but sleep on your own premises. On others, a group of RVers form a moving field trip, moving along like a wagon train, communicating via CB radios or cell phones as they travel and making stops along the way.

For information: Elderhostel, 11 Avenue de Lafayette, Boston, MA 02111; 877-426-8056 or 617-426-7788; www.elderhostel.org.

GRANDPARENTS/GRANDCHILDREN CAMPS

See Chapter 10 for summer camps and other vacations designed for grandparents and grandchildren who want to spend time together.

VOLUNTARY ASSOCIATION FOR SENIOR CITIZEN ACTIVITIES (VASCA)

VASCA is a nonprofit organization that offers scholarships to elderly low-income residents of New York City who are over the age of 55 to attend an adult camp for a week or two in the summer. Located in New York, New Jersey, Connecticut, and Pennsylvania, the seven camps, sponsored by nonprofit organizations and foundations, are small rustic country retreats, lakeside resorts or big sprawling complexes. Two accommodate the disabled and the blind.

For information: VASCA, 151 W. 30th St., New York, NY 10001; 212-216-9137; www.vasca.org.

YMCA/YWCA

The Y runs many camps, most of them for children, but some also offer inexpensive weeks for adults. For example, the YMCA of the Rockies operates a resort, Snow Mountain Ranch, with a special program in mid-August for active adults over the age of 50 at its Camp Chief Ouray in Granby, Colorado. The High Point YMCA's Camp Cheerio, in the Blue Ridge Mountains of North Carolina, sets aside three weeks a year for campers over 50, who live in the same cabins and pursue the same activities as the kids do the rest of the summer.

For information: Call your local YMCA or YWCA for information about camps in your area.

17

Shopping Breaks, Taxes, Insurance, and Other Practical Matters

In this chapter you won't find suggestions for interesting vacation possibilities or unusual places to explore. Instead, you'll get useful information about benefits and services that could be coming to you simply because you are now sufficiently mature to take advantage of them.

SAVE MONEY IN THE STORES

All over the U.S. and Canada today, and increasingly the rest of the world, retailers are now offering discounts and other special privileges to older customers. That's because they have come to realize that these huge numbers of consumers—many with considerable money in their pockets—know the value of a dollar, are extremely fond of bargains, and tend to have the will and the time to hunt them down.

GOLDEN OPPORTUNITIES

Log on to seniordiscounts.com, a website that lists hundreds of local and national age-related deals all over the country, including your own hometown. Name the city, state, and business category that interests you, and you'll get a list that includes the amount of the discount, age requirement, address, telephone number, and sometimes even a map.

For information: SeniorDiscounts.com, 1401 Central Ave., Albuquerque, NM 87104; 877-924-2023 or 505-924-2222; www.seniordiscounts.com.

In fact, the older population has begun to expect reduced prices and to become loyal customers of the shops that offer them.

Stores vary on the age at which you may take advantage of their special offers, but most start you off at 60. Some give you 10 or 15 percent off every day, while others reserve one day a week or a month for their senior discounts. Grocery stores, too, are getting into the act and so are many specialty food stores.

Most large chains of pharmacies also have plans that will save you money. For example, if you are 55 or more, both Rite Aid and CVS are ready to give you a 10 percent discount on prescription drugs when you pay in cash. Longs Drugs, a group of drug stores in the western U.S., offers its Longs Senior Advantage program to customers at age 55 or 65 (depending on the state) who are not covered by insurance, saving them 10 to 50 percent on cash prescriptions. Eckerd's Senior Rewards Card allows 55-plus customers in Texas and Florida to earn 10 percent credit on all cash-paid prescriptions, the credit to be used toward the purchase of any merchandise in the store.

Major department stores, such as Bloomingdale's and Lord and Taylor, occasionally feature senior savings days, when everything costs 10 or 15 percent less for customers over 60. Banana Republic gives customers 62 and older 10 percent off every day. Kohl's Department Stores schedules periodic senior days, always on a Wednesday and announced in local newspapers, when you get 10 percent taken off the cost of all your purchases. Ross Dress for Less, with about 500 stores in 22 states, gives shoppers 55+ the same 10 percent but does it every Tuesday. Many of Modell's sporting-goods stores take 10 percent off for seniors every day of the week.

What all this means is that it never hurts to ask wherever you shop whether there are good deals available to you.

GETTING HELP ON YOUR TAX RETURNS

Assistance in preparing your tax returns is available free from both the Internal Revenue Service and AARP.

The IRS offers Tax Counseling for the Elderly (TCE) for people over 60 and Voluntary Income Tax Assistants (VITA) for younger people who need help. Trained volunteers provide information and will prepare returns at thousands of sites throughout the country. Watch your local newspaper for a list of sites in your area or call 800-TAX-1040 during the tax season, January 2 to April 15.

Or you may enlist the help of AARP's Tax-Aide Service at more than 10,000 sites nationwide where, in the ten-week

HELP FROM THE IRS

The IRS publishes a useful free booklet, *Tax Information for Older Americans* (Publication No. 554). Get it from your library or local IRS office or call 800-TAX-FORM. You can also read it or download it—along with all tax forms, reports, and other useful publications—from the IRS website: www.irs.gov.

period before April 15, about 30,000 volunteers help low- and moderate-income members of AARP to prepare their tax returns. Volunteers will even go to your home, when necessary, if you are physically unable to get to a site. To locate an office in your community, call 888-227-7669. Or call your regional or state AARP offices. Or check the website: aarp.org/taxaide. Have your membership number and zip code handy and also your calendar, as an appointment is required.

SAVE ON AUTO AND HOMEOWNERS INSURANCE

Among the nice surprises waiting for you on your 50th or 55th birthday is the possibility of paying less for your automobile and homeowners insurance. So see if you can take advantage of your age when you shop for a new policy or renew an existing one.

Mature drivers get breaks because, as a group, they tend to be cautious drivers, much more careful than the younger crowd, having shed their bad habits such as speeding and reckless driving. And, although older drivers total more accidents per mile, they drive fewer miles, have fewer serious accidents, use their seat belts, usually don't operate their cars to commute to work every day in rush-hour traffic, and tend to stay off the roads at night and in bad weather. Therefore, statistically, they have fewer serious accidents per driver than other risk categories do, at least until they are over the age of 75.

An additional discount—usually 10 percent—applies on some of your automobile coverage in most states when you successfully complete a state-approved defensive-driving course. Among the programs is AARP's 55 Alive Driver Safety Program (call 888-227-7669 for information), an eight-hour classroom refresher that specifically addresses the needs of older drivers with physical and perceptual changes that affect their driving. Open to both AARP members and nonmembers at a current cost of $10 per person, and taught by volunteers, the course is given locally all over the country. Defensive-driving courses are

HOW TO FIND ELDER SERVICES

For contact information about community services for older adults in your state and local area, such as senior centers, home health services, housing, transportation, legal assistance, or adult day care centers, call the **Eldercare Locator** at 800-677-1116 or go online to www.eldercare.com. This nationwide governmental resource will help older adults and their families find local services for seniors. Call between 9 A.M. and 8 P.M. (Eastern Time) Monday through Friday and explain the problem. Be prepared to provide the name, address, and zip code of the person needing help, as well as a brief description of the assistance you are seeking.

FOR MEDICAL EMERGENCIES

If you have a chronic medical condition, drug or food allergies, special needs such as a surgical implant, or take medications on which your life depends, consider joining MedicAlert, an emergency medical information service that is especially useful when you're traveling. Members wear metal bracelets or neck chains engraved with their personal ID number, key medical facts, and the telephone number of the 24-hour Emergency Response Center. In an emergency, attending medical personnel can call for essential medical information, as well as names and phone numbers of personal physicians and family members.

The cost is $35 to enroll, then $20 a year thereafter. Members may update their records as often as necessary at no extra charge.

For information: MedicAlert, 2323 Colorado Ave., Turlock, CA 95382; 800-633-4298 or 209-668-3333; www.medicalert.org.

offered by other groups, including local high schools and the AAA.

Homeowners over a certain age are also considered better risks for insurance claims than younger people because they spend more time at home where they can keep an eye on things and take care of their property. So some companies offer them reductions on premiums.

Although discounts are wonderful and we all love to get them, they aren't everything. Always shop the bottom line when you buy insurance. You may be able to save hundreds of dollars just by shopping around but you should know what you are getting for your money. If one company charges higher premiums for comparable coverage and then gives you a discount, you have not profited. Get quotes from at least three insurers, going over your list of drivers, vehicles, and specific coverage needs.

Be sure to ask for the discounts that may be coming to you because agents don't always volunteer this information. In addition to your age-related discount, ask about others. Some insurers offer discounts for insuring more than one car on the same policy, clean driving records, antitheft devices, low mileage, more than one policy with the same company, and longtime coverage. And watch out for policies that bump up your costs again when you turn 70.

Remember that insurance regulations and the possibility of age-related discounts differ from state to state as well as company to company. That means you must do your homework to find out whether savings are in your future.

BENEFITS FROM BANKS

Almost all banks today offer special incentives and services to their older customers, often starting at age 50. These include privileges such as a low minimum-balance requirement; free safe-deposit boxes; and elimination of monthly service charges, per-check charges, fees for traveler's checks, cashier's checks, or money orders. Some banks even throw in discount eyewear and pharmacy service, accidental-death insurance, social activities, group excursions, seminars, and newsletters.

Bank and state regulations differ, so it pays to be a comparison shopper to make sure you're getting the best deals available in your community.

LEGAL ASSISTANCE

Call upon your local area senior agency, which is required by law to provide some legal assistance to older citizens. Yours may help you untangle some puzzling legal problems or, at least, tell you what services are available to you. Or contact your local bar association for information about referrals or pro bono programs. The National Academy of Elder Law Attorneys (520-881-4005 or www.naela.com) will also help you find an attorney who specializes in working with older clients and their families.

FREE LEGAL SERVICES

Members of AARP who need the services of an attorney or have a legal question can get a free 30-minute initial consultation with a lawyer in your community who is associated with the AARP Legal Services Network. They can also have simple wills, powers of attorney, and living wills drawn up for them at low fixed fees and take advantage of a 20 percent reduction off the attorney's usual rates for other legal services.

For information: 800-424-3410; www.aarp.org/lsn.

For a list of participating LSN attorneys in your area, call 800-424-3410 or write LSN Fulfillment, PO Box 100084, Pittsburgh, PA 15233. Or look in your local Yellow Pages in the Associations, Attorneys, or Lawyers sections under the heading AARP-Legal Services Network. Another alternative is to visit the LSN website at www.aarp.org/lsn.

18

Volunteer for Great Experiences

If, perhaps for the first time in your life, you have time, expertise, talent, and energy to spare, consider volunteering your services to organizations that could use your help. Plenty of significant work is waiting for you, and more and more older Americans are volunteering as a way of finding fulfillment both before and after retirement. If you are looking for a good match between your abilities and an organization that needs them, take a look at the programs described here, all of them specifically seeking the experience and enthusiasm of older adults.

You can also visit www.seniorcorps.org, the website of Senior Corps, the umbrella organization for three federal volunteer programs, RSVP, Foster Grandparents, and Senior Companions, where you can search for volunteer opportunities by your zip code and interests.

But, first, keep in mind:

When you file your federal income tax, you may be allowed to deduct unreimbursed expenses incurred while volunteering your services to a charitable organization. You may be able to deduct program fees and reasonable costs for transportation, parking, tolls, meals, lodging, and uniforms. You may not be able to take off all of your travel expenses, meals, and lodging, however, when you spend a significant amount of personal or vacation time before, during, or after a service program, or if you get benefit from your service, such as academic credit.

CARIBBEAN VOLUNTEER EXPEDITIONS (CVE)

You can do valuable and meaningful work in the Caribbean helping local agencies to preserve the architectural heritage of the islands. Caribbean Volunteer Expeditions (CVE) takes volunteers there for a week at a time where you spend the mornings working on archaeological digs or documenting historical plantations, windmills and other structures. Afternoons are free for explorations of the island and visiting museums and historic sites. Volunteers pay their own airfare and costs for housing and food, although sometimes lodging costs are reduced or even free. No need for architectural expertise but, if you have it, it will be appreciated.

For information: CVE, Box 388, Corning, NY 14830; 607-962-7846; www.cvexp.org.

ELDERHOSTEL SERVICE PROGRAMS

Elderhostel Service Programs tap the experience and expertise of older adults (55 or over) in short-term volunteer projects in the U.S. and Canada, and other countries of the world. Teams of hostelers are paired with nonprofit organizations for a wide variety of service activities, from historical preservation to teaching English to natural-resources conservation, working with children with special needs, participating in archaeological research, and even helping to build affordable housing. No special skill or experience is required, and training is provided on the job. A 55 or older volunteer may be accompanied by an adult who is younger.

Many institutions and organizations—far too many to list here—collaborate with Elderhostel to put mature Americans, retired or not, to work for one to three weeks per session. These are hosted by such diverse groups as Habitat for Humanity, Oceanic Society Expeditions, the U.S. Forest Service, Global Volunteers, Cross-Cultural Solutions, Appalachian Mountain Club, Hole in the Woods Ranch, the Center for Bioacoustics, the Museum of Science and Industry in Chicago, Grand Canyon National Park, and many more.

The fee you pay to participate varies with each program and includes full room and board, equipment, social and cultural events, and, in most cases, airfare.

For information: Elderhostel, 11 Avenue de Lafayette, Boston, MA 02111; 877-426-8056 or 617-426-7788; www.elderhostel.org.

EXPERIENCE CORPS

Started in 1995 and now in more than two dozen cities, Experience Corps is a national Civic Ventures program that provides schools and other youth organizations with older

WORKING FOR THE ENVIRONMENT

Environmental Alliance for Senior Involvement (EASI) is a nonprofit coalition of many senior and environmental organizations that tap the talents, expertise, experience, and enthusiasm of older adults to help protect and improve the environment. Volunteers in every state and 20 foreign countries now work on a wide range of environmental activities that include water quality monitoring, forest management, radon testing, brown fields revitalization, stream corridor restoration, community gardens, homeland security, and much more.

For information: EASI, PO Box 250, Catlett, VA 20119; 540-788-3274; www.easi.org.

adults who serve as tutors and mentors, help with homework, provide attention to children with special needs, and foster the development of youngsters. Volunteers are 55-plus, work part-time, half-time, full-time, or as needed, and do not require special previous experience.

For information: Experience Corps, Civic Ventures, 425 Second St., San Francisco, CA 94107; 415-430-0141; www.experiencecorps.org.

FAMILY FRIENDS

A national program sponsored by the National Council on Aging, Family Friends recruits volunteers over the age of 55 to work in many locations around the country with children with disabilities, chronic illnesses, or other problems. The volunteers act as caring grandparents, helping the families in whatever ways they can, mostly dealing with children, perhaps foster children or adoptees, at home but occasionally in hospitals, homeless shelters, or Head Start centers. They are asked to serve at least four hours a week and commit themselves to the program for at least a year. Volunteers are reimbursed for expenses incurred.

The local projects are funded by the federal government; corporations; foundations; and local, county, city, or state governments.

For information: Family Friends Resource Center, 409 Third St. SW, Washington, DC 20024; 202-479-6675; www.family-friends.org.

FOSTER GRANDPARENTS

Foster Grandparents devote their volunteer service to children with special or exceptional needs. They provide emotional support to victims of abuse and neglect, mentor troubled teenagers and young mothers, care for premature infants and children with physical disabilities and severe illnesses, and tutor children who lag behind in reading. Volunteers must be 60 or older; meet certain income-eligibility guidelines; and serve 20 hours a week, usually 4 hours a day Monday through Friday, in facilities in their own neighborhoods.

For this, they receive—in addition to the immense satisfaction—modest tax-free stipends to offset their costs, some meals during service, reimbursement for transportation, an annual physical examination, and accident and liability insurance while on duty.

For information: Contact your local Foster Grandparents program or the Corporation for National Service, 1201 New

York Ave. NW, Washington, DC 20525; 800-424-8867; www.seniorcorps.org.

JEWISH NATIONAL FUND (JNF) CAARI PROGRAM

Each winter, the Jewish National Fund's CAARI program (Canadian American Active Retirees in Israel) sends a group, made up of retired adults age 50 and above, to Israel to participate in an interactive educational program that ranges from 2 to 12 weeks in length. The group meets Israelis of all ages, learns about the current situation first-hand, and experiences life through Israeli eyes. The participants attend lectures, tour the country, and volunteer in schools, hospitals, community agencies, and JNF's forests.

For information: JNF CAARI Program, Missions Dept., 42 E. 69th St., New York, NY 10021; 888-563-0033, ext. 284; www.jnf.org.

NATIONAL EXECUTIVE SERVICE CORPS

This nonprofit organization performs a unique service. It helps other nonprofit organizations solve their problems by providing retired executives with extensive corporate and professional experience to serve as volunteer consultants. Its services are offered in five basic areas—education, health, the arts, social services, and religion—and the assistance covers everything from organizational structure and financial systems to marketing and funding strategy. Volunteers' expenses are covered.

For information: National Executive Service Corps, 120 Wall St., New York, NY 10005; 212-269-1234; www.nesc.org.

NATIONAL PARK SERVICE

If you love the outdoors and have the time, volunteer to work for the National Park Service as a VIP (Volunteers-in-Parks). VIPs are not limited to over-50s, but a good portion of them are retired people with time, expertise, talent, and interest in forests and wilderness. You may work a few hours a week or a month, seasonally or full-time, and may or may not—depending on the park—wear a uniform or get reimbursed for out-of-pocket expenses. The job possibilities range from working at an information desk to serving as a guide, maintaining trails, driving a shuttle bus, painting fences, designing computer programs, patrolling trails, making wildlife counts, writing visitor brochures, and preparing park events.

For information: Contact the VIP coordinator at the national park where you would like to volunteer and request an application. Or write to Volunteer Coordinator, National Park Service, 1849 C St. NW, Ste. 3045, Washington, DC 20240; 202-565-1050; www.nps.gov/volunteer.

NATIONAL TRUST WORKING HOLIDAYS

Britain's National Trust runs hundreds of "working holidays" in England, Wales, and Northern Ireland, inviting volunteers to exchange work for an interesting and low-cost holiday. The Trust, which oversees Britain's historic and environmental treasures, organizes small groups to lend a hand for one- or two-week sessions in such tasks as restoring historic buildings, clearing ponds, or maintaining footpaths. Most programs accept anybody over 18, but several—the Oak Plus Projects—are reserved for enthusiasts between 50 and 70 who are willing to tackle outdoor work.

Lodging is in simple farmhouse accommodations and the work is paced to allow ample time to relax, take in the local attractions, or go for a stroll.

For information: The National Trust, PO Box 84, Cirencester, Glos, GL7 1ZP, England; www.nationaltrust.org.uk/volunteering.

PEACE CORPS

It may surprise you to learn that the Peace Corps is a viable choice for idealists of any age. There is no upper age limit for acceptance into the Peace Corps, and since its beginning in 1961, thousands of older volunteers have brought their talents and experience to almost 100 countries all over the world. To become a volunteer, you must be a U.S. citizen and meet basic legal and medical criteria. Some assignments require a college or technical-school degree or an experience equivalent. Married couples are eligible and will be assigned together. Service is typically for two years after three months of training.

What you get in return for your hard work is the chance to travel; an unforgettable living experience in a foreign land; basic expenses; housing; plus technical, language, and cultural training. You will also have the opportunity to use your expertise constructively in fields such as agriculture, business, environment, health, education, and community development.

For information: Peace Corps, 1111 20th St. NW, Washington, DC 20526; 800-424-8580; www.peacecorps.gov.

SENIOR ENVIRONMENTAL EMPLOYMENT (SEE) PROGRAM

The SEE Program, administered by the U.S. Environmental Protection Agency (EPA), establishes cooperative agreements with six national organizations to recruit qualified people 55 and over to help with environmental problems. The recruits, who work part-time or full-time in EPA offices or in the field, are paid by the hour in jobs ranging from secretarial and clerical work to highly specialized technical and scientific positions. All are designed to assist the agency in protecting and/or cleaning up the environment.

For information: U.S. EPA, Arial Rios Blg., SEE Program, 1200 Pennsylvania Ave., Washington, DC 20460; 202-564-0415; www.epa.gov/epahrist/see/brochure.

RETIRED AND SENIOR VOLUNTEER PROGRAM (RSVP)

RSVP matches the interests and skills of men and women over the age of 55 with volunteer opportunities in their own communities. Volunteers—who may serve anywhere from a few to more than 40 hours a week—may choose to tutor children, renovate homes, teach English to immigrants, plan community gardens, deliver meals, make hospital visits, work in day-care centers, or do whatever their own communities need. They are not paid but receive supplemental insurance while on duty, a preservice orientation, and on-the-job training from the agency or organization where they are placed.

For information: Contact your local or regional RSVP office or Corporation for National Service, 1201 New York Ave.

NW, Washington, DC 20525; 800-424-8867; www.senior corps.org.

SENIOR COMPANIONS

Senior Companions help older adults, who are frail, have disabilities, or have serious or terminal illnesses and need extra assistance to live independently in their own homes or communities. They provide companionship and friendship to isolated seniors, assist them with simple chores, and provide needed transportation. Volunteers must be 60 or older; meet certain income eligibility guidelines; and serve 20 hours a week, usually 4 hours a day Monday through Friday. Although they are not paid, they receive a modest tax-free stipend, reimbursement for transportation, some meals during service, on-duty accident and liability insurance, and an annual physical examination.

For information: Corporation for National Service, 1201 New York Ave. NW, Washington, DC 20525; 800-424-8867; www.seniorcorps.org.

SERVICE CORPS OF RETIRED EXECUTIVES (SCORE)

A national organization, SCORE offers free counseling for fledgling small businesses by working and retired executives with expertise in a range of areas including finance, management, and marketing. Its volunteers serve as mentors in one-on-one counseling, computer counseling, seminars, and workshops. SCORE currently has a membership of about 10,500 men and women and 389 chapters all over the country.

For information: Contact your local U.S. Small Business Administration office or SCORE, 409 Third St. SW, 6th floor,

FORTY PLUS

Offices in 20 cities throughout the U.S. comprise **Forty Plus**, a nonprofit cooperative of unemployed executives, managers, and professionals, men and women, who have earned at least $40,000 a year. Their objective is to help members conduct effective employment searches and find new jobs. There is no paid staff. The members do all the work and help pay expenses. They must commit themselves to attend weekly meetings and spend at least two days each week working at the club and assisting others in their search for work.

In return, members are assisted in examining their career skills and defining their goals, counseled on résumé writing and interviewing skills, helped to plan marketing strategy, and given job leads. They may also use the premises as a base of operations, with phone answering and mail service, computers, and reference library.

Forty Plus currently maintains offices in New York City and Buffalo, New York; Oakland, San Diego, San Jose, and Los Angeles (with a branch in Laguna Hills), California; Fort Collins, Colorado Springs, and Lakewood, Colorado; Columbus, Ohio; Dallas and Houston, Texas; Murray, Ogden, and Provo, Utah; Philadelphia, Pennsylvania; Bellevue, Washington; Washington, D.C.; St. Paul, Minnesota; and Honolulu, Hawaii.

For information: Addresses of locations and descriptive materials are available from Forty Plus of New York, 149 5th Ave., New York, NY 10010; 212-358-7646; www.fortyplus-nyc.org.

Washington, DC 20024; 800-634-0245 or 202-205-6762; www.score.org.

SERVICE OPPORTUNITIES FOR OLDER PEOPLE (SOOP)

SOOP, sponsored by the Mennonite Mission Network and other organizations, provides a way for older people of all persuasions to contribute their experience and skills in a variety of locations throughout the U.S. and Canada. You may sign up for a few weeks or up to six months, living at the site and working to help others in need in whatever way you can, from teaching, building, and child care to home-making, farming, and administering. Once you decide on the kind of work and time commitment you prefer, you make plans with a location coordinator for your assignment and housing. Volunteers usually pay for their own travel, food, and lodging.

For information: Mennonite Mission Network, PO Box 370, Elkhart, IN 46515; 574-294-7523; www.mennonitemis sion.net.

SHEPHERD'S CENTERS OF AMERICA (SCA)

An interfaith, nonprofit organization of older adults who volunteer their skills to help seniors in their communities, SCA has about 90 centers in 26 states. Supported by Catholic, Jewish, and Protestant congregations as well as businesses and foundations, the centers operate many programs designed to enable older people to remain in their own homes as active participants in community life. They also encourage intergenerational interaction. Centers offer such in-home services as Telephone Visitors, Family Friends,

Meals on Wheels, Handyhands Service, and Respite Care, all provided mostly by volunteers. Programs at the centers include other services, day trips, classes, and courses as well as support groups and referrals. Membership is open to anyone over the age of 55.

For information: Shepherd's Centers of America, 1 W. Armour Blvd., Ste. 201, Kansas City, MO 64111; 800-547-7073; www.shepherdcenters.org.

SIERRA CLUB

The Sierra Club, the largest grassroots organization in the country, plans several service trips a year for seniors. On the one-week trips, all meals are included, but you must take your own equipment and provide your own transportation to and from the site. Depending on the place you

JOB PROGRAM FOR OLDER WORKERS

Senior Community Service Employment Program (SCSEP), a federally funded program, recruits unemployed low-income men and women over the age of 55, assesses their employment strengths, and places them in paid jobs in community-service positions. At the same time, the enrollees begin training in new job skills and receive such help as counseling, physical examinations, group meetings, and job fairs while the agency tries to match them with permanent jobs in the private and public sector. If you qualify and are looking for a paying position, this agency is worth a try.

For information: SCSEP, National Council on the Aging, 409 Third St. SW, Washington, DC 20024; 800-424-9046 or 202-479-1200; www.ncoa.org. Or contact your local, county, or state Office for the Aging.

choose, you'll spend your time helping to reconstruct and maintain trails, plant vegetation, assist with archaeological digs and surveys, count birds, and more.

Remember that membership in the Sierra Club costs you less if you are a senior—$24 a year while younger adults pay $39. Two seniors in the same household can join for $32 a year for the same membership that costs $47 for younger people.

For information: Sierra Club Outings, 85 Second St., San Francisco, CA 94105; 415-977-5521; www.outings.sierra club.org.

VOLUNTEER SENIOR RANGER CORPS

The Volunteer Senior Ranger Corps program, already operating in about a dozen national parks, is a new program established by the National Park Service and its partners. It gives grants to parks to help them recruit senior volunteers and enhance relationships with local communities. Those at least 50 years of age may apply by contacting the park where they'd like to work. Each participating park—such as Glacier National Park, Delaware Water Gap National Recreation Area, and Fire Island National Seashore—determines its own projects for the volunteers. To date, the projects include such activities as trail monitoring, investigating archaeological sites, restoring native plants in overused areas, and teaching groups of urban children how to fish.

For information: National Park Service, www.nps.gov/volunteer.

VOLUNTEERS FOR ISRAEL

In this volunteer work-and-cultural program in Israel for adults 18 and older, you'll put in eight-hour days for two to three weeks, working alongside members of the Israel Defense Forces. You'll sleep in a segregated dormitory and work in small groups at a reserve or supply military base, doing whatever needs doing most at that moment. You may serve in supply, warehousing, or maintenance of equipment or in social services in hospitals. You'll wear an army uniform with a "Civilian Volunteer" patch. Board, room, and other expenses are free, but you must pay for your own partially subsidized airfare.

For information: Volunteers for Israel, 330 West 42nd St., Stes. 16–18, New York, NY 10036; 212-643-4848; www.vfi-usa.org.

OPERATION ABLE

If you're over 40 and in the market for a job but don't know where to start looking for one, hook up with **Operation ABLE**, a nonprofit organization affiliated with a network of agencies that will help match you with a likely employer. You're in luck if you live in the Chicago area, where there are many regional offices and a job hotline (312-782-7700), a referral service for job seekers in the Chicago area. But there is also a network of independent ABLE-like organizations, modeled after the original, in several other cities, including Boston; Los Angeles; Lincoln, Nebraska; Rockville, Maryland; Southfield, Michigan; and St. Albans, Vermont.

Operation ABLE tries every which way to get you into the working world. It provides job counseling, group training activities, and individual career assessment and guidance; teaches job-hunting skills; matches older workers with employers; operates a pool of temporaries; and offers many other services.

For information: Operation ABLE, 180 N. Wabash Ave., Chicago, IL 60601; 312-782-3335; www.jobhotline.org.

VOLUNTEERS IN TECHNICAL ASSISTANCE (VITA)

VITA provides another avenue for helping developing countries. A nonprofit international organization, VITA provides volunteer experts who respond—usually by direct correspondence—to technical inquiries from people in these nations who need assistance in such areas as small-business development, energy applications, agriculture, reforestation, water supply and sanitation, and low-cost housing. Its volunteers also perform other services such as project planning, translations, publications, marketing strategies, evaluations, and technical reports and often become on-site consultants.

There is no minimum age, but you must have enough time to serve.

For information: Volunteers in Technical Assistance, 1600 Wilson Blvd., Ste. 710, Arlington, VA 22209; 703-276-1800; www.vita.org.

19

The Over-50 Organizations and What They Can Do for You

When you consider that there are more people in this country over the age of 55 than there are children in elementary and high schools, you can see why we have powerful potential to influence what goes on around here. As the demographic discovery of the times, a group that controls most of the nation's disposable income, we've become a prime marketing target. And, just like any other large group of people, we've got plenty of needs.

A number of organizations in the U.S. and Canada have been formed in recent years to act as advocates for the 50-plus population and to provide us with special programs as well as opportunities to spend our money on their products or services. Here is a brief rundown on them and what they have to offer you. You may want to join more than one of them so you can get the best of each.

AARP

AARP offers so many benefits that you'd be mighty foolish not to join as soon as you turn 50 and become eligible for membership in this 35-million-member organization that serves as an advocate for the older population and has become one of the most effective lobbying groups in the country. Its newsletter, *AARP Bulletin*, and a bimonthly magazine, *AARP The Magazine*, go to more homes than any other publications in the U.S. The cost of membership is $12.50 for a year, $21 for two years, or $29.50 for three years (and that includes your spouse or companion who may be under 50). Overseas members pay $28 per year.

Here are some of AARP's benefits:

- Group health insurance, life insurance, automobile insurance, homeowners insurance, mobile-home insurance, long-term-care insurance
- A broad assortment of money-saving discounts on airfares, cruises, hotels and motels, auto rentals, vacation packages, entertainment, legal services, online services, and more. To view them, see www.aarp.org/privileges
- A mail-order pharmacy service that delivers prescription and nonprescription drugs
- A motoring plan that includes emergency road and towing services, trip planning, and other benefits
- A national advocacy and lobbying program at all levels of government to develop legislative priorities and represent the interests of older people
- About 3,400 local chapters with their own activities and volunteer projects
- Special programs in a wide range of areas such as consumer affairs, legal counseling, financial information,

housing, health advocacy, voter education, employment planning, independent living, disability initiatives, grandparent information, and public benefits

- Tax-Aide, a program conducted in cooperation with the IRS that helps lower- and moderate-income members with their income tax returns
- 55 ALIVE Driver Safety Program, an eight-hour course offered nationwide to improve your driving skills and, in many states, help you qualify for a multi-year discount on auto insurance premiums
- Legal Services Network, which assists members in finding prescreened attorneys to help with legal problems
- Free publications on many subjects relevant to your life

For information: AARP, 601 E St. NW, Washington, DC 20049; 800-424-3410 or 202-434-AARP; www.aarp.org.

ALLIANCE FOR RETIRED AMERICANS

This organization, created by a coalition of the AFL-CIO, affiliated unions, and community-based organizations, started out in 2001 with 2.5 million members and is rapidly growing because all retired members of participating unions and members of the former National Council of Senior Citizens are automatically enrolled. Its purpose is to mobilize millions of older people to make their voices heard for public policies that will "protect and preserve programs vital to the health and economic security of older Americans." Annual dues of union retirees are paid by their unions; others pay a membership fee of $10 a year.

For information: Alliance for Retired Americans, 888 16th St. NW, Ste. 4000, Washington, DC 20006; 888-373-6497; www.retiredamericans.org.

CANADA'S ASSOCIATION FOR THE FIFTY-PLUS (CARP)

Canadians over the age of 50 are invited to join CARP, a 50-plus lobbying group with over 400,000 members, retired and employed. For a membership fee of $15.95 (Canadian) a year for singles or couples, members get many benefits, including discounted rates on out-of-country health insurance, long-term care insurance, extended health and dental plans, and automobile and home insurance. They can also take advantage of an expanded travel program with an auto club and discounts on airfares, travel packages, hotels, and car rentals. Members may also participate in the activities of local chapters in their own communities.

CARP publishes a lively, informative magazine called *FiftyPlus*, with six regular issues per year, that publishes articles on a wide range of subjects such as health care, travel, hobbies, politics, and people. CARP is a major advocate, national and provincial, on issues of great concern to mature Canadians. Free financial seminars are held frequently throughout the country.

For information: CARP, 27 Queen St. East, Ste. 1304, Toronto, ON M5C 2M6; 800-363-9736 (in Canada) or 416-363-8748; www.50plus.com.

CANADIAN SNOWBIRD ASSOCIATION (CSA)

CSA is an organization with about 93 million members, mainly seniors and retirees, who travel outside Canada for up to six months of the year. As their advocate and lobbying group, CSA addresses issues of concern to Canadian seniors such as health care, absentee voting rights, cross-border problems, residency requirements, U.S. tax laws for Canadians wintering abroad, and estate tax rules on Canadian-owned vacation property in the U.S. And it endorses travel insurance as well as out-of-country health insurance.

Membership costs $20 (Canadian) per household a year, and benefits include a magazine, travel offerings, an automobile club, a currency-exchange program, home and automobile insurance, and social gatherings in popular snowbird locations such as Florida, Arizona, Texas, and California.

For information: Canadian Snowbird Association, 180 Lesmill Rd., North York, ON M3B 2T5; 800-265-3200 or 416-391-9000; www.snowbirds.org.

CATHOLIC GOLDEN AGE (CGA)

A Catholic nonprofit organization that is concerned with issues affecting older citizens, such as health care, housing, and Social Security benefits, CGA has well over a million members and more than 200 chapters throughout the country. It offers many good things to its members, who must be over 50. These include spiritual benefits, such as masses and prayers worldwide, and practical benefits, such as discounts on hotels, campgrounds, and car rentals.

Other offerings include group insurance plans, pilgrimage and group travel programs, and an automobile club. A new benefit program is Access to Care that offers discounts on the cost of long-term care facilities, assisted-living facilities, and home health care. Another is the Health Care Card that allows members to save money on the costs of prescriptions as well as on vision, dental, and hearing services. Membership costs $8 a year or $15 for three years.

For information: Catholic Golden Age, RD2, Box 249, Olyphant, PA 18447; 800-836-5699; www.catholicgoldenage.org.

GRAY PANTHERS

A national organization of about 20,000 intergenerational activists, the Gray Panthers work on multiple issues that include peace, jobs for all, antidiscrimination (ageism, sexism, racism), family security, the environment, campaign reform, preservation of social security, health care, and housing. They are active in more than 50 local networks across the U.S. in their efforts to promote social justice. Annual membership is $20.

For information: Gray Panthers, 733 15th St. NW, Ste. 437, Washington, DC 20005; 800-280-5362 or 202-737-6637; www.graypanthers.org.

MATURE OUTLOOK, CANADA

Canadians over 50 can join Sears' Mature Outlook program and get a multitude of benefits, including discount coupons for Sears products and services purchased in the stores, through the catalog, or with Sears HomeCentral; discounts on hotels and rental cars; 10 percent off at Sears Optical and Sears Restaurants and Nabob Cafes; travel offers; and a subscription to *New Outlook* magazine. Annual membership is $19.99 (Canadian) for Sears Cardholders, $24.99 for noncardholders.

For information: Mature Outlook, PO Box 4200, Sta. A, Toronto, ON M5W 3A8; 800-265-3675 (800-650-9950 for service in French); www.sears.ca.

NATIONAL ASSOCIATION OF RETIRED FEDERAL EMPLOYEES (NARFE)

As you can probably gather, this is an association of more than 400,000 federal government retirees, current employees, and their spouses. The primary mission of NARFE is to protect the earned benefits of retired federal employees, and has become an active lobby program in Washington and the states. Annual membership costs $25, plus local chapter dues. Members receive *Retirement Life*, a monthly magazine and are entitled to discounts and special services.

For information: NARFE, 606 N. Washington St., Alexandria, VA 22314; 800-627-3394 or 703-838-7760; www.narfe.org.

NATIONAL EDUCATION ASSOCIATION (NEA–RETIRED)

With a membership of more than 200,000 retired education employees from teachers to school bus drivers, NEA-Retired acts as an advocate for their special interests such as pensions and health care and supports public education through legislative lobbying as well as reading programs, mentoring, and intergenerational activities. Among its benefits of membership are life, health, disability, and casualty insurance programs; savings and investment plans; credit and loan programs; and discounts, educational guides, and a bimonthly magazine, *Active Life*. Join for $15 a year or $100 for life, plus local dues that vary depending on your state.

For information: NEA-Retired, 1201 16th St. NW, Washington, DC 20036; 202-822-7149; www.nea.org/retired.

OLDER WOMEN'S LEAGUE (OWL)

OWL is a national nonprofit organization that has local chapters dedicated to achieving economic, political, and social equality for older women. Anyone, of any age, is allowed to join. OWL provides educational materials, training for citizen advocates, and informative publications dealing with the important issues—such as Social Security, health care, retirement benefits, employment discrimination—that face women as they grow older. Annual dues are $25.

For information: OWL, 666 11th St. NW, Washington, DC 20001; 800-825-3695 or 202-783-6686; www.owl-national.org.

THE RETIRED OFFICERS ASSOCIATION (TROA)

This group is open to anyone who has been a commissioned or warrant officer in the seven U.S. uniformed services. Members receive lobbying representation on Capitol Hill and an excellent magazine that features articles on matters of special interest to them. They may also take advantage of a number of benefits, including discounts on car rentals and motel lodgings, a travel program with "military fares" to many overseas destinations, sports tournaments, a mailorder prescription program, group health and life insurance plans, and a car lease-purchase plan. A loan program allows members to borrow funds for the education of their children and grandchildren, to be paid back after graduation.

TROA also has many autonomous local chapters with their own activities and membership fees. Annual dues are $20. Auxiliary members (spouses, widows, or widowers) pay $15 a year.

For information: The Retired Officers Association, 201 N. Washington St., Alexandria, VA 22314; 800-245-8762 or 703-549-2311; www.troa.org.

Index